RED AZALEA

Red Azalea

LIFE AND LOVE IN CHINA

ANCHEE MIN

VICTOR GOLLANCZ

LONDON

First published in Great Britain 1993
by Victor Gollancz
A Cassell imprint
Villiers House, 41/47 Strand, London WC2N 5JE

A catalogue record for this book is
available from the British Library.

ISBN 0 575 05529 4

Photoset in Great Britain by
Rowland Phototypesetting Ltd, Bury St Edmunds, Suffolk
and printed in Great Britain by
St Edmundsbury Press Ltd, Bury St Edmunds, Suffolk

To Qigu

ACKNOWLEDGMENTS

Thank you:

Sandra Dijkstra, my agent, for your discovery.

Joan Chen, my comrade-in-arm, for your inspiration.

Xian-ming Yuan, for your enlightenment since Shanghai 51st Middle School.

Michele Dremmer, for your affection.

Diana and Richard K. M. Eu, my aunt and uncle, Mr S. G. Lee, Harris Meyer and Deborah Mihm, for your sincere support.

Michele Smith for helping me with my English since I arrived in the United States.

Vincent Yip, my brother-in-law, for being my 'walking dictionary'.

Yan-Fang Jiang and Ci-Feng Zhang, my parents-in-law, for babysitting Lauryan.

Julie Grau, for your energy and for your faith in the book. Dan Frank, my editor, thank you.

AUTHOR'S NOTE

I have translated the Chinese names according to their original meaning instead of transcribing them phonetically. I have changed some names in order to protect lives.

PART
ONE

紅

杜

鵑

I was raised on the teachings of Mao and on the operas of Madam Mao, Comrade Jiang Ching. I became a leader of the Little Red Guard in elementary school. This was during the Great Proletarian Cultural Revolution when red was my colour. My parents lived like – as the neighbours described them – a pair of chopsticks, always in harmony. My father was an instructor of industrial technique drawing at Shanghai Textile Institute, although his true love was astronomy. My mother was a teacher at a Shanghai middle school. She taught whatever the Party asked, one semester in Chinese and the next in Russian. My parents both believed in Mao and the Communist Party, just like everybody else in the neighbourhood. They had four children, each one a year apart. I was born in 1957. We lived in the city, on South Luxuriant Road in a small two storey townhouse occupied by two families. The house was left by my grandfather who had died of tuberculosis right before I was born.

I was an adult from the age of five. That was nothing unusual. The kids I played with all carried their family's little ones on their backs, tied with a piece of cloth. The little ones played with their own snot while we played hide and seek. I was put in charge of managing the family because my parents were in their working units all day, just like everyone else's parents.

I called my sisters and brother my children because I had to pick each one of them up from kindergarten and nursery school while I myself was only a kindergartner. I was six when my sister Blooming was five, my second sister Coral was four and my brother Space Conqueror was three. My parents made careful choices in the names they gave us. They were considered eccentric because the neighbours named their children Guard of Red, Big Leap, Long

March, Red Star, Liberation, Revolution, New China, Road of Russia, Resist US, Patriotic Forerunner, Matchless Red Soldier, etc. My parents had their own ideas. First they called me Lin-Shuan, Rising Sun at a Mountain. They dropped it because Mao was considered the only sun. After further contemplation, they named me Anchee, Jade of Peace. Also, it sounded like the Chinese translation of the English word 'angel'. They registered me with it. Blooming and Coral were named after the sound of 'Chee' (jade). There were two reasons why my parents named my brother Space Conqueror: one was that my father loved astronomy; the second was to respond to Mao's call that China would soon erect its own spaceship.

As I understood it, my parents were doing work that was saving the world. Every evening, I would pick the children up and fight with the kids on the block all the way home. It was like eating a regular meal that I got a purple cheek or a bloody nose. It did not bother me too much. Although I was scared of crossing at traffic lights and dark alleys, I learned not to show my fear because I had to be a model for the children, to show them what bravery meant. After I arranged for the children to play by themselves in the living room, I went to set up the stove to cook dinner. It always took me a long time to light the stove because I did not understand that wood and coals needed air to burn. I stuffed the stove as I sang songs of Mao quotations. One time, when I tried many times and the stove would not light, I lost my patience. I went out to play, thinking that the stove was not burning. Then a kid came and told me that there was smoke coming out of our house window. This happened three times.

I tried to put the children to sleep while the sky was still bright. The children's little feet kicked the cotton blankets and made new holes over the old. The blankets soon became rags. When the room quietened down I would lean on the windowsill staring at the entrance to the lane, waiting for my parents to appear. I watched the sky turn deep blue, Venus rising, and I would fall asleep by the window.

*

14

In 1967 when I was ten years old we moved. It was because our downstairs neighbour accused us of having a bigger space than they had. They said, How can a family of six occupy four rooms while a family of eleven has only one? The revolution is about fairness. They came up with chamber pots and poured shit on our blankets. There were no police. The police station was called a revisionist mechanism and had been shut down by the revolutionaries. The Red Guards had begun looting houses. No one answered our call for help. The neighbours just watched.

The downstairs neighbour kept bothering us. We cleaned the shit night after night, swallowed insults in meek submission. The downstairs family became uncontrollable. They threatened to harm us children when our parents were not at home. They said their second daughter had a history of mental illness, therefore they could not be responsible for what she was going to do. The second daughter came up and showed me an ax that she had just sharpened. She said she could chop my head in two like a watermelon. She asked me if I would like her to do it. I said, You wait here and I'll tell you whether I would like it or not later. I grabbed my sisters and brother and we ran and squeezed ourselves into a closet all day.

One day, when my mother stepped in the door after work, the second daughter jumped on her. I saw them wrestle in the stairwell. Mother was pushed, crushed on the floor, and was slashed with the scissors. I was in shock. I stood right next to my mother and saw blood pouring down her face and wrists. I wanted to scream but I had no voice. The second daughter went downstairs and cut her own wrists with the scissors. She then rushed out to a curious crowd outside the door, bloody hands raised high in the air. She shouted, Look at me, I am a worker who was attacked by a bourgeois intellectual. Comrades, this is a political murder. Her family members came out. They shouted, A debt of blood must be paid by blood.

My father said we must move. We must escape. He wrote little notes describing our house and what we would like in exchange.

He stuck the notes on the tree trunks by the streets. The next day a truck arrived by our door fully loaded with furniture. Five men got out of the truck and said they had come to exchange their house with ours. My father said we hadn't looked around for our choice yet. The men said, Our house is perfect for you and it's ready for you to move in. My father said we didn't know what it looked like. The men said, Go and take a look at it now, you will like it. My father asked how many rooms. They said, Three, very nice, Shanghai standard. My mother said, Do you know that our downstairs neighbours' second daughter is mentally ill? The men said it would not be a problem. They said they were a father and sons, all workers at a Shanghai steel factory. The sons needed rooms to get married. They wanted the rooms in a hurry. My father said, Please let us think about it. The men said, We'll wait outside your door while you make up your mind. My father said, You can't do that. The men said, No problem. My parents decided to take a look at the men's house on Shanxi Road.

I was asked to guard the house while my parents were gone. I was doing my homework when I saw the men start to unload their furniture. After that they began to move our furniture. I went up to them and said, My parents aren't back yet. The men said they would like to help us while they still have the truck. There's nowhere you can borrow such a truck by the time you think you're ready to move, they said. Are you going to move all this stuff with your bare little hands?

When my parents got back, most of our furniture was packed on their truck. My mother said, This is not what I want, you can't force us to move. The men said, We're workers, we don't play mind-games. You advertised, we came with a good offer. It's Sunday, our only day off. We don't like to be fooled. We beat the second daughter downstairs because she fooled us. She confessed that she's normal and her family just wanted to have more rooms.

My father took my mother and the children aside. He said, We must get away. Let's move, forget about fairness. So we did. We moved to Shanxi Road in the Xu-Hui district. It was a row of townhouses. Our floor was a two-room apartment shared by three families. The apartment was owned by the government. The three families had to share one toilet. We occupied the front of the floor. Besides a drawing room, we had a porch and a kitchen. The family who occupied the back of the floor had five members. They lived in one room and their stove was right next to the public toilet. I did not like it because it often happened that when I had a shit they would be cooking. The third family on the floor lived in a back-porch converted space. They were very quiet people.

My father said, Let's settle down. Think of it this way, things could be worse, we could have been killed. At least it's safe here. We all agreed and felt better. Upstairs was a big family with six children. Their third daughter was my age. Her official name was Sun Flower but she was called Little Coffin at home because she was as thin as a skeleton. She came down and asked me if I would like to join her family's Mao study seminar every evening after dinner. I said I had to ask my father. My father said no. He said he did not want to have a revolution at home. It surprised me. I spent a night wondering whether my father was a hidden counter-revolutionary and whether or not I should report him.

Little Coffin was disappointed when she heard that I would not attend their family's Mao study seminar. She went back upstairs and I heard her family begin singing 'Red in the East, rises the sun, China has brought forth a Mao Tse-tung . . .' I admired her family. I wished we could do the same thing.

We girls were arranged to sleep on the porch while my brother slept in the kitchen. My mother missed our old house terribly. She missed having a toilet of our own.

The morning after we had moved, Monday, I remember, I was woken by a loud electric bell. I leaned out of the window and looked down. I discovered that our downstairs neighbour was a cable and wire hardware workshop. When the loud electric bell rang at seven-thirty, a crowd of women would rush in. Heads were moving like bees crowding into a nest. There were about two hundred women working downstairs and in the back lane under a roof-shed that covered one third of the back lane. The women used to be housewives. They had no education but were good at working with their hands. Here they wired and welded all day. They brought their own lunches and ate them in the yard. From my window I could see what they ate, mostly preserved salty fish and tofu. Some of them were given milk coupons because the wires they were welding carried poisonous chemicals. The smell of these chemicals came upstairs when they laid the wires out in the yard.

The women downstairs liked to chat, quarrel and sing Comrade Jiang Ching, Madam Mao's, operas. The neighbours described the women as Big Fight Mondays Wednesdays and Fridays, Small Quarrel Tuesdays Thursdays and Saturdays. They had loudspeakers in each room. In the afternoon there was a voice reading from Mao works, from articles in the *People's Daily* and *Red Flag Magazine*. By three-thirty, when we got back from school, we would hear an exercise music tape being played. The women would get out, rank themselves and occupy the whole lane doing ten minutes of stretching. I often leaned on the windowsill with my sisters and brother watching them. We started to know the women's nicknames, such as Chow-Di – Draw-A-Brother, Lai-Di – Gain-A-Boy, Shuang-Di – Double-Boy, Yin-Di – Win-A-Boy and Bao-Di – Guarantee-A-Boy. The names disturbed me. Though I could not link myself to those names, the idea began to sink into my mind that to be born a girl was a sad thing. The workshop ran three shifts. The wiring machine was on day and night. My father had a hard time bearing the noise. He could not sleep. He went down to complain but it was useless. The women needed to work, the boss said. It was a revolutionary task.

The children of the lane often went to watch the women wiring. The women sanded the wires before moulding them. They gave us sandpaper and we sanded the wires. We had fun. The

18

women told us that the wires would be shipped to Vietnam. What we were doing was a national secret. The women won award certificates from the government. They framed the biggest certificate on the wall. It said, 'Honour and Glory to Wu-Lee Hardware Workshop'.

I went to Long Happiness Elementary School. The school was six blocks away from where we lived. My new classmates laughed at me because I always wore the same jacket with holes everywhere. I wore it all seasons. It was one of my cousin's old clothes. Blooming usually wore the clothes after I grew out of them, with patches at the collars and elbows. Coral took over. More patches. The clothes melted, though she was careful. She knew Space Conqueror was waiting for his turn. Space Conqueror always wore rags. The neighbourhood children called him 'Flea'. It made me feel very guilty.

The children in the new neighbourhood were unfriendly. They attacked us often. We were called 'Rags' and 'Fleas'. My father said to us, I can't afford to buy you new clothes to make you look respectable, but if you do well in school you will be respected. The bad kids can take away your school bag but they can't take away your intelligence.

I followed my father's teaching and it worked. I was accepted as a member of the Little Red Guard and was soon appointed head of the Little Red Guard because of my good grades. I was a natural leader. I had early practice at home. In those years learning to be a revolutionary was everything. The Red Guards showed us how to destroy, how to worship. They jumped off buildings to show their loyalty to Mao. It was said that physical death was nothing. It was light as a feather. Only when one died for the people would one's death be heavier than a mountain.

My parents never talked about politics at home. They never complained about the labour they were assigned to do. By 1971 my father was no longer a college instructor: he was sent to work in a printing-shop as an assistant clerk. Although my mother had a university degree, she was sent to work in a shoe factory. It was a political demand for one to be a member of the working class said her boss. The Party called it a re-education programme. My parents were unhappy about their jobs but they behaved correctly for us, because if they were ever criticized it would affect our future.

My mother was not good at being someone she was not. Her colleagues said that she had been politically clumsy. One day at school when she was ordered to write the slogan 'A long long life to Chairman Mao' on wax paper, she wrote it as 'A no no life to Chairman Mao'. In Chinese, 'a long long life' translates as 'ten thousand years of no ending', so there was a character 'no' in it. Mother got the characters mixed up and it became 'no years of no ending'. It was an accident my mother said. She had a severe headache when she was ordered to do the job. She was not allowed to rest when her blood pressure was high. She did not understand why she wrote it the way she did. She always loved Mao, she confessed. She was criticized at the weekly political meeting that everyone in the district had to attend. They said she had an evil intention. She should be treated as a criminal. My mother did not know how to explain herself. She did not know what to do.

I drafted a self-criticism speech for my mother. I was twelve years old. I wrote Mao's famous quotations. I said, Chairman Mao teaches us, 'We must allow people to correct their mistakes.' That's the only way great Communism is learned. A mistake made by an innocent is not a crime. But when an innocent is not allowed to correct her mistake, it is a crime. To disobey Mao's teaching is a crime.

My mother read my draft at her school meeting and she was forgiven. Mother came home and said to me that she was very lucky to have a smart child like me.

But the next week Mother was caught again. She used a piece of newspaper that had Mao's picture on it to wipe her shit in the toilet room. We all did our wiping with newspaper in those days because very few people could afford toilet paper. Mother showed a doctor's letter at the masses' weekly meeting. It proved that her blood pressure was extremely high when the incident took place. She was not forgiven this time. She was sent to be reformed through hard labour in a shoe factory. The factory made rubber boots. Each pair weighed ten pounds. Her job was to take the boots off the moulds. Eight hours a day. Every evening she came home and collapsed.

When Mother stepped through the door she would slide right down on a chair. She sat there, motionless, as if passed out. I would have Blooming get a wet towel and a jar of water, Coral a bamboo fan, Space Conqueror a cup of water, and I myself would take off Mother's shoes. We then waited quietly until she woke up, and we would begin our service. Mother would smile happily and be served. I would do the wiping of her back, with Blooming fanning. Coral would re-soak the towel and pass it back to me while Space Conqueror changed the water. By then we would hear our father's steps on the staircase. We would expect him to open the door and make a mock-face.

We often ran out of food by the end of the month. We would turn into starving animals. In hunger, Coral once dug out a drug bottle from the closet and chewed down pink-coloured pills for constipation. She thought they were sweets. Her intestines were damaged. Space Conqueror gorged fruit skins and cores he picked from the rubbish box on the street. Blooming and I drank water while longing for the day to end.

Mother received her salary on the fifth day of each month and we would wait for her at the bus station on that day. When the bus door opened, Mother popped down with her face glittering. We would jump on her like monkeys. She would take us to a nearby bakery to have a full meal. We would keep taking in food until our stomachs became as hard as melons. Mother was the happiest woman on earth at those moments. It was the only day she did not look ill.

My father did not know how to make shoes, but he made shoes for all of us. The shoes he made looked like little boats because the soles he bought were too small to match the top. He drilled and sewed them together anyway. He used a screwdriver. Every Sunday he repaired our shoes, his fingers wrapped in bandages. He did that until Blooming and I learned how to make shoes with rags.

One day Mother came home with a lot of drug bottles. She came from the hospital. She had tuberculosis and was told to wear a surgical mask at home. Mother said that in a way she was pleased to have the disease because she finally got to spend time with her family.

I became a Mao activist in the district and won contests because I was able to recite the Little Red Book. I became an opera fan. There were not many forms of entertainment. The word 'entertainment' was considered a dirty bourgeois word. The opera was something else. It was a proletarian statement. The revolutionary operas created by Madam Mao, Comrade Jiang Ching. To love or not love the operas was a serious political attitude. It meant taking sides: to be or not to be a revolutionary. The operas were taught on radio and in school and were promoted by the neighbourhood organizations. For ten years. The same operas. I listened to the operas when I ate, walked and slept. I grew up with the opera. They became my cells. I decorated the porch with posters of my favourite opera heroines. I sang the operas wherever I went. My mother heard me singing in my dreams, she said that I was pickled in the operas. It was true. I could not go on a day without listening to the operas. I pasted my ear close to the radio, figuring out the singer's breaths. I imitated her. The aria was called 'I won't quit the battle until all the beasts are killed'. It was sung by Iron Plum, a teenage character in an opera called *Legend of the Red Lantern*. I would not stop singing the aria until my vocal chords hurt. I went on pushing my voice to its highest pitch:

My dad is a pine tree, his will is strong
A hero of indomitable spirit, he is a true Communist
I follow you,
Walk up with you and never hesitate.
I raise the red lantern high,
The light guides me on.
I follow you to beat the beasts,
My generation and the next . . .

I was able to recite all the librettos of the operas: *The Red Lantern, Outwit of the Tiger Mountain, Sha-Jia Pond, The Harbour, A Raid on White Tiger Regiment, The Red Detachment of Women, Song of the Dragon River.* My father could not bear my loud wailing with the radio, he always yelled, Are you hanging yourself in the kitchen?

紅 杜 鵑

G randma from the countryside brought us a young hen. The Old Tailor next door was impressed by a mass of dark brown feathers by her mouth when he first saw her. He said, She has Karl Marx's beard! The hen was then named Big Beard. Big Beard was Grandma and Grandpa's pet. They had had her since she was two days old. When Grandma was too poor to afford her, she had a hard time killing her for a meal. She brought her to Shanghai and told us to eat Big Beard for her. Big Beard is too young to produce eggs, said Grandma. A hen is worthless if she cannot produce eggs. Big Beard made a go-go-go sound and inclined her head when she heard the comments. Her crown was very very red, like a piece of burning coal. Steam it with sorghum wine, said Grandma. You won't find any taste like that. We asked

Grandma to have Big Beard with us but she shook her head quickly and said, You eat it, I am allergic to chicken meat. She took up her luggage and walked, almost ran, away. Her small feet could hardly catch her steps.

So who was going to kill Big Beard? Not me, said my father. I am not even interested in eating it since you let me see it . . . Father stared at Big Beard. Big Beard inclined her head from side to side and made a go-go-go sound, then soothed her feathers with her mouth. Father went back to his desk. Big Beard flapped her wings towards Mother. Oh no, not me, said Mother, I can't kill anything, you know. She looked at me, so did the children. I knew what they were saying: You are the bravest. You should be the butcher.

I said, I will. No big deal. I've made good dishes out of live pigeons, crabs and frogs. A hen, in ten minutes, I could have its feathers pulled off, just like the way I always watched those ducks get sliced by the neck in the food market. The butchers hung them by the feet, let their blood drip clean, sank them in boiling water, took them out and mopped off the feathers.

My sisters and brother nodded at me. They never doubted my determination. Mother said, Take it to the yard, just don't let me hear anything. Wait, she pulled my sleeve. Maybe we should give it to the people upstairs. Why? we all asked. I just hate to see my children kill. This was Mother. She made us miss a lot of fun. She made us free the birds we caught, the kitten we found. I said, We'll do it in the yard. There won't be any noise. This hen was worth at least five yuan in the market. A person's five-day salary, just think about it. Mother went quiet as I took Big Beard by the wings. Big Beard made more go-go-go sounds as she struggled in my hands. Space Conqueror said, Don't cry, it's not that bad, we're sending you to Karl Marx where you can compare beards together. I said, Shut up, Space Conqueror, go and get me the big scissors. Before Space Conqueror took off, I was suddenly bitten. Big Beard, the hen, bit me. Her mouth was like a pair of scissors. I loosened my grip. She flew up and down by the stair-

24

case. After hitting the ceiling a few times, she crashed on the cement yard.

She lay there, the hen, Big Beard, on her stomach, on the cement yard, with one of her wings dangling on the side, limp. Go . . . go . . . go . . . she shivered, trying to stand up again. She fell, dragging the wing around. We looked at each other, then at Big Beard. Her wing is broken, said Coral. Space Conqueror passed me the big scissors. I said, No, I can't kill her now. She is wounded. Not me, said Blooming. Nor me, said Coral. No way will it be me, Space Conqueror said and began to cry. You always take advantage of me. He ran towards the window. Raising his head he yelled, Mother, they are taking advantage of me again!

We decided to postpone the killing. We wouldn't do it until Big Beard's broken wing was healed. We made a home for Big Beard in the kitchen by the sink. We went out to find her dry straw. We made a nest-like wreath. She sat on it quietly. We watched her for hours on end. She sat there, her head under her wing, her little body hot. The heat came from under her feathers. She's having a fever, said Mother. She's infected. What, what should we do? We all became nervous. I have my antibiotic pills, but I don't know if . . . It will be good for Big Beard if it's good for a human, said Blooming. Big Beard acts almost like a human. She really does, said Coral, smoothing the hen's feathers. Look, she knew she would be killed so she went to crush herself and broke her wing.

We were all tapping the hen carefully with our fingers. Big Beard looked at us gently. Go-go-go-go. Go-go-go-go. She's in pain, Mother, we all said. Please give her the antibiotic pills.

Mother put a spoonful of antibiotics into Big Beard's mouth as we held her body. Coral and Space Conqueror held the feet, Blooming and I the wings. Big Beard was cooperative. After that she shit around the kitchen then went to sleep when we began our dinner. We couldn't eat the dinner. The hen made our small kitchen smell of shit. Big Beard occupied the whole corner of the kitchen, we could only crowd into our seats. We were all thinking about the sick hen as we ate. I would like to see you keep the kitchen clean, I mean keep the smell away, said Mother. Do you hear me? She looked at us. We raked the rice into our mouths. Do you hear your mother? said Father. Or I will give the hen away tonight.

We begged and promised that we would keep the kitchen clean. We went out to our neighbours to get stove ashes. We covered Big Beard's shit with ashes and shovelled it into the bin. We fed Big Beard with worms, chopped bones, rice and all kinds of vegetables. She gained weight. Her crown became redder. We talked to her, sang songs to her, hoping she would produce eggs soon. But she disappointed us. She grew prettier, her feathers shining and her claws strong, but still no eggs. We lost interest in serving her. You clean! I pointed at Blooming. You clean! Blooming pointed to Coral. You! Coral to Space Conqueror. Space Conqueror pointed us to Mother, Mother, they are taking advantage of me again!

Kill the hen! ordered my father. I said I needed to study for an examination this weekend. We do too, said the children. Then do it on Monday, said Father. All right, Monday, I promised.

I sharpened the scissors on Monday at noon. There was no one home. I stared at Big Beard. She stared back. She looked nervous. She was searching around and was unusually anxious. Her face was so red. She went to sit on the wreath then stood up and walked around, back and forth, back and forth. I got curious. I moved closer to observe her. She did not like it. She went to hide herself under a chair near a drainage pipe. I sensed that she wanted privacy. I did not want to leave. I stood up trying to think of a way to watch her without being seen. There was a mirror above the sink. I had an idea. I climbed on top of the kitchen table and lay on my back. I turned the mirror to an angle where I could see Big Beard and she would not see me.

After about five minutes, Big Beard got up from the wreath. She looked around as if to make sure there was no one in the kitchen. She used her mouth to arrange the straw in the wreath and began to spread her legs. She was in a funny pose, not kneeling and not standing. Her tail began to bend down to cover her anus. She stayed in that pose. Her body swelled. She was pushing inside. Was she producing an egg? I held my breath and stared at the mirror. Big Beard disappeared in the mirror, she moved to an angle where I could not see her. I did not want to scare her, so I waited patiently. A few minutes later, Big Beard got into the scene again and turned towards me at a perfect angle. I saw her anus was enlarged, and a pinkish-white thing was coming out. It's an egg! Big Beard spread her legs further, her face turning purple. She went back to the funny pose, pushed and pushed. Finally she stood up. I saw an egg in the wreath.

I jumped down from the table and carefully picked the egg from the wreath. It was warm. The shell was thin, almost transparent. There were blood dots on the shell. I looked at Big Beard. She looked back at me modestly. I hugged her as she began to sing. Go-go-go La! Go-go-go La! Her cackle was so loud, so proud.

Coral carried Big Beard to the bed. She thought this would provide her with a good rest after such a hard labour. We all kneeled in front of the bed and talked to Big Beard. We passed the egg around. Space Conqueror got a pen and I wrote the date on the egg. Blooming went to find a box and carefully put the egg in with soft papers and stored it under her bed.

When our parents got in we told them the big news. We said that since Big Beard started to produce eggs there was no reason to kill her any more. Eggs were the most expensive thing in the market. My parents agreed but said they would not eat Big Beard's eggs. We said we would save the eggs for house guests.

Big Beard became the centre of our attention. Each day after school we went to dig worms. Space Conqueror climbed the trees for bigger worms. Big Beard became picky in taste. She began to take only live worms. She produced one egg every two days and soon the box was full.

But Big Beard's good life did not last. That summer the neighbourhood Party committee launched a Patriotic Public Health

Campaign and all the dogs, ducks and chickens had to be killed in three days. We tried to hide Big Beard but we could not shut her up. Every time she dropped an egg she had to pronounce her mother's pride. The committee, a group of retired old people, came to our door to shout slogans to mobilize us. We pretended not to hear them at first. When they came nearer, waving their little paper flags in their hands, we got nervous. We held Big Beard under the window and covered her with blankets. The old people shouted their voices hoarse and their breaths broken. The slogan was, 'Do not raise duck and hen in the city!' It later became, 'Do not raise duck . . .' The old man who was leading the shout lost his breath here; he stopped, catching his breath, he went on, '. . . raise hen in the city!' The slogan shouters did not care what they shouted, they just repeated where the old man had stopped, so they went, 'Do not raise duck!' After the old man regained his voice they followed, 'Raise hen in the city!'

The head of the neighbourhood Party committee came to talk with me. He asked why I was not behaving as a head of the Little Red Guard should. He asked if I still wanted to be voted a Mao's Loyalist in the coming year. I understood what I had to do. I promised to kill Big Beard the next morning. He said that he and his committee would come and check on me by seven-thirty. He wanted to have Big Beard's head.

I had a bad sleep as I had expected. I got up at dawn. Big Beard was already up eating her breakfast in the dark. Hearing me come in, she made her go-go-go sound. I took the scissors and picked up Big Beard by the wings. I went down to the yard. Upstairs Little Coffin had already come back from the food market. I asked her what time it was. She replied that it was five to seven. I kept telling myself, No big deal, Big Beard is only a hen, an animal, an enemy of public health. I raised up the scissors and put the scissors back down. I went back upstairs to fetch a bowl to collect Big Beard's blood. It was seven-fifteen. I came back down to the yard and realized I had forgotten another thing. I went back upstairs to boil water. I let Big Beard free in the yard. She seemed glad. Shaking her feathers she used her mouth to chop open my fist. She was playing with me. I went back up and the water was boiling. I took the hot-water container down and placed it next to the bowl. I grabbed Big Beard but she struggled away as if she sensed some danger. I chased her. She kneeled down in front of me. I picked her up and folded her head under her wing. I was using my full strength. I began to pull her beard off. My hands were weak. I made myself ignore it. I kept pulling until Big Beard's neck showed. I picked up the scissors. My arms were stiff. It was seven-twenty-five. Big Beard pulled her head out from under her wing. She looked at me, her face was red. She kept struggling. I heard the neighbourhood committee's drum beating in the next lane. I folded Big Beard's head back under her wing. I raised my scissors and aimed at her neck. She struggled violently. It was seven-thirty. The bell of the Wu-Lee Hardware Workshop rang; the women poured in. The committee people arrived at the door, the slogan-shouting was like waves rising and falling. I clapped the scissors. Big Beard pulled her head out and made a go-go-go sound. She pushed an egg out of her body.

I could not look. I brought the scissors down. When I could look again I saw Big Beard flying over everybody's head, dripping blood on her way. My sisters and brother were looking down from the window. Big Beard was on a tree, almost as high as our window, then she dropped down on the white cement ground.

I ran upstairs. I said I could not touch the hen again. No one in my family would. Big Beard lay dead on the cement yard, next to the bowl and a container of boiled water. The egg was stepped on. When the water got cold Little Coffin came to me and asked what I was going to do with the hen. It's going to spoil, she said. I begged her to take it. I said it would make a good dish to go with wine. I knew her father and grandfather were alcoholics. She took it.

I went upstairs after dinner. Little Coffin's family was in a Mao seminar. Big Beard had become a handful of bones lying in a bin in the corner. Little Coffin told me that Big Beard tasted excellent.

紅 杜 鵑

In school, Mao's books were our texts. I was at the head of the class on the History of the Communist Party of China. To me, history meant how proletarians won over the reactionaries. Western history was a history of capitalist exploitation. We hung portraits of Marx, Engels, Lenin and Stalin next to Mao in our classrooms. Each morning, we bowed to them as well as bowing to Mao, praying for a long long life for him. My sisters copied my compositions. My compositions were collected slogans. I always began with this: 'The East wind is blowing, the fighting, drumming, is beating. Who is afraid in the world today? It is not the people who are afraid of American Imperialists. It is the American Imperialists who are afraid of the people.' Those phrases won me prizes. Space Conqueror looked up to me as if I were a magician. For me, compositions were nothing; it was abacus competitions that were difficult. I wrote compositions for my brother and sisters, but I felt I had not much in common with the children. I felt like an adult. I longed for challenges. I was at the school day and night promoting Communism, making revolution by painting slogans on walls and boards. I led my schoolmates in collecting pennies. We wanted to donate the pennies to the starving children in America. We were proud of what we did. We were sure that we were making red dots on the world's map. We were fighting for the final peace of the planet. Not for a day did I not feel heroic. I was the opera.

I was asked to attend the school's Revolutionary Committee meeting. It was 1970, and I was thirteen years old. I discussed how to carry on the Cultural Revolution at our Long Happiness Elementary School with the Committee people, the true revolutionaries. When I raised my hand and said I would like to speak, my face would no longer flush. I knew what I was talking about. Phrases from the *People's Daily* and *Red Flag* magazine poured out of my mouth. My speeches were filled with an impassioned and noble spirit. I was honoured. In the early seventies my being a head of the Little Red Guard at middle school brought our family honour. My award certificates were my mother's pride, although she never hung them on the wall. My name was constantly mentioned by the school authorities and praised as 'Study Mao Thoughts Activist', 'Mao's Good Child' and 'Student of Excellence'. Whenever I spoke through a microphone in the school's broadcasting station, my sisters and brother would be listening in their classrooms and their classmates would look at them with admiration and envy.

The school's new Party secretary, a man named Chain, was a worker's representative from the Shanghai Shipping Factory. He was about fifty years old, extremely thin, like a bamboo stick. He taught me how to hold political meetings. He liked to say, We have to let our little general play a full role in the Cultural Revolution and give full scope to the initiative of the Little Red Guards. He told me not to be afraid of things that I did not understand. You must learn to think like this, he said: If the earth stops spinning, I'll continue to spin.

It was the first week of November when Secretary Chain called me in. He told me excitedly that the committee had finally dug out a hidden class enemy, an American spy. He said, We are going to have a meeting against her, a rally which two thousand people will be attending. You will be the student representative to speak against her. I asked who it was. Wrinkling his eyebrows, the Secretary pronounced a shocking name. It was Autumn Leaves, my teacher. I thought I had heard Secretary Chain wrong. But he nodded at me slowly confirming that I heard him exactly right.

31

I sat down. I actually dropped down on the chair. My legs all of a sudden lost their strength.

She was a thin, middle-aged lady and was seriously near-sighted. She wore a pair of dark glasses and had a hoarse voice and a short temper. She loved Chinese, mathematics and music. The first day she stepped into the classroom she asked all the students if any of us could tell what her name 'Autumn Leaves' meant. No one was able to figure it out. Then she explained it. She said that there was a famous poem written in the Tang Dynasty about autumn leaves. It praised the beauty and significance of the falling leaves. It said that when a leaf fell naturally, it symbolized a full life. The touch of the ground meant the transformation of a ripe leaf to fresh mud. It fertilized the seeds through the winter. Its pregnancy came to term with the next spring. She said that we were her spring.

She was an energetic teacher who never seemed to be tired of teaching. Her methods were unique. One moment she raised her arms to shoulder-level and stretched them out to the sides, making herself look like a cross, when explaining infinity; the next moment she spoke with a strong Hunan accent when explaining where a poet was from. Once she completely lost her voice while trying to explain geometric progression to me. When she finally made me understand, she laughed silently like a mute with her arms dancing in the air. When I thanked her she said she was glad that I was serious about learning. She set me up as the example for our class and then the entire grade. When she knew that I wanted to improve my Chinese, she brought me her own books to read. She was this way with all her students. One day when it was raining hard after class, she gave students her raincoat, rain shoes and her umbrella as they went home. She herself went home wet. The next day she had a fever, but she came to class and struggled on, despite her fever. By the time she finished her lecture, she had lost her voice again. There was no way I could picture Autumn Leaves as an American spy.

As if reading my mind, Secretary Chain smiled and asked me if I had ever heard the phrase, 'Raging flames refine the real gold.' I shook my head. He said, It is time for you to test yourself out to see whether you are a real revolutionary or an armchair revolutionary. He recited a Mao quotation. 'To have a revolution is not like having a dinner party, not like painting a pretty picture or making embroidery. It is not that easy and relaxing. Revolution is an insurrection in which one class overthrows the other with violent force.'

I found my words were blocked by my stiff tongue. I kept saying, Autumn Leaves is my teacher. Secretary Chain suggested that we work on my problem. He lit a cigarette and told me the fable of 'A Wolf in Sheep's Skin'. He said Autumn Leaves was the wolf. He told me that Autumn Leaves's father was a Chinese American who was still living in America. Autumn Leaves was born and educated in America. Secretary Chain said, The capitalist sent his daughter back to China to educate our children. Don't you see this as problematic?

For the next two hours Secretary Chain convinced me that Autumn Leaves was a secret agent of the Imperialists and was using teaching as a weapon to destroy our minds. Secretary Chain asked whether I would tolerate that. Of course not, I said. No one can pull our proletarians back to the old society. Good, said Secretary Chain tapping my shoulders. He said he knew I would be a sharp spear for the Party. I raised my head and said, Secretary, please tell me what to do. He said, Write a speech. I asked what I should write. He said, Tell the masses how you were mentally poisoned. I said that I did not quite understand the words 'mentally poisoned'. Secretary Chain said, You are not mature enough to understand that yet. He then asked me to give an opinion on what kind of person I thought Autumn Leaves was. I told him the truth.

Secretary Chain laughed loudly at me. He said that I had already become a victim of the spy who had almost killed me with the skill of the wolf who killed the sheep leaving no trace of blood. He punched his fist on the table and said loudly, That in itself is wonderful material to be discussed! I felt awkward. He stopped laughing and said, You shouldn't be discouraged by your immaturity.

He made me feel disappointed with myself. Let me help you, he suggested. He asked me the name of the books she loaned me. *An Old Man of Invention*, I began to recall, *The Little Mermaid* and *Snow White*. He asked for the author's name. I said it was something like Andersen.

Secretary Chain suddenly raised his hand in the air and furrowed his brow. He said, Stop, this is it. Who is Andersen? An old foreign man I guess, I replied. What were his fairy tales about? About the lives of princes, princesses and little people. What does Andersen do now? he asked. I do not know, I replied.

Look how careless you are! Secretary Chain almost yelled at me. He could be a foreign spy! Taking out a little glass vial, Secretary Chain put a few pills into his mouth. He explained that it was the medicine for his liver pain. He said his liver was hurting badly but he could not tell his doctor about it because he would be hospitalized immediately. He said his pain was getting worse but he could not afford to waste a second in the hospital. How can I disappoint Chairman Mao, who put his trust in people like us, the working class, the class that was even lower than the pigs and dogs before the Liberation?

His face was turning purple. I suggested that he take a rest. He waved me to go on as he pressed his liver with his hands to endure the pain. He told me that he did not have much schooling. His parents died of hunger when he was five. His brother and little sister were thrown into the sea after they died of cholera. He was sold to a child dealer for fifteen pounds of rice. He became a child worker in a shipping factory in Shanghai and was often beaten by the owner. After the Liberation, he joined the Party and was sent to a workers' night school. He said, I owe our Party a great deal and I haven't worked hard enough to show my appreciation.

I looked at him and was touched. His pain seemed to be increasing. His fingers pressed against his liver harder, but he refused to rest. You know we found Autumn Leaves's diary and it had a paragraph about you, he said. What . . . what did she say about me? I became nervous. She said that you were one of the very few children who were educable. She put quotation marks around 'educable'. Can you think of what that means? Without waiting for my reply Secretary Chain concluded, It is obvious that Autumn Leaves thinks that you can be educated into her type, her father's type, the Imperialists' type. He pointed out that the purpose of writing this diary was to present it to her American boss as proof of her success as a spy.

My world turned upside down. I felt deeply hurt and used. Secretary Chain asked me whether I was aware of the fact that I was set up as a model by Autumn Leaves to influence the others. Her goal is to make you all *betray* Communism! I felt the guilt and anger. I said to Secretary Chain that I would speak tomorrow. He nodded at me. He said, Our Party trusts you and Mao would be very proud of you.

Pull out the hidden class enemy, the American spy Autumn Leaves! Expose her under the bare sun! the crowd shouted as soon as the meeting started. I was sitting on the stage on one of the risers. Two strong men escorted Autumn Leaves on to the stage facing the crowd of two thousand people including her students and colleagues. Her arms were twisted behind her. She was almost unrecognizable. Only a few days had passed since I had seen her, but it seemed as though she had aged ten years. Her hair had suddenly turned grey. Her face was colourless. A rectangular board reading 'Down with American Spy' hung from her neck. Two men forced her to bow to Mao's portrait three times. One of the men bent her left arm very hard and said, Beg Chairman Mao for forgiveness now! Autumn Leaves refused to say the words. The two men bent her arms up backwards. They bent them harder. Autumn Leaves's face contorted in pain and then her mouth moved. She said the words and the men let her loose.

My mouth was terribly dry. It was hard to bear what I saw. The string of the heavy board seemed to cut into Autumn Leaves's skin. I forgot what I was supposed to do – to lead the crowd to shout the slogans – until Secretary Chain came to remind me of my duty.

Long live the great proletarian dictatorship! I shouted, following the slogan menu. I was getting more and more scared when I saw Autumn Leaves struggling with the two men who had been trying to press her head towards the floor while she tried to face the sky. When her glasses fell off, I saw her eyes close tightly.

Secretary Chain shouted at her. The crowd shouted Confess! Confess! Secretary Chain took the microphone and said that the masses would not have much patience. By acting this way Autumn Leaves was digging her own grave.

Autumn Leaves kept silent. When kicked hard, she said that she had nothing to confess. She said she was innocent. Our Party never accuses anyone who is innocent, said Secretary Chain, and yet the Party would never allow a class enemy to slip away from the net of the proletarian dictatorship. He said now it was time to demonstrate that Autumn Leaves was a criminal. He nodded at me and turned to the crowd. He said, Let's have the victim speak out!

I stood up and felt dizzy. The crowd began clapping their hands. The sunlight was dazzlingly bright and was hurting my eyes. My vision became blurred and I saw a million bees wheeling in front of me sounding like helicopters. As the crowd kept clapping, I moved to the front of the stage. I stopped in front of the microphone. Taking out the speech I had written last night, I suddenly felt a need to speak with my parents. I was afraid. I had not gone home last night but slept in the classroom on the table with other Little Red Guards. Five of us wrote the speech. I regretted not having my parents go over the speech with me. I took a deep

36

breath. My fingers were shaking and would not obey me in turning the pages.

Don't be afraid, we are all with you, Secretary Chain said in my ear as he came to adjust the height of the microphone. He placed a cup of water in front of me. I took the water and drank it down in one breath. I felt a little better. I began to read.

I read to the crowd that Autumn Leaves was the wolf in sheep's skin. I took out the books she loaned me and showed them to the crowd. As I was delivering my speech, I saw from the corner of my eye that Autumn Leaves had turned her head in my direction. She was murmuring. I became nervous but managed to continue. Comrades, I said, now I understand why Autumn Leaves was so kind to me. She was trying to turn me into an enemy of our country, and a running dog of the Imperialists! I read on.

There was some slogan-shouting, during which I glanced secretly at Autumn Leaves. She was breathing hard and was about to fall. I stood, my limbs were turning cold. I tried to remove my eyes from Autumn Leaves, but she caught them. I was terrified when I saw her staring at me without her glasses. Her eyes looked like two ping-pong balls that almost popped out of her eye sockets.

The crowd shouted, Confess! Confess! Autumn Leaves began to speak slowly to the crowd with her hoarse voice. She said that she would never want to turn any of her students into the country's enemy. She broke into tears. Why would I? she repeated again and again. She was losing her voice. She began to swing her head trying to project her words but no sound came out. She said that her father loved this country and that was the reason she came back to teach. Both her father and she believed in education. Spy? What are you talking about? Where did you get this idea? She looked at me.

If the enemy doesn't surrender, let's boil her, fry her and burn her to death! Secretary Chain shouted. The crowd followed, shouting and waving their fists. Secretary Chain signalled for me

37

to go on. But I was trembling too hard to continue. Secretary Chain walked to the microphone from the back of the stage. He took over the microphone. He told the crowd that this was a class enemy's live performance. It had given us an opportunity to learn how deceitful an enemy could be. Can we allow her to go on like this? No! the crowd shouted.

Secretary Chain was ordering Autumn Leaves to shut up and accept the criticism of the revolutionary masses with a correct attitude. Autumn Leaves said that she could not accept any untrue facts. Autumn Leaves said that a young girl such as me should not be used by someone with an evil intention.

You underestimated our Little Red Guard's political awareness, Secretary Chain said with a scornful laugh. Autumn Leaves demanded to speak to me. Secretary Chain told her to go ahead. He said that as a thorough-going dialectical materialist he never underestimated the role of teachers by negative example.

As the crowd quietened down, Autumn Leaves squatted on her heels to seek her glasses on the floor. When she put her glasses back on she started to question me. I was scared. I did not expect that she would talk to me so seriously. My terror turned into fury. I wanted to get away. I said, How dare you put me in such a spot to be questioned like a reactionary? You have used me in the past to serve the Imperialists; now you want to use me to get away from the criticism. It would be a shame if I lost to you!

Autumn Leaves called my name and asked if I really believed that she was an enemy of the country. If I did not think so could I tell her who assigned me to do the speech. She said she wanted the truth. She said Chairman Mao always liked to have children show their honesty. She asked me with the exact same tone she used when she helped me with my homework. Her eyes were demanding me to focus on them. I could not bear looking at her eyes. They had looked at me when the magic of mathematics was explained; they had looked at me when the beautiful Little Mermaid story was told. When I won the first place in the Calculation with Abacus Competition, they had looked at me with joy; when I was ill, they had looked at me with sympathy and love. I had not realized the true value of what all this meant to me until I lost it for ever that day at the meeting.

I heard people shouting at me. My head felt like a boiling teapot. Autumn Leaves's eyes behind the thick glasses now were like gun barrels shooting at me with fire. Just be honest! Her hoarse voice raised to its extreme. I turned to Secretary Chain. He nodded at me as if to say, Are you going to lose to an enemy? He was smiling scornfully. Think about the snake, he said.

Yes, the snake, I remembered. It was a story Mao told in his book. It was about a peasant who found a frozen snake lying in his path on a snowy day. The snake had the most beautiful skin the peasant had ever seen. He felt sorry for her and decided to save her life. He picked up the snake and put her into his jacket to warm her with the heat of his body. Soon the snake woke up and felt hungry. She bit her saviour. The peasant died. Our Chairman's point is, Secretary Chain said as he ended the story, that to our enemy we must be absolutely cruel and merciless.

I turned to look at the wall-sized portrait of Mao. It was mounted on the back of the stage. The Chairman's eyes looked like two swinging lanterns. I was reminded of my duty. I must fight against anyone who dared to oppose Mao's teaching. The shouting of the slogans encouraged me.

Show us your standpoint, Secretary Chain said. He passed me the microphone. I did not know why I was crying. I heard myself calling for my parents as I took the microphone. I said, Mama, Papa, where are you? The crowd waved their angry fists at me and shouted Down! Down! Down! I was so scared, scared of losing Secretary Chain's trust, and scared of not being able to denounce Autumn Leaves. Finally, I gathered all my strength and yelled hysterically at Autumn Leaves with tears in my throat: Yes, yes, yes, I do believe that you poisoned me; and I do believe that you are a true enemy! Your dirty tricks will have no more

39

effect on me! If you dare to try them on me again, I'll shut you up! I'll use a needle to stitch your lips together!

Ten years later, after the Cultural Revolution, when I heard that Autumn Leaves was invited back after retirement to the Long Happiness Elementary School as a senior adviser, I went to visit her, intending to apologize.

Since I knew Autumn Leaves had a habit of working early in the office, I went at seven o'clock in the morning in late spring. The shadow of tree leaves projected by the sun on the ground looked like a huge net. As I walked through the campus, I thought that a beaten street-dog must feel the way I was feeling: sick, tired and cheap.

The stage where I delivered my speech was still there but was washed greenish and had rotted through the years. As I stepped into the building where I used to attend classes, I could feel my blood start to run fast and my legs get heavy. I pulled myself to the fifth-grade office. The door was wide open. Autumn Leaves was sitting alone in front of her desk, reading. I felt time had stopped. Nothing had changed a bit. I had never grown up.

I could not make myself move. I stood for a while trying to get my courage together. Autumn Leaves looked the same although all her hair had turned white. Her heavily wrinkled hands trembled slightly as she turned a page. Feeling my presence, she put down the book. Raising her eyes behind the thick glasses, she looked at me. The pupils – how familiar they were to me! My heart pumped so hard that I could hear thunder rolling in my chest. Her eyes turned cold and hard as she seemed to recognize me. When she turned her head slowly away, I went up and told her my name and the reason I had come.

There was a silence. The intensity in her eyes began to subside, I heard the familiar hoarse voice say, 'I am very sorry, I don't remember you. I don't think I ever had you as my student.'

紅 杜 鵑

When I was seventeen, life changed to a different world. The school's vice principal had a talk with me after his talks with many others. He told me that he wanted to remind me that I was a student leader, a model to the graduates. The policy was there, as strict as maths equations. He told me that I belonged to one category. The category of becoming a peasant. He said it was an unalterable decision. The policy from Beijing was a holy instruction. It was universally accepted. It was incumbent upon me to obey. He said he had sent four of his own children to work in the countryside. He was very proud of them. He said many more words. Words of abstractions. Words like songs. He said when one challenges the heaven, it brings pleasure; when one challenges the earth, it brings pleasure; when one challenges one's own kind, it brings the biggest pleasure. He was reciting the poem by Mao. He said a true Communist loves to take challenges. She would take them with dignity. I was seventeen. I was inspired. I was eager to devote myself. I was looking forward to hardship.

I listened to the stories of the neighbourhood. My next-door neighbour wrote from his village and said that he had purposely hammered his finger at work in order to claim injury for a chance to be sent back home. Little Coffin's big sister went to the northern border and wrote that her roommate was shot as a traitor when she tried to escape to the USSR. My cousin who went to Inner Mongolia wrote and said that his close friend died while putting out a mountain fire. He was honoured as a hero: he saved the village's grain storage at the expense of his life. My cousin said the hero made him understand the true meaning of life so he decided to spend the rest of his life on horseback in Mongolia to model himself after the hero.

Among the gossip, I heard that the Li family's daughter was raped by a village head in the South-west province; the Yang family's son was honoured for killing a bear that had eaten his coworker in a forest at a northern farm. These families were upset. They took the horror stories to the local Party administrators. The letters were shown. But the families were told not to believe such monstrous lies because they were made up by enemies who feared the revolution spreading. The Party authorities showed the families pictures of the places where their children had gone; pictures of prosperity. The families were convinced and comforted. The family upstairs sent their second and third child to the countryside. Little Coffin's parents were honoured with certificates and red paper flowers for the family had sent three children to the countryside. Their doors and walls were pasted with big poster-sized letters of congratulation.

Finally, my name appeared on the school's Glorious Red List – I was assigned to the Red Fire Farm which was located near the shore area of the East China Sea. The next day, I was ordered to go to a city building to cancel my Shanghai residency.

It was a cold afternoon. The city building had no lights. The clerks worked in the shadows. It was in the shadows that I began my heroic journey. The officer passed me back my family's resident registration book. I saw my name blotted out by a red stamp. The red stamp, the symbol of authority. That afternoon, I felt like a bare egg laid on a rock. Maybe I would come to a real birth or maybe I would be smashed by the paw of some unfamiliar creature. I realized at that moment that it was much too easy to sing, 'I'll go where Chairman Mao's finger points'. I remembered how I sang that song. I never realized what I was singing until that day.

I sat in the dark. And my family sat with me. And the day came.

PART TWO

紅杜鵑

O n the morning of the fifteenth of April 1974, my family accompanied me to the People's Square. Ten huge trucks were parked in the centre of the square. Red flags with characters the colour of gold were tied to the side of every truck proclaiming 'Red Fire Farm'. The flags were blown to their full size, as bright as the colour of fresh blood.

I registered. A woman of about twenty-five, with short hair cut to the ears and half-moon-shaped eyes, greeted me. She was warm. She introduced herself as Comrade Lu. She said congratulations to me repeatedly and leaned over my shoulder and said, Be proud of yourself! She smiled. The half-moon eyes became quarter moons. She shook hands with me and tied a red paper flower to the front of my blouse. She said, Hey, Smiling, we are family now.

I got on a less-crowded truck. My father passed me my suitcases. Mother looked ill. Blooming and Coral went to hold her arms. Space Conqueror stared at me. His deep-set eyes were two wells of chaos. My father waved at me and forced a smile. Now get out of here, he said, trying in vain to be funny.

My family stood in front of me, as if taking a dull picture. It was a picture of sadness, a picture of never-the-same. I was out of the picture.

I wanted to tell my family to leave because the longer they stayed the more bitter I grew. But I was not able to say anything. I was too sad to say anything. But I was seventeen. I had courage. I turned towards the direction where the wind blew from. I said to the future, Now I am ready, come and test me!

When the trucks pulled away, the crowd moaned. It was a bad scene. Parents would not let go of their children's arms. I looked away. I thought of my heroic past, how I had always been proud to be a devoted revolutionary. I forced myself to feel proud, and that way I felt a little better. Comrade Lu saw me, saw that I did not wave goodbye to my family. She came to my side and said, Good guts. She asked us to sing a Mao quotation song. She led, 'Go to the countryside, go to the frontier, go to where our country needs us the most . . .'

We began to sing with Lu. Our voices were dry and weak like old sick cows. Lu waved her arms hard, trying to speed up the singing. People paid no attention to her. It was a moment when memory takes root. The moment youth began to fade. I stared at my parents who stood like frosted aubergines – with heads hanging weakly in front of their chests. My tears welled up. I sang loudly. I screamed. Lu said into my ear, Good guts. Good guts. Her arm was holding the flag of Red Fire Farm. The trucks advanced, facing the blowing wind. The dust blurred, the image of Shanghai faded.

On the truck, no one introduced themself to the others. Everyone sat right next to their luggage, listening to the roaring sound of the wind. We sat, as if mourning. In a few hours, we were greeted by the night stars of the sky. I started to miss my father. I thought of the night he dragged me, Blooming, Coral and Space Conqueror out of our beds at midnight to observe the Milky Way and the stars. He wanted us to be astronomers. The dream he had not had a chance to complete himself. It was as clear as tonight, the sky, the Milky Way, Jupiter, Mars, Venus and a man-made earth satellite in orbit . . .

It was in drowsiness that I smelled the East China Sea. Lu told us that we had arrived at Red Fire Farm. It was late afternoon. There was an ocean of endless sea-reeds. The trucks spread out in different directions. Like a little spider our truck crawled into the green. The sky felt so murky and short. Short like a reachable ceiling.

I got off the truck with tingling legs. In front of me were two rectangular grey-brick barracks standing on each side of me. Between the barracks there was a long public sink with many taps.

I saw people walk in and out of the barracks. People who looked tired, bored, in dusty clothes, with greasy hair. They paid no attention to us.

I was picking up my suitcases when I heard someone shout suddenly: Assemble! The commander is coming!

Commander? Was I in a military camp? Confused, I turned to Lu, who was staring tensely towards the east. Her smile had disappeared completely. She looked hard. I followed her eyes towards the open field. A small figure appeared on the horizon.

She was tall, well built and walked with authority. She wore an old People's Liberation Army uniform, washed almost white, and gathered at the waist with a three-inch-wide belt. She had two short thick braids. She had the look of a conqueror.

Stopping about five feet away from us, she smiled. She began to examine us one by one. She had a pair of fiery intense eyes, in which I saw the energy of a lion. She had weather-beaten skin, thick eyebrows, a bony nose, high cheekbones, a full mouth in the shape of a water chestnut. She had the shoulders of an ancient warlord, extravagantly broad. She was barefoot. Her sleeves and trousers were rolled halfway up. Her hands rested on her waist. When her eyes focused on mine, I trembled for no reason. She burned me with the sun in her eyes. I felt bare.

She began to speak. Her words carried no sound. People quietened down and a whisper-like voice was heard. Welcome, you new soldiers to Red Fire Farm who join us as . . . She cleared her throat and spat out the words one by one . . . as our fresh blood. She said she welcomed us to break out of the small world of our personal concerns to be part of an operation on such a grand scale. She said that we had just made our first step of the Long March. Suddenly raising her voice, she said that she wanted to introduce herself. She said, My name is Yan Sheng. Yan, as in discipline, Sheng as in victory. You can call me Yan. She said she was the Party secretary and commander of this company. A company that was making earth-shaking changes in everything. She lowered her voice again to a whisper. She said she did not really have much to say at an occasion

47

like this. But she did want to say one thing. Then she shouted, Don't any of you shit on my face! Don't any of you disappoint the glorious title of 'The Advanced Seventh Company', the model of the entire Red Fire Farm Army! She asked whether she had made her point clear. And we, startled, said, Yes!

Fanning her hand in front of her nose as if to get rid of some bad smell, she asked whether we wished not to be as weak as we were. She repeated her question again. She wanted to hear us say *yes*! in the proper manner of a soldier. And we shouted in one enthusiastic voice.

She said, That's better, and then smiled. Her smile was affectionate. But it lasted only three seconds. She looked hard again and told us that the farm had 13,000 members and our company four hundred. She said that she expected every one of us to function as a cog in a big revolutionary machine. Keep yourself up. Run, run and run, said she, because if you stop, you rust. She wanted us to remember that although we would not be given formal uniforms, we would be trained as real soldiers. She said, I never talk nonsense, never. This phrase of hers stuck in my mind for a long time, for it was expressed in such a rough-necked way.

As if blanketed by shock, no one moved after Yan called us to be dismissed. Lu raised her hand at Yan. And Yan took a step back from the ranks and introduced Lu as her deputy commander.

Lu said that she had a couple of things to say to the ranks. She marched in front of the ranks. Big smiles piled up on her face before she opened her mouth. With a surgical voice she said that although she was newly transferred to this company, she was an old member of the Communist Party family. She started to recite the history of the Communist Party beginning with its very first establishment meeting on a small boat near Shanghai. She talked and talked until the sun drew back its last ray and we were covered by the descending fog.

I was assigned to house number three, occupied by females. My room was about nine by fourteen feet, with four bunk beds.

I had seven roommates. The only private space was within the mosquito net that hung from thin bamboo sticks. The floor was packed earth.

The next day we were ordered to work in the rice fields. The leeches in the muddy water frightened me. A girl named Little Green was working alongside me. A leech was on her leg. When she tried to pull the leech out it went deeper. It soon disappeared into the skin leaving a black dot on the surface. She screamed in horror. I called up an experienced soldier named Orchid for help. Orchid came and patted the skin above the leech's head. The leech backed itself out. Little Green was very appreciative for my help and we became good friends.

紅 杜 鵑

Little Green was eighteen. She had the bed next to mine. She was pale, so pale that exposure to the sun all day did not change the colour of her skin. Her fingers were thin and fine. She spread pig shit as if she were arranging jewellery. She walked gracefully, like a willow in a soft breeze. Her long braids swayed on her back. She looked down at the floor whenever she spoke. She was shy. But she liked to sing. She told me that she was brought up by her grandmother, who used to be an opera singer before the Cultural Revolution. She inherited her voice. Her parents were assigned to work in remote oil fields because they were intellectuals. They came home once every year on New Year's eve. She never got to know her parents much but she knew all the old operas, though she never sang old operas in public. In public she sang 'My Motherland', a popular song since Liberation. Her voice was the platoon's pride. It helped us to get through the tough labour, through the days we had to get up at five and work in the fields until nine at night.

She was daring. Dared to decorate her beauty. She tied her braids with colourful strings while the rest of us tied our braids with brown rubber bands. Her femininity mocked us. I watched her and sensed the danger in her boldness. I used to be a head of the Red Guard. I knew the rules. I knew the thin line between right and wrong. I watched Little Green. Her beauty. I wanted to tie my braids with colourful strings every day. But I did not have the guts to show contempt for the rules. I had always been good.

I had to admit that she was beautiful. But I and all the other female soldiers said she was not. We tied on brown rubber bands. The colour of mud, of pig shit, of our minds. Because we believed that a true Communist should never care about the way she looked. The beauty of the soul was what should be cared about. Little Green never argued with anyone. She did not care what we said. She smiled at herself. She looked down on the floor. She smiled, from the heart, at herself, at her colourful string and was satisfied. No matter how tired she got, Little Green always walked forty-five minutes to a hot-water station and carried back water to wash herself. She cleaned the mud off her fingernails, patiently and gaily. Every evening, she washed herself in the net while I lay in my net, watching her, with my paw-like fingernails laid on my thighs.

Little Green proudly showed me how she used remnants of fabric to make pretty underwear, finely embroidered with flowers, leaves and birds. She hung a string next to the little window between our beds on which she could hang her underwear to dry. In our bare room the string was like an art gallery.

Little Green upset me. She upset the room, the platoon and the company. She caught our eyes. We could not help looking at her. The good-for-nothings could not take their eyes off her, that creature full of bourgeois allure. I scorned my own desire to display my youth. A nasty desire, I told myself a hundred times.

I was seventeen and a half. I admired Little Green's guts. The guts to redesign the clothes we were issued. She tapered her shirts at the waist; she remade her trousers so that the legs would look longer. She was not embarrassed by her full breasts. In the early evening, she would carry the two containers of hot water, her back straight, chest full. She walked towards our room singing. The sky behind her was velvet blue. The half-man-half-monkey male soldiers stared at her when she passed by. She was the Venus of the farm's evening. I envied and adored her. In June, she dared to go without a bra. I hated my bra when I saw her, saw her walking towards me, bosoms bouncing. She made me feel withered without ever having bloomed.

The days were long, so long. The work was endless. At five in the morning we were cutting the oil-bearing plants. The black seeds rolled on to my neck and into my shoes as I laid the plants down. I did not bother to wipe the sweat that was dripping and salted my eyes. I did not have the time. Our platoon was the fastest in the company. We soared like arrows. We advanced across the fields in staircase formation. When we worked, we were sunk into the sea of the plants. We barely straightened our backs. We had no time to straighten our backs. Little Green did, once in a while. She upset us. We threw unfriendly words out. We said, Shame on the lazybones! We did not stop until Little Green bent down to work again. We did this to every-one but Yan. Yan was a horse-rider. We were her horses. She did not have to whip us to get us moving. We felt the chill of a whip on the back when she walked by and examined our work. I watched her feet moving past me. I dared not raise my head. I paid attention to what my hands were doing. She stopped and watched me working. I cut and laid the plant neatly. I tried not to let the black seeds rain down. She passed by and I let out a breath.

*

A pair of Little Green's prettiest hand-embroidered underwear was stolen. It was considered an ideological crime. The company's Party committee called a meeting. It was held in the dining hall. Four hundred people all sat on little wooden stools. In rows. The question regarding the theft was brought up by Yan. No one admitted to the theft. Lu was indignant. She said she could not bear such behaviour. She said the fact of what was stolen shamed us all. She said the Party should launch a political campaign to prevent such behaviour from taking place. She said it should be more the fault of the company leaders than of the soldiers. Yan stood up. She apologized for being soft on watching her soldiers' minds. She apologized to the Party. She criticized Little Green for vanity. She ordered her to make a confession. She told Little Green that in the future she should not hang her underwear near the window.

Little Green was washing her fingernails in the evening. She tried to wash off the brown, the fungicide that had stained her nails. She used a toothbrush. I lay on my hands. I watched her patience. Little Green said that she was disappointed in Yan. I thought she was more human than Lu, said Little Green. Lu is a dog, I do not expect her to show elephant's tusks. But Yan was supposed to be an elephant. She is supposed to have ivory instead of jigsaw-patterned dog teeth.

I made no comment. I was unaware of when I had become Yan's admirer. Like many others in the company, I guarded her automatically. During field breaks we gossiped legendary stories of Yan. I learned from Orchid that Yan had joined the Communist Party at eighteen. When she had arrived five years ago, the land of Red Fire Farm had been barren. She had led her platoon of twenty Red Guards in reclaiming it. Orchid was among them. Yan was famous for her iron shoulders. To remove the mud to build irrigation channels, she made twenty half-mile trips in a day, carrying over a hundred and sixty pounds in two hods hanging from a shoulder pole. Her shoulders swelled like steamed bread. But she continued carrying the hods. She allowed the pole to rub her bleeding shoulder. She believed in will power. After a year, her blisters were the size of thumbs. She was the number one weight-lifter in the company. Orchid told the story as if Yan were a god.

I saw Yan carry large loads in the afternoon. She piled reed upon reed on her head until she looked like she had a hill on her shoulders, with only her legs moving underneath. She had a man's muscles. Her feet were like animal paws.

The older soldiers never got tired of describing one image of their heroine. A few years ago, after the grain storage there was a fire. Straw huts and fields of ripe crops were burned and all the Red Guards cried. Yan stood in front of the ranks with one of her braids burnt off, her face scorched and her clothes smoking. She said that her faith in Communism was all she needed to rebuild her dream. The company built new houses in five months. She was worshipped. She was more real than Mao.

Late at night, when I listened to the sound of Little Green washing herself, I imagined Yan with a burnt-off braid, her skin scorched by fire raging behind her . . . Yan had become the protagonist in my opera. I began to sing 'Red Detachment of Women'. Little Green hummed with me, then the other roommates. I was singing the song of Yan. Yan was the heroine in real life. In singing, I wanted to reach her, to become her. I wanted to become a heroine. I adored Little Green as a friend but I needed Yan to worship.

The willow outside the window swayed hard. The leaves tapped on the glass. The night was windy. Tomorrow would be another hard day. Depression sunk in. I pushed my thoughts to Yan. She inspired me, gave significance to my life. Little Green's disappointment over Yan did not diminish my admiration for her. I needed a leader to get me up. My back was sore. My fingernails were all brown, my skin cracked. But my focus was on Yan. In thinking of her I fell into sleep.

I started to imitate Yan's way of walking, talking and dressing. I was not aware of what I was doing. My belt was two inches wide. I wished it was one inch wider. I cut my long braids short, short to the length of Yan's braids. I tried to carry as much as I could when our platoon was sent to dig a new irrigation channel. I allowed my shoulder pole to rub my bleeding blisters. When the pain drilled into the heart, I forced myself to think of Yan, to think of the way she dealt with the pain.

To impress Yan, I gave speeches in every night's self-confession and criticism meeting. I put my weakness on the table. Everyone did the same. We helped each other to examine our thoughts, to get rid of the incorrect ones. We believed if we failed to do so, our hearts would be murdered by bourgeois evil spirits. Mao had warned us that those bad spirits were everywhere, hiding and waiting for the right time to get us. The class struggle must be talked about every day, every month and every year, said Mao. We discussed our characters, talked about how to improve ourselves and remain decent. We talked about building a stronger will. A will of magic. A will of ever-victory. I did not realize until later that these were the days of significance, days of ardent love and days of satisfaction. I was enthusiastic at these meetings. Though Yan didn't seem to notice me, I was not discouraged. I rode on my sincerity and believed that I would finally win her trust.

I was among those ordered to attend a military training programme organized by the farm's headquarters. I was glad that I was considered politically reliable. The programme was a series of intensive courses on shooting, handling grenades and combat. Yan said she would not pass us until we pickled in our own sweat. We were also called to go on midnight searches when we had to pull ourselves out of bed and be ready to leave with our rifles and flashlights in three minutes.

One night in the early summer, I was awakened at midnight

by an emergency call. The platoon leader called for me at my window and within minutes I was off with the group.

The air felt like water, soothing my face. We moved briskly, almost jogging, through the reeds. When we reached the wheat fields, a loading order was given in a whisper.

I snapped awake – this was the first order to use live ammunition, something serious had happened. I loaded my gun.

And then I heard Yan's voice. She ordered us to lie down, then to advance. It was a killer's voice.

We began crawling through the wheat. It was hard to see. The wheat whipped us, leaving its tiny needles all over me. I held my gun tightly. The male soldier in front of me stopped crawling and passed back a stand-by order.

I lay there holding my breath and listening. The insects began to sing and the wheat smelled sweet. The night was still. Mosquitoes began to bite me through my clothes. There was a noise in the distance. Then silence. I thought the noise had been my imagination. After about a minute, I heard the noise again. It was two sounds. One was a man's and the other was a woman's murmuring. I heard a soft and muted cry. And then my shock: I recognized the voice as Little Green's.

My only thought was that I couldn't let Little Green be caught like this. She was my best friend, the only air in our stifling room. She had never told me anything about being involved with a man, though I could understand why: it would be shameful to admit. A good female comrade was supposed to devote all her energy, her youth, to the revolution; she was not permitted even to think about a man until her late twenties, when marriage would be considered. I thought about the consequences that Little Green would have to bear if she were caught. I could see her future ruined right here. She would be abandoned by society and her family disgraced. I crawled forward towards the noise. A firm hand immediately pressed me down to the ground. It was Yan. I struggled, trying to fight her off. But she was too strong. Her grip was firm as a rock. She seemed to know exactly what was going on.

The murmuring and hard breathing became louder. Yan clenched her teeth together and drew in a breath. I felt the force of her body. In a second she loosened her grip on my back and shouted suddenly, Now!

It was as if a bomb had exploded next to me. Yan turned her flashlight on Little Green and the man. About thirty other flashlights, including mine, were switched on at the same time.

Little Green screamed. It broke the night. She was in her favourite shirt – the one embroidered with pink plum flowers. The lights shone on her naked buttocks. Her scream pierced me to the core. My heart in slices.

The man with Little Green was skinny, wore glasses and looked very bookish. He pulled up his pants and tried to run. He was caught immediately by the group led by Deputy Commander Lu, who pulled out her rifle and held it to the bookish man's head. He was not from our company, but I remembered having seen him at the market. He had smiled at Little Green, but when I asked whether she knew him, she said no.

Little Green was trembling and weeping. She scrambled back and forth for her clothes, trying to cover her buttocks with her hands.

I lowered my flashlight.

Yan slowly approached the man. She asked him why he had to do that to Little Green. Her voice was trembling. To my surprise, I saw her eyes glisten with tears.

The man bit his lip. He did not say anything.

Yan threw her belt down and ordered the male soldiers to beat the man. She walked away but stopped and said that she would be pleased if the soldiers could make the man understand that today's woman was no longer the victim of man's desire. She took off her jacket to cover Little Green. She said to her softly, Let's go home.

The bookish man did not look guilty. As the kicking and whipping began, he struggled not to cry out.

I returned to the barracks with the other female soldiers. From a distance we could hear muted cries from the man and Lu shouting, Death to the rapist! Little Green could not stop whimpering.

A public trial was held in the dining hall. Little Green had undergone four days of 'intensive mind re-brushing'. On a makeshift stage, Little Green declared in a high, strained voice that she had been raped. The paper from which she read slipped out of her hands twice. Her bookish lover was convicted. I will never forget his expression when the death sentence was announced. As if waking from a nightmare, he looked suddenly relaxed. His bruised purple face had brightened when Little Green walked into the hall.

I sat next to Yan. I heard her exchanging words with Lu. They said that the man was too deeply poisoned by bourgeois thoughts. Yan sighed in a sad tone. Lu said that the good thing was that the Party had managed to stop the poison from spreading. Yan agreed and said that at least she had saved Little Green. Lu gave a short speech to end the trial. The overturned cart in front serves as a warning to the carts behind, she said to the company.

Little Green's scream remained in my ear for a whole week. I thought about talking to Little Green but felt too guilty to face her.

No one talked about the man after the execution, although he was on everyone's mind. Little Green stopped washing. Months passed. Still she had not washed. There were complaints about her smell. When I carried back two containers of hot water and asked if she would allow me to wash her underwear for her, she took a pair of scissors and cut them into strips. She chopped off her long braids and stopped combing her hair. Mucus dripped from her lips. At night, she sang songs off-key. Then it got worse. She would not quit singing after midnight. She sang old operas.

One after another. She played with the curtains of the nets in the room. Mosquitoes got into the nets. The roommates became furious. They tied Little Green up on her bed. But she laughed and then sang louder. The roommates spat on her face and told her to shut up. But she went on until daybreak. When we woke up, all the shoes were gone. Little Green took them. She threw the shoes into a pond behind the company's storage. Little Green was going mad, but no one wanted to face the thought. I could not describe my feelings. I had destroyed her. We murdered her. We were mad. We strangled her into madness.

The roommates reported her behaviour. Yan refused to believe Little Green was insane. She shut us all up. She asked Orchid, Lu and me to go with her, to send Little Green to the farm's hospital.

We escorted Little Green on a tractor. Four of us holding her as if carrying an animal to a slaughterer's. Yan had her jacket on Little Green. She protected her from the strong wind and covered her as if she were a newborn.

The doctors performed many tests on Little Green but could not figure out what was wrong with her. They told Yan that nothing more could be done and asked her to take Little Green back. Yan roared. She threatened that she would accuse them all of being reactionaries if they did not come up with an acceptable diagnosis. The doctors pleaded with her. Finally they referred Little Green to a Shanghai hospital where she was diagnosed as having had a nervous breakdown.

When Little Green returned from the hospital months later, I did not recognize her. The drugs that she had been prescribed had made her gain weight. She was as fat as a bear.

She was again given a bed in my room, where she sat quietly most of the day staring in one direction. Her pupils sometimes moved upwards into her skull as if to read her own brain. Her hair was matted. I thought of the evenings when she would wash her hair after dinner and comb and dry it as the sun set. I remembered the song she sang well, 'My Motherland'.

There are girls like beautiful flowers,
Boys with strong bodies and open minds.
To build our new China,
we are happily working and sweating together . . .

紅 杜 鵑

I spent the night of my eighteenth birthday under the mosquito net. A nameless anxiety had invaded me. It felt like a sweating summer afternoon. Irritatingly hot. The air felt creamy. It was the ripeness of the body. It began to spoil. The body screamed inside trying to break the bondage. I was restless.

The reeds were sprouting underneath my bed. I had to cut them because they pricked through my bamboo mat and had scratched my cheek the night before. I had to stop them or they would hurt me. They had hurt me before. And I had weeded them by the roots. But the reeds were indestructible. They were excessive, salt-proof. When I thought they were gone, they were back. They grew from nowhere. It must be the salt. The salt empowered the reeds, I thought. They worked hand-in-glove. They were the true Red Fire Farmers.

I got out from the bed and squatted. I pulled the reeds out and broke each of them in two. I got back in my net, sealed the curtain, clapped to death three mosquitoes. I pinched them down and looked at the bloody spots on the net. The restlessness over-took me like the growing back of the reeds, from nowhere. It was the body. That must be it. Its youth, the salt. The body and the restlessness worked hand-in-glove. They were screaming in me, breaking me in two.

I used a small mirror to examine my body, to examine the

details of its private parts. I listened to my body, carefully. I heard its trouble, its disturbance. It had been trying to capture something, a foreign touch, to soothe its anxiety, but in vain. The body demanded to break away from its ruler, the mind. It was angry. It drove me to where I did not want to go: I had begun having thoughts about men. I dreamed of being touched by many hands. I was disgusted with myself.

It was violent. My body was in hunger. I could not make it collaborate with me. I tossed all night, loneliness wrapped me, anxiety distressed me. I lay on my back, as if stretched on prison bars. My hands all over my body, I did not know how to gain back peace. I could feel a monster growing inside, a monster of desire. It grew bigger each day, pushing my other organs aside. I was defenceless. I could see no way out. The mosquito net was a grave with a little spoiled air. Feeling wounded, I could not cry. I had to guard myself because no one else cried in the room. Had my roommates nothing in common with me? The mosquitoes bit me. I looked for them. They parked in the corners of the net. They were fat and clumsy after bloodsucking. I aimed, clapped. The mosquito flew away. I waited, chased, waited, aimed again and attacked. I clapped one. It lay flat in my hand, bloody and sticky. The mosquito's blood. My blood. I chased mosquitoes every night. Pinched them all to death. Bloody spots on the net pronounced my success. I played with long-legged mosquitoes. I admired the creatures' elegance. I would allow one to land on my knee and watch it as it bit me. I watched it insert its tiny straw-like mouth into my skin, feeling its bite. I let it suck, suck to its satisfaction. Then I pinched it with two fingers, firm, and watched its dark brown blood drip.

The killing of mosquitoes didn't put my mind to rest. My mind was no longer the mind I knew. It was no longer the perfect stainless mind. I began to have thoughts of those disgraced girls, the girls of my middle-school years. As a head of the class I was assigned to sit by them to help them get on the right track. Those girls had bad reputations. They were their families' shame. I was supposed to correct them and influence them. Though it was never explained to me what was wrong with them, it was known that they were called 'La-Sai' – a slang word which indicated that the girls had done shameful things with men and were condemned by those who were moral. These girls had no self-respect. They were called 'porcelain with scars'. No one wanted them. They looked forward to no future. They had no future. They were garbage. Placing them next to me showed the generosity of the Communist Party. The Party abandoned no sinners. The Party saved them. I represented the Party.

Sitting next to these girls for seven years I learned how their hearts were chewed by shame. I learned never to put myself in their position, I learned to stay clear of men. I looked up to the model women the society praised. The heroines in the revolutionary operas had neither husbands nor lovers. The heroine in my life, Yan, did not seem to have anything to do with men either. Did she too feel restless? How did she feel about her body? Recently, she seemed more serious than before. She stopped giving speeches at the meetings. She put on a long face and it remained cloudy all week. I saw her trying to talk to Little Green. Little Green reacted weirdly. She played with reeds or the buttons on Yan's uniform absentmindedly. She laughed hysterically. Yan looked painfully confused. She shook Little Green's shoulders. She begged her to listen. But she was talking to a vegetable.

Late in the evening after I finished sharpening my sickle I went back to my room and sat by Little Green. My roommates were all busy. Like silkworms spinning silk, they were knitting sweaters, bags and scarves. No one talked.

I went to sit in my net and closed the curtain. I looked at the net ceilings. Loneliness penetrated me. I was no different from the cow I had been working with. I told myself to bear with life. Every day we were steamed by the sun, kneeling on the hard land, planting cotton seeds and cutting the reeds. It dulled me. My mind had become rusted. It seemed not to be functioning. It produced no thoughts when the body sweated hard. It floated in whiteness. The brain was shrinking in salt, drying under the sun.

The cotton seeds we planted climbed out of the soil, like premature creatures with wild reeds all around them. When they first sprouted they looked like little men with brown caps. They were cute in the early morning, but by noon they were devastated by the bare sunshine and many of them died in the evening before the fog brought them moisture. When they died or began to die, the brown caps fell on the ground and the little men bent sadly. The ones that survived stretched and grew taller. They struggled on for another day. In a week these caps came off and the little men's heads split themselves in half. These were the first two leaves of the plants. At Red Fire Farm they never grew to be what was expected of them because the crazy bully reeds sucked all the water and fertilizer. The reeds spread out their arms and took all the sunshine. The cotton plants would bend to the side, they lived in the shadow of the reeds. Their flowers were pitiful. They looked like pinkish-faced widows. The fruit — the cotton balls they finally bore — were stiff nuts, thin, crooked, chewed by insects, hiding in the hearts of the plants. It was cotton of the lowest quality. Not even qualified to be rated. If some did qualify, they were rated four. We would pick them and put them into bags and ship them to a paper-making factory instead of a fabric-making factory.

I felt as if I was one of those stiff nuts. Instead of growing I was shrinking. I resisted the shrinking. I turned to Orchid. I was thirsty. Orchid was eager to make friends with me. She invited me to sit on her bed. She chatted about patterns for knitting. She talked nonstop. She told me that it was her fourth time knitting the same sweater. She showed me the details of the patterns and said that once she finished it, she would take it apart and reknit it, using the same yarn again. She said knitting was her biggest pleasure in life. She must knit. Nothing else interested her. She fixed her eyes on the needles. She did not go beyond that. Her moving fingers reminded me of a cricket chewing grass. I stared at the yarn being eaten, inch by inch. I suggested we talk about something else, for example, opera. She refused to hear me. She kept talking while her hands were busy working on the sweater. The cricket chewed the yarn, inch by inch, hour after hour, day in, day out. I began to talk about the opera. I sang, 'Let's Learn from the Green Pine Tree on Top of the Tai Mountain'. Orchid dozed off. She slid down into her net. She snored, loudly. She made me want to murder her. Imagining that this was how I would have to live the rest of my life drowned me in madness.

I saw her setting out alone for the fields in the late evenings carrying a jar. One day in heavy fog, I decided to follow her. I waited in the sea of reeds. She came, carrying a brown-coloured jar. She sought something at the root of the reeds. She was trying to catch poisonous water-snakes. She was quick and nimble. She put the snakes in the jar. I followed her. Mile after mile. Led by the myths she radiated. I hid and smelled the reeds, the sea, the fog and the night. I followed her the next day. Miles in the reeds. My sleep got better. I was curious about Yan's intention, her reason for risking her life to catch the snakes.

It had poured all day. We were ordered to wait in the room until the sky cleared up. As I sat, I prayed to the God of Weather to have the rain last as long as possible. Only when it rained were we allowed to rest. When it did rain, I would be so relieved. I would run out of the room, lift up my face, stretch my arms towards the sky to feel, to taste and to say thank you to the rain. I would let the rain pour on my face, sink into my hair, go down my neck, waist, legs, my toes.

As I sat by the window I got lost in my thoughts, staring at the willow tree. The rain turned to mao-mao-yu, 'cow-hair-rain', as the peasants called it. I stared at a window opposite mine. It was the window of the room of the company heads. Yan's window. The window intrigued me. I often wondered how the people lived behind that window. I knew them well in uniforms but not in their mosquito nets. What about their nights? Were any of their nights like mine?

The opposite window opened. I backed myself into my net. I watched through the curtain. It was the commander. She stuck an arm out. She was feeling the rain. She raised her chin towards the grey sky. Her eyes shut. She held that pose. It was such a private pose. Between her and the sky. Was she feeling the same way I was feeling: lonely and depressed? After Little Green went mad, my worship for Yan had turned sour. My sorrow for Little Green had transformed itself into anger towards Yan. I decided that Yan was no longer worth my respect. She was the murderer, although so was I. But she did it intentionally, and that was unforgivable. I executed her decision. Yet there was a stubbornness that grew inside of me. I found myself refusing to think that Yan was not worthy of my respect. For some strange reason, I felt that I still needed Yan to be my heroine. I must have a heroine to worship, to follow, to act as a mirror. It was how I was taught to live. I needed it the same way Orchid needed knitting, to survive, to get by.

I developed a desire to conquer Yan. More truthfully, to conquer myself, because Yan symbolized my faith. I wanted her to tell me what it was that drove her to take such cruel action against Little Green; I wanted to tear away her Party secretary's mask, to see what was inside her head. I wanted her to surrender. I was obsessed.

She suddenly turned in my direction and stopped. She saw me staring at her. She put a finger into her mouth and whistled. Yan, the commander, whistled to order everyone to get back to work in the fields. She whistled. She drove away my thoughts. She closed the window without a wave of her hand, a word, a nod, a hint of anything.

The rain had stopped. The sky was loaded with heavy dark clouds. The clouds looked as if they were about to fall upon our heads. The clothes I put out to dry before going to bed were wet and muddy. I took them down from the string and put them on, then dragged myself to the field.

We were transplanting rice-shoots. We worked for three hours without a break. I was working the edge of the field and noticed a trace of blood in the muddy water. I tracked the blood and found Orchid down on her knees in the water, her pants bloody red. Orchid always had problems with her period. It could last for half a month, bleeding her to exhaustion. She told me that she hadn't understood what her period was when it first came. She felt too ashamed to ask anyone for advice. She stuffed un-sterilized clothes into her pants. The blood was blocked but she got an infection. I asked her why she hadn't told her mother or a friend about it. She said her mother was in a labour camp and her friend knew even less than she. Her friend was not sure whether Chairman Mao was a man or a woman.

I asked Orchid why she had not asked the platoon leader for a day off. She said she did. She was rejected. The head sent her to Lu and Lu said that the transplanting had to be completed by midnight or we would lose the season. I told Orchid that I thought Lu was an armchair revolutionary who demanded other people be Marxists when she herself was a revisionist. Orchid disagreed. She said Lu was tough on herself too. She said that Lu had never taken a day off when her period came. Orchid said Lu had serious cramps every time. Orchid once saw Lu crying and twisting on the toilet because of the pain. I did not know what to say. I told Orchid that I would help her as soon as I finished with my own planting.

The rain started again and got heavier. I worked fast so I could go to help Orchid. My arms and fingers were moving as if they were not mine. Standing to stretch my back, I noticed Yan, a few plots away. She moved like a dancer: passing the rice-shoots from left hand to right and inserting the shoots into the mud in perfect time with her steps backward. Her wet clothes were pasted to her body.

I did my best to compete. Yan responded to the challenge. She

65

toyed with me, like a cat does a mouse. She sped up and I fell far behind; then she suddenly slowed down to allow me to catch up, before surging ahead again. She finished with one plot, then went to the next without turning her head.

The sky turned darker. A loudspeaker broadcast Mao quotation songs. The soldiers were exhausted like plants whipped by a storm. Two huge bright lights were carried to the fields and steamed bread was brought out. The soldiers crawled towards the bread baskets. Lu stopped us. She yelled, No dinner until the work is completed. Our stomachs had begun to chew themselves. But we dared not talk back to Lu, the deputy of the Party secretary. We feared her. Then there was the commander's voice. A voice of thunder: What kind of fool are you? Doesn't your common sense tell you that man is the engine when food is his fuel? Yan waved her arm as if to shovel us to the bread. Go now, she shouted. We ran like pigs to the trough.

Orchid was in tears when I finally went to help her, and a long way behind. We chewed our bread while we planted the shoots. We finished at ten o'clock. Orchid thanked me, crying with relief. She said her mother would have wanted to kill herself if she had witnessed this. In frustration I told Orchid to shut up. I said if Yan could do this so could we. We were not the only ones who were living this type of life. There were hundreds and thousands of youths in the same shoes. Orchid nodded. She used her sleeve to wipe off her tears. I was sorry for her. I did not like her pitifulness. As I dragged her out of the fields, a meeting was called.

One of the lights was being moved to the plot where we had worked, millions of mosquitoes swarming into its ray. Lu shouted for attention. She wanted to talk about the quality of the day's work. She passed the loudspeaker to Yan. Yan was coated with mud. Only her eyes were sparkling. She ordered the light to be moved to illuminate a particular spot where dozens of rice-shoots were floating on the water. The work was poorly done all the way to the edge of the field. Someone did a nice job here, Yan said sarcastically. The shoots will all be dead before daybreak. She wanted us to look at the dying shoots. To look hard. She said the shoots were her babies.

The soldiers began to survey the field nervously. The word broke out that the section responsible for the careless planting was platoon number four – our territory. I knew it was the area I had worked as I tried to keep up with Yan.

Lu ordered the person responsible to step out of rank and receive public criticism. Orchid sensed my fear, and grabbed my hand tightly. Lu said, No one leaves until the mistake is admitted.

As I gathered my courage and was about to step out, Yan suddenly said that she preferred to let the comrade correct her own mistake.

The fields had become quiet in the moonlight. The drizzle had stopped and the air was still. The insects resumed their nightclub singing. The fragrance of the plants wafted over me. The moon moved out of the clouds. I planted my feet in the mud and began to redo the work. My feet were swelling. I sang a Mao quotation song to fight off sleep.

> I've made up my mind
> Not to fear death.
> Overcoming all the difficulties,
> I strive for victory
> I've made up my mind . . .

The sky was piled with orange clouds when I awoke. The sun had yet to rise. I lay in the mud, joints sore, knowing I hadn't finished the work. The thought of having to resume my work brought pain to my back. Leeches parked on my legs. I had no energy to pat them off. They sucked my blood until they were satisfied and fell off. I was in despair. Yet I knew there was no way to escape. I had to finish my work. I had no guts to face the Party's abandonment. I feared being disgraced.

67

I forced myself to sit up. I looked around and thought I was dreaming. My work had been done. It had been done all the way to the edges. I looked towards the sun. There was someone. Someone about thirty yards away, pacing the field.

My tears welled up, because I saw Yan. She was pacing in the sun. She was the sun. My cold heart warmed.

I stood up and walked towards her.

She turned around, hearing me approach.

I stopped in front of her. I could not say anything.

She nodded at me then bent down to finish the last few patches. She washed her hands in the irrigation channel. She saw the leeches on my legs and told me to pat them off. She said that Orchid came to her last night and told her everything. She said she was pleased that I stayed all night in the fields. She said I did what I was supposed to do. She unknotted her braids, bent and washed them in the channel. She squeezed the water from her hair and flung her head. She combed her hair with her fingers and braided it. She said when she had found me I looked like a big turtle. She thought I had fainted or something. She paused and said that I made her feel guilty because I could have caught a disease like arthritis. It would be the Party's loss if I did.

I rubbed my eyes, trying to look fresh.

She looked me in the eyes, a thread of a smile on her face. She said she had guessed that I was strong willed. She said she liked strong-willed people. She looked at the sun for a while. She said, I want you to be the leader of platoon number four. She would arrange to move me to her room so that I could discuss problems with the company heads. She then walked quickly back towards the barracks.

I stood in the sunshine, feeling, feeling the rising of a hope.

紅 杜 鵑

I moved in with Yan and six other platoon heads. Yan and I shared a bunk bed, I occupied the top. The decoration in Yan's net was a display of Mao buttons, pinned on red-coloured cloth, about a thousand different kinds of them, from different historical stages. I was impressed. Yan put them up during the day and took them down at night. The room was the same size as the room I had lived in before. It served as a bedroom, conference room and makeshift dining room. It was also a battle front. Although Yan was officially in charge and Lu was her deputy, Lu wanted much more. She wanted Yan's position. She was obsessed. She called meetings without agendas. We had to obey her. We had to sit through her meetings in our drowsiness. She liked to see people obey her. To feel powerful was a drug she needed. Only in meetings could she feel that she was as in control of other people's lives as she was of her own. She made warnings and threats at the meetings. She enjoyed our fear. She aimed at all our possible mistakes. She waited, had been waiting, for a precise moment, to catch a mistake and beat it into submission. She had been trying to catch Yan. Her incorrectness. I could tell that she would have pushed Yan off a cliff if she had a chance.

Lu's full name was Ice Lu. She was the daughter of a revolutionary martyr. Her father was killed by the Nationalists in Taiwan. He was murdered when carrying out a secret assignment. Her mother suffered this loss to her death. She died three days after giving birth. It was a terrible winter. Strong wind, like a knife, cut through the skin. She named her baby Ice. Ice was raised under the Party's special care. She grew up in an orphanage funded by the Party leaders. Like Yan, she was also a founder of the Red Guard. She had gone to visit Mao's hometown in Hunan

69

where she had eaten leaves from the same tree Mao had eaten from when besieged and pinned down in the valley by the Nationalists some thirty years ago.

Lu showed me a skull she had discovered in the backyard of a house in Hunan. She said it was a Red Army martyr's skull. She pointed to a hole in the forehead of the skull and told me that it was a bullet hole. She fondled the skull with her fingers, going in and out of the eye holes, touching its jaws. The strange expression on her face caught my breath. She told me that an old village lady buried the martyr secretly. Twenty years later, the skull had risen above the soil. The old lady dug it out and gave it to Lu when she learned that her father had been a martyr too. Lu often thought it could have been her own father's skull.

I stared at the skull, trying to comprehend its attractiveness to Lu. Maybe the threatening spirit? Maybe the coldness that only death could carry? Lu had a look that matched her name. Her look was chilly. Her enthusiasm did not feel warm. She spoke slowly, pronouncing each syllable clearly. She had a long face, the shape of a peanut. Her expression was determined and judgemental. Her features were located evenly on her face. Slanting eyes, icy, like a painted ancient beauty. But her beauty was ruined by her forever-correctness. Her half-moon-shaped eyes were no longer warm and sweet to the soldiers. Our respect for her was that of mice for a cat.

Lu liked action. She did not know hesitation. She attacked and invaded. It was her style to catch and chop. Stand by, aim and shoot, as she always liked to say. But that did not impress me. On the contrary, it distanced me. She had a fixed mind. A mind full of dead thoughts. She observed me. In coldness. In suspicion. It started the moment I moved in. Her smile carried warnings. She gave me a copy of her Mao study notes. Her handwriting was extremely square. I wished my calligraphy was like hers, but her writing bored me. Her mind was a propaganda machine. It had no engine of its own. I told her so when she asked me for an opinion. I did not say her mind was a propaganda machine, but I suggested she oil the engine of her mind. She said she liked my frankness. She said people had been telling her lies. She was lied to by a bunch of hypocrites. She hated hypocrites. She said the country was filled with hypocrites. The Party in many respects was run by hypocrites. She said it was her duty to fight against hypocrisy. She would spend the rest of her life correcting the incorrect. She asked me to join the battle. I did not fully understand what she meant, but I did not say so. I said, Yes, of course. Hypocrites were bad in any case. She asked, Do you smell hypocrites in our room?

Our roommates came back after dining. They were singing and joking. They joked about how they punished those lazybones, the ones who refused to be content with their lives as peasants. The roommates quietened down when they heard Lu speaking about hypocrites. One after another, like fish, they shuffled into their own nets. There were sounds of groping. It reminded me of vampires in graves chewing human bodies.

Lu continued speaking. It was like a theatrical performance. As a daughter of a revolutionary martyr, I'll never forget how my forefathers shed their blood and lay down their lives for the victory of the revolution, said Lu. I'll never fail to live up to their expectations. I hope that all of you, my comrades-in-arms, will supervise my behaviour. I welcome any criticism you have for me in the future. The Party is my mother and you're all my family.

She tried to be a living opera heroine, but I would never see her that way.

I had a hard time imagining how Lu could sleep nose-to-nose with that skull every night. I began to have nightmares after I figured out that the skull was right next to my bed, since my bed and Lu's were connected to each other. I dared not complain. My instinct told me not to because I was sure Lu would take my complaint as an insult. How could I afford to be quoted as someone who was afraid of a martyr's skull?

71

Lu watched everyone and recorded her observations in her red plastic notebook. She made monthly reports to headquarters. I have learned my political skills from my family, she often said. Once she proudly told us about her family: her adopted parents were Party secretaries in the military, her adopted sister and two brothers were Party secretaries at universities and factories. All her relatives had the honour of staying in private hospitals when they were sick. Their rooms were next to the Prime Minister's.

Lu made political dunce caps. She would always single out one person to wear one at meetings. She always had her way. Phrases from *Red Flag* magazine and the *People's Daily* dropped out of her mouth like a waterfall. She reminded me of how it would be if sheep were living with a wolf. She told me one day that a mirror was a symbol of self-love – a bourgeois extra. I dare not argue back. I said, Of course, and hid my little mirror inside my pillow cover. I knew Lu could make me a reactionary if she wanted. She had already made a number of people reactionaries. She sent them to work at jobs like blasting a mountain to make rice paddies, or digging up earth to make an underground channel. She arranged for their lives to be forfeited. Those who survived resembled Little Green. No one escaped from paying the price if they talked back to Lu. Not even a bug. I feared Lu so much.

Strangely enough, on the other hand, Lu tried hard to impress the soldiers by washing our clothes and sharpening our sickles and hoes. She visited each room every night, tucking in our blankets, making sure that no one left an arm or leg out to catch cold. She would send her entire salary anonymously to a comrade's sick parents. She did that often. She was greatly praised. Lu liked to say, I don't mind being the cloth used to wipe the greasiest corner of the kitchen for the Communist Party. She was good at saying things like that. We said we appreciated her caring. We had to. Very much. We put words of praise down on the monthly report to be sent to headquarters. That was what Lu wanted from us. The soldiers knew this by heart.

She pointed out Yan's incorrectness whenever possible. She

72

said Yan was too soft on brain-reformation, too loose on the company's budget, too impatient in conducting the company's Mao study seminar. Yan fought back angrily, but she was a poor mouth fighter. She was not Lu's rival. She spoke incoherently. In desperation, she would curse. Swear word after swear word, all kinds – spoiled rice-shoot, pig ass, mating worm, etc. Lu enjoyed seeing Yan in awkward predicaments. She liked to push her into a verbal corner and beat her hard. She attacked her ruthlessly. She showed the company that Yan was uncivilized, only capable of swearing. She then would say, Why don't we report the case upstairs and let them decide who's right and who's wrong? Always, Yan would give up, withdraw, because she did not want to ruin her image as a secretary of a 'well-united Party branch', as Lu well knew.

Lu knew that I was a fan of operas. She used to ask me to sing a piece or two during field breaks. She said it soothed her addiction. I sang loudly. I called up my platoon to sing with me. Lu enjoyed it. We both did. But things changed after the Little Green incident. I could no longer sing anything. When Lu asked me to sing again, I could not put myself in the mood. I tried and my mind was full of Little Green's voice singing 'My Motherland'. My eyes would go to Little Green, who like a silent spirit floated in and out of the fields and rooms. The soldiers took turns taking care of her. We tried to hide the truth from her family. We imitated her handwriting and wrote to her grandmother. Our trick did not last. Her grandmother recognized the fake handwriting. She wrote to the Party committee of the company demanding to be told the truth. She said if she had not been restricted (she was put in a detention house where she was considered an enemy) she would have come to check Little Green out herself immediately. Yan took the time to write back to her. I proofread the letter to polish Yan's grammar and tone. It was a hard letter to write. Yan tried to explain what had happened. I could see Yan struggle through the writing. She did not really explain. She could not. She could not say we were the ones who had murdered her granddaughter. Yan said Little Green was very ill. She was suffering a mental distraction. But she was in good hands now. She had been taken care of. The farm had been looking for new medicine and treatment for her. It was a weak letter. It expressed nothing but guilt. It asked the grandmother to keep the big picture in mind, to see that it was just one incident. Hundreds of thousands of youths were assigned to the countryside by the Party. 'Certain sacrifice is required when working with stamina for the prosperity of the country,' Yan ended the letter by quoting Mao.

Yan looked exhausted. Blue ink was on her fingers and lips. I made a clean copy of her letter and gave it back to her. She went to the farm's headquarters to get a stamp and mail it. That night she said to me, When I die I will be sliced into pieces by the demons in hell. She said she could see it clearly now.

Lu told me that I was a good sprout. Worthy enough to be selected as one of her 'pillars of the state'. Her slogan-talk got on my nerves. I disliked it. Superficiality pervaded her speech. She tried to dominate everything. Many times she demonstrated her political and ideological expertise in meetings by giving long dissertations on the history of the Party. She wanted to be admired so much. She did it to remind Yan that she had none of the skills required of a leader. She succeeded in embarrassing her. I saw Yan's awkwardness. She sat in the corner, rubbing her hands. Frustrated. I felt sorry for Yan. It made me like her more. I liked her awkwardness. I adored her clumsiness.

Neither the headquarters' heads nor the soldiers were responding to Lu's exhibited leader's skills. Seasons passed and Lu was still where she had always been. Although Lu did not like to deal with frustration, she was a good fighter. She picked more fights with Yan, pointed out her imperfections in front of the ranks. Yan became even more furious. She wanted to eat Lu up. It took me half a month to figure out the words Yan had muttered when insulted by Lu. She called Lu a mother of fart. When Lu wished to extend a meeting in order to sharpen the soldiers' minds, Yan said,

Let's sharpen the hoes first. Lu said, You're going to get crushed in a blind alley if you only pay attention to pushing your cart forward without watching which track you're on. Yan said dryly, Let's get crushed. Lu said, As you make your bed, so you must lie on it. Yan said, Damn, I should do something to sharpen my teeth.

I often felt that Lu had more than two eyes when she watched or spoke with me. Lu once said that she would like to cultivate me to join her special advanced activist study team. I did not say that I was not interested, but I must have betrayed lack of interest. She said she was greatly disappointed. I said I would do my best to stay close to her team. I promised to borrow her Mao study notes. She said she knew my reason for not joining her. She said it was bad to live under someone's shadow. She said she would hate to leave a stone in her shoes. She said if one did not come to her political senses, one would lose her political future.

Though it was important for me to look noble to my troops, I made my choice to ignore Lu's warning. I felt that I must stand by Yan. By supporting Yan, I would cast myself as the lesser of two evils in a bad play. I never wanted to be a soldier at the Red Fire Farm. I felt like a slave. Yan was my reason, my faith to go on. Yan made me feel at least that we were achieving something; the impossible, as it now seemed, but it was still something.

To make Yan proud, I assigned the hardest tasks to our platoon – applying manure, taking night shifts, digging canals. I told my soldiers that my ambition was to make the platoon well known in the company, so everyone would have the best chance to be considered for membership of the Communist Youth League. The soldiers believed in me. Orchid even quit her knitting. By the end of the year, my platoon was selected as the Vanguard Platoon, and was given a citation at the entire farm meeting. I was accepted into the Communist Youth League.

At the oath ceremony, Yan walked onstage to congratulate me. She shook my hands and squeezed them in her carrot-like fingers. Laughing, she whispered that she could not wait to have me join the Party. She said that I must become a Party member. She said,

I could make it happen to you next spring. She said she would like to see it happen very much. I was excited. I could not say a word. I squeezed her hands back, hard. For many nights afterwards, before going to sleep, I replayed the ceremony in my head. I dreamt of Yan laughing. I realized how much I liked it.

After the busy summer season ended, the soldiers were allowed a little time for themselves after dinner. The spare time made me feel empty in the heart. I missed Little Green terribly. I would comb her hair and wash her clothes, but although her body was getting back to its original shape – she was once again slim like a willow – her mind seemed to have gone for ever. Nothing I tried made her respond to me. She still wore the shirt with the plum flower on it – the one she had on the night she got caught – but it had holes under the armpits and elbows. The shirt reminded me of the night – I'll never forget it – when I had my gun pointed at her. I did not know how other people were living with this guilt, if there was any guilt. No one talked about it. The company pretended it had never happened. Little Green was given light jobs working as a storage guard and was given coupons for sugar and meat. Yan was strange in the way she treated Little Green. She grabbed her and gazed into her eyes. She observed her anxiously. She tried to talk to Little Green when everyone else had quit a long time ago.

Little Green had become dangerous to herself. Once I caught her swallowing tiny stones. Orchid also caught her eating worms. I reported the incidents to Yan. From then on, I often saw Yan follow Little Green around the fields late in the evening. They were like two lost boats drifting over the sea in a dense fog.

She still went to catch the poisonous snakes. And I still followed her. Her secretiveness and my curiosity became a melody of the farm's night.

I began to dislike going into my mosquito net. It was too quiet. I avoided my bed and walked on a narrow path through the reeds. As the daylight faded, I found myself at the farm's Brick Factory. Thousands of ready-to-bake bricks were laid out in patterns. Some stacks were eight feet high, some leaning as if about to fall, and some had already fallen. I could hear the echo of my own steps. The place had the feel of ancient ruins.

One day there was another sound among the bricks, like the noise of an Erhu, a two-stringed banjo. I picked out the melody – 'Liang and Zhu', from a banned opera; my grandmother used to hum it. Liang and Zhu were two ancient lovers who committed suicide because of their unpermitted love. The music now playing described how the two lovers were transformed into butterflies and met in the spring again. It surprised me to hear someone on the farm able to play it with such skill.

I followed the sound. It stopped. I heard steps. A shadow ducked by the next lane. I tailed it and found the Erhu on a brick stool. I looked around. No one. Wind whistled through the patterned bricks. I bent over to pick up the instrument, when my eyes were suddenly covered by a pair of hands from behind.

I tried to remove the hands. Fingers combated. The hands were forceful. I asked, Who is this? and there was no reply. I reached back to tickle. The body behind me giggled. A hot breath on my neck. I cried out, Yan?

She stood in front of me, smiling. She held the Erhu. You? Was it you? You played Erhu? I looked at her. She nodded, did not say anything. Though I still could not make my mind connect the image of the commander with the Erhu player, I felt a sudden joy. The joy of a longing need met. A lonely feeling shared, and turned into inspiration. In my mind, I saw peach-coloured petals descend like snow and bleach the landscape. Distant valleys and hills melted in one. Everything wrapped in purity.

She sat down on the stool and motioned me to sit next to her. She kept smiling and said nothing. I wanted to tell her that I had not known she played Erhu, to tell her how beautifully she played, but I was afraid to speak.

She picked up the Erhu and the bow, retuned the strings, bent her head towards the instrument and closed her eyes. Taking a deep breath, she stroked the instrument with the bow – she started to play 'The River'.

The music became a surging river in my head. I could hear it run through seas and mountains; urged on by the winds and clouds, tumbling over cliffs and waterfalls; gathered by rocks and streaming into the ocean. I was taken by her as she was taken by the music. I felt her true self through the Erhu. I was awakened. By her. In a strange land, faced by a self I had not got to know, and the self I was surprised, yet so glad, to meet.

Her fingers ran up and down the strings, creating sounds like rain dropping on banana leaves. Then her fingers stopped, and she held her breath. Her fingertips touched and then stayed on the string. The bow pulled. A thread of notes was born, telling of an untold bitterness. Slowly she vibrated the string. Fingers dipped out sad syllables. She stroked the bow after a pause. The notes were violent. She raised her head, eyes closed and chin tilted up. The image before me became fragmented: the Party secretary, the heroine, the murderer and the beautiful Erhu player . . .

She played 'Horse Racing', 'The Red Army Brother is Coming Back' and finally 'Liang and Zhu' again.

We talked. A conversation I had never before had. We told each other our life stories. In our eagerness to express ourselves we overlapped each other's sentences.

She said her parents were textile workers. Her mother had been honoured as a Glory Mother in the fifties for producing nine children. Yan was the eighth. The family lived in the Long Peace district of Shanghai where they had one wood-framed room and shared a well with twenty other families. They had no toilet, only a night-stool. It was her responsibility to take the night-stool to a public sewage depot every morning and clean it. I told her that we lived in better conditions. We had a toilet, though we shared it with two other families, fourteen people. She said, Oh yes, I can imagine your morning traffic. We laughed.

I asked where she had learned to play Erhu. She said her parents were fans of folk music. It was her family tradition that each member had to master at least one instrument. Every one in her family had a speciality, in lute, Erhu, Sheng with reed pipes or trumpet. She was a thin girl when she was young so she chose to learn Erhu. She identified with its vertical lines. Her parents saved money and bought her the instrument for her tenth birthday. The family invited a retired Erhu player to dinner every weekend and asked him to drop a few comments on Erhu to the child. The family hoped that Yan would one day become a famous Erhu player.

She was fifteen years old when the Cultural Revolution began in 1966. She joined the Red Guard and marched to Beijing to be inspected by Chairman Mao at Tienanmen Square. As the youngest Red Guard representative, she was invited to watch an opera, newly created by Madam Mao, Jiang Ching, at the People's Great Hall. She liked the three-inch-wide belts the performers were wearing. She traded her best collection of Mao buttons for a belt. She showed me her belt. It was made of real leather and had a copper buckle. It was designed by Comrade Jiang Ching, my heroine, she said. Have you read Mao's books? she asked. Yes, I had, I said, all of them. She said, That's wonderful, because that's what I did too. I memorized the Little Red Book and know every quotation song.

I told her that I was a Red Guard since elementary school, although my experience was much less glorious than hers, but I would not be fooled about how much one knew about Mao quotation songs. She smiled and asked me to give her a test. I asked if she could tell where I sang.

'The Party runs its life by good policies—'

Page seven, second paragraph! she said.

'If the broom doesn't come, the rubbish won't automatically go away—'

Page ten, first paragraph!

'We came from the countryside—'

Page a hundred and forty-six, third paragraph!

'The world is yours—'

Page two hundred sixty-three, first paragraph!

'Studying Chairman Mao's works, we must learn to be efficient. We should apply his teachings to our problems to ensure a fast result . . .'

She joined my singing.

'As when we erect a bamboo stick in the sunshine, we see the shadow right away . . .'

Where are we? I shouted.

Vice-Chairman Lin Biao's Preface for Mao Quotations, second edition! she shouted back and we laughed, so happily.

We were still talking when we reached the barracks. We stood in the dark, filled with incredible delight. Be careful, she said. I nodded and understood: avoid Lu's attention. We took separate paths and went back to our room.

I could not sleep that night. The room and the mosquito net felt very different from yesterday. Yan did not speak to me in the room, but there was life and fresh air. I felt spring. The growth of the reeds under the beds for the first time became tolerable. I thought I would like the green in the room. Would Yan? She was in the bunk beneath me. There was so much that I wanted to share with her. But I dare not talk to her. Lu's bed was next to ours. We, eight people, sleeping in one room, compartmented by mosquito nets.

I heard Yan tossing. Would she awaken Lu? Lu would be jealous of us, of our delight. I felt sorry for her. I wished I could be her friend. It was sad that the only thing she was close to was the skull. I felt sympathy for her for the first time. It was a funny feeling. What made me care for Lu? Yan? Lu was two years older than Yan. She was twenty-five. She wanted so much. She wanted to control our lives. What was she doing with her youth?

Wrinkles had climbed on her face. Soon she would be thirty, and forty, and she would still be at Red Fire Farm. She said she loved the farm and would never leave. I wondered how anyone could love this farm. A farm that produced nothing but weeds and reeds. A complete darkness. A hell. Lu spoke no truth. She did not know how. Did she have feelings? Feelings that Yan and I shared tonight? She must have. She was young and healthy. But who dared to be dear to her? Who truly cared for her besides flattering her for her power? Who would she be sharing her feelings with? Would she marry? What a funny thought to think of Lu being married. Men in the company were afraid of her. They yielded to her, accepted her dominance. Men surrendered before they faced her. The shadow of her appearance chased men away. They treated her like a poster on a wall. They showed her their admiration but framed her on their mind's wall. I saw loneliness in Lu's eyes. The eyes that stared into fields on rainy days. The eyes of thirst.

Lu went to bed late. She sat on a wooden stool studying Mao's works. Every night she practised this ritual. She took about ten pages of notes each night. She was the last one to go to bed and the first to get up. She cleaned the room and the hall. I love to serve the people, she liked to say. She quoted Mao's teaching when she was praised. She would say, I did only what the Chairman taught me. She would recite, 'It is not hard for a person to do a couple of good things for others; it is hard for a person to spend his entire life doing good things for others.'

I found Lu's behaviour frightening. Her rigidness exposed her single-minded ambition for power. I became more careful, more polite towards her. I selected words carefully when I spoke with her. We talked around each other. She tried to grasp the core of my mind. She knew that neither of us could control the other. She was displeased. She sensed my intimacy with Yan, immediately, like a dog to a smell. She came to me one day after work and said, I know why you have been looking excited, you are such a thief. I said, I don't understand what you mean. She smiled and nodded. She told me to go on duty to inspect the soldiers' suitcases room by room. She went with me. She told me to rummage about the articles to look for obscenity. As we were walking back to our room after duty she said suddenly, Do you remember what you said last night? I almost stumbled over a rock. She hit my guilty conscience. I said, How would I know whether I had said anything? I was sleeping – how could I know? But you know, I just heard it, she said with an insidious smile. Just heard it, she repeated. Her words felt like bugs climbing up my back.

Lu opened the door to let me in first, then she followed and closed the door. Tell me, what's been on your mind? She looked at me as if I was a fly and she was a spider, as if we fought in the net she weaved. I said, I've got to go and wash my clothes. I haven't had clean clothes to wear for a week. I must hurry because I have a platoon meeting to hold. She looked at me, my dirty clothes, my bare feet. She said, I thought you were a sincere person. I said, I am a sincere person. She said, But not to me. I want you to be aware of your growing sophistication. You're losing your purity. The purity which I saw when I first picked you in Shanghai. Remember what I told you about what I liked about you? Remember I had asked you to keep what's good in you? I said, I have been keeping the goodness and will carry on keeping it but now I have to wash my clothes. She stepped back to let me walk through the door. Don't pretend that you don't understand me, she said. If you sincerely want to become a member of our Party, it won't do you any good if you refuse to be honest with me.

As I washed my clothes I thought about how easily Lu could destroy me by making false reports and dropping ambiguous words into my dossier which only the Party bosses had access to. Words that could bury me alive. Words that once in the dossier would never be changed. They would follow me even after death. The dossier determines who I am and who I will be. It would be the only image of me the Party considered real and trustworthy.

As the Party secretary, Yan had the power to do the same as Lu, to manipulate people. But Yan never liked to play tricks. She believed in justice, no matter how unjust her justice was to me. She tried not to give expression to a personal grudge – a principle Mao had set for every Party member. She tried not to do that to Lu, though she wanted to very much. She never added extra salt or vinegar in her reports to headquarters. I was moved by this when I read her reports as I copied them for her. It brought me closer to her. I saw no such quality in Lu. Lu often volunteered to work longer hours in the fields doing all the good things anyone could think of, but she would never forgive anyone who had stepped on her toes by disagreeing with her at meetings or destroying her orders. I'll pinch him like pinching a bug if anyone has the guts to make a fool of me, she said to our faces. I'd be glad to give the enemy a taste of the iron fist of the proletarian dictatorship.

紅 杜 鵑

Lu brought back a dog from the headquarters. His name was 409. 409 was a military-trained German Shepherd. It was said that he could do anything. 409's mission was to watch a pig named Tricky Head. Tricky Head, a male pig weighing almost two hundred pounds, was the company's big headache. He was the trickiest of his group. The company did not have enough fine animal feed. The pigs were given half fine feed and half coarse grain. One day the farmhands found that a few of the bags of fine feed were gone – one of the pigs must have eaten them, but they could not figure out which one. Two days later, another few bags of fine feed were gone. This time the farmhands noticed that the pigs were eating the undigested shit of Tricky Head. They suspected that Tricky Head was the thief. They targeted him and caught him in the middle of his theft. The strange thing about Tricky Head was that he had the face of a dog and he acted like a dog. He could jump out of the pen and into the grain storage and afterwards, when he had had enough fine feed, he would run back to the pen and pretend nothing had happened. He did not eat any less at the last feeding of the day. He was bigger than the others.

Lu adored 409. She spent all her savings and bought the dog dry meat. She trained him and rewarded him. 409 soon became very attached to her. They would take a walk by the sea every night. Lu became more pleasant than she used to be. 409 was mean to everybody but Lu. Lu was proud of 409's loyalty. She encouraged his meanness. She often recited one particular Mao quotation to 409. She ordered 409 to sit by her feet then she would say, 'Isn't it a key question that one must learn to be able to tell who is his friend and who is not?' 409 would bark a yes to her and he would be rewarded with a piece of dry meat. Then Lu would go on, 'Is it not a capital question that one must answer as a true revolutionary: who is the people's friend and who is not?' 409 would bark again and receive another piece of meat.

When he stood on his feet he was as tall as Lu. Lu often had him walk on his back legs while he put his front legs on her shoulders. One day when Lu was out at headquarters for a meeting, 409 wailed all day. It sounded like an old woman crying. By noon he began to hit himself against the wall. Two male soldiers shut him in a pigpen and he hurled himself into the bars until they broke in half. No one could stop him until Lu got back. Seeing that the dog could not do without her, Lu broke into tears.

409 was a terrible watchdog. The soldiers said that he must have had a past-life relationship with Tricky Head – the two animals got along the moment they met. They stared at each other uncertainly then went to smell each other and accepted each other. Was it because Tricky Head had the face of a dog? They sat by

each other like brothers. They played in the pigpen. When it came to stealing the fine feed, not only did 409 not stop Tricky Head, he helped him rake out the feed from the bags so Tricky Head could eat faster. When the farmhands came, 409 put on a sincere face as if he had fought to guard the feed but failed.

Yan did not like 409. She called him a traitor. She kicked him and suggested that Lu send him back to the headquarters. Lu reluctantly said yes. As if knowing Lu's feelings, 409 went up to her and put his tongue all over her face.

Lu begged Yan to let 409 stay. She showed Yan the dog's file. It said that 409 had good credit in his war records. She said, Give me two weeks to train him to watch Tricky Head. I promise he'll be as good as he was promised to be. Yan said that the fine feed was running short. The company could not afford to lose one more bag. The other pigs were going to starve. Lu took night shifts to watch the animals. 409 was still the same. Lu could not get him to behave correctly. Yan was upset and ordered Lu to send 409 away. The same day, the day when 409 was supposed to be sent away, Lu caught Tricky Head stealing the fine feed. She went to Yan and said that sending the dog away was not going to stop Tricky Head. Why don't we kill Tricky Head instead of sending the dog away? She was permitted.

Lu had the pig killed for supper. Tricky Head was in everyone's bowl. 409 chewed the pig bones, and afterwards he went to look for Tricky Head everywhere. He smelled Tricky Head's pen and stayed in the sawdust until Lu called him out. Lu was happy, she combed 409's back hair with her fingers. Lu spent hours with 409, putting her whole hand in his mouth and making him do all kinds of tricks.

Lu took 409 to local villages where he could mate. 409 was nice to the female dogs but mean to their owners. It was said that he would mate with the female dog and afterwards, in expressing his pleasure, he tore the owner's pants. He jumped on them, stood on his back legs and barked. The villagers said that he woke up the dead. The villagers told Lu never to bring 409 around again. Lu just laughed. She did not know just how serious the villagers were.

Early one evening when Lu brought 409 back from a nearby village, 409's face was turning green. He vomited and vomited. Lu tried to feed him water and porridge but 409 could take nothing in. I was sharpening the hoes when Yan came to me with the news. Yan said, Lu is singing an opera. I went to the grain storage where 409 usually slept. Before I saw 409 I heard Lu's sobbing. 409 was lying in Lu's bosom, dead. Lu sobbed like a village widow. A vet was standing next to them. Yan came and passed Lu a wet towel. As Lu wiped her face Yan asked the vet about the poisoning. The vet said that it was in a steamed-bread. The villagers did it, said Lu. They are reactionaries, she added clenching her teeth. We must make them pay for it. Yan did not respond to her at first. After dinner when she noticed Lu was still sitting by 409, Yan said, If I were you I wouldn't have taken him to mate so much.

Lu buried 409 by the river. When our platoon went to work hoeing the fields the next dawn, Lu was already at work. She had swollen eyes. I asked her if she slept well last night and she said that she had sat by the grave the whole night. At break-time she asked me to accompany her to the grave to visit 409. I went with her. I was moved by her sadness. I did not know Lu was capable of being sad. She kneeled in the mud and planted wild flowers on top of the grave. She sobbed as she was doing so. I took her up by the arms and she leaned on my shoulders. She thanked me. I wished that I could do more for her. She looked at me and said, I've lost my only friend, my best friend. What am I going to do? Her tone scared me. I dared not say a word. I looked at her. She stared into the fields. The wind blew her hair up from its roots. She murmured to herself, I will, I will. You will have new friends, I said. She looked at me suspiciously. You see, 409 never lied to me, she said.

Lu knew I was not really saying what I meant. She knew I did not want to be her friend. I could not tell her that I was afraid of her being too capable. She had the quality of a murderer, and that was what kept me away.

Lu and I worked shoulder to shoulder all day. We exchanged few words. I was thinking of Yan, her hearty laughter. Lu was quick at work. Her slim figure moved like a mountain goat on a cliff, her every move was precise and sufficient. Like a mountain goat, she had thin ankles and thin wrists, and it enabled her to run faster and bend quicker. She was an ardent worker. She was a hard-liner. But to me she was like a stage light: she was bright in the dark, but when the sun rose, she lost her brightness. She faded in the sunshine, and Yan was the sun.

Yan and I betrayed no intimacy in public. We silently washed each other's clothes and took tripe to fill hot-water containers for each other. We became accustomed to each other's eye signals. Every couple of days, we would go separately to meet at the Brick Factory. Yan would make excuses such as checking the quality of the day's work. I would take the thickest Mao book and my notebook and pretend to find a place to study by myself. We shuttled through the reeds, hand in hand. She taught me how to make whistles with reeds. She would roll up a piece of reed to make a green trumpet. She told me to blow when she blew hers. We made music of the reeds, of the evening. We messed with each other's tones and laughed when the tone sounded like the cough of an old man.

Even when winter came, we continued to meet. Sitting by the bricks, Yan would practise her Erhu: I would just lie back and listen. We began to talk about everything, including that most forbidden subject – men.

Yan said that according to her mother, who hated her father, most men were evil. Mother said that she wouldn't ever have produced nine children with father if she had not wanted to respond to the Party's call, 'More population means more power'. Men take pleasure in seducing and raping women, she concluded.

I remembered how Yan had taken off her belt that night and

ordered the male soldiers to beat the bookish man. I understood where her hatred for men had come from. I said her father did not represent every man. Yan insisted he did. She then told me about her five brothers, all in their twenties, all tall and strong. They talked obscenely at midnight while the whole family of eleven slept in the same room. Her elder brother talked about tricking a neighbourhood girl to come into the room, seducing her on the bed while his four brothers watched through a door slit. I asked how her parents reacted to this. Yan said they refused to believe it. They accused Yan of misreporting. The brothers beat her up and her parents watched and thought they did the right thing. That was the main reason she left her family for Red Fire Farm.

Yan asked me how I felt about men. I said, If you want to hear the truth you might be shocked. She said she was ready and promised to continue to be my friend no matter what I told her. I told her a story. A story I had never told anyone. It happened during a Red Guards' meeting when I was sixteen. There had been a power failure and, as we were waiting in the dark, a hand touched my back. Trembling, it slowly moved around my side to touch my breast. I was shocked but allowed the hand to stay for about a minute and then stood up and moved to another seat. When the lights came back on I turned. I saw three boys sitting behind me, all about my age. One of them looked nervous and pale. I knew him – a straight-A student, a popular calligrapher who had a girlish face.

I thought that I had lost my purity. I was ashamed of myself.

Why didn't you yell? Why didn't you push his hand away? Yan asked. I told her I didn't know why myself. I told her that actually my body felt good. She was stunned. She sat in silence for a long time. She put her face in her palms.

The reeds swayed like the sound of whispering. *Sah-sah-sah, sah-sah-sah.* I watched Yan, the way she gathered her courage. She asked whether I knew the difference between the sexual organs of a grown man and a boy. I had seen a picture of it in an acupuncture book. It was drawn as an upside-down teapot. Yan nodded and said that was good enough. She sat for a while longer. Blushing, she told me that she had something to confess. I waited. She said, Never mind. I said, You don't trust me. It's not that, she said. I said, What is it? She took a breath and said that she really couldn't. She couldn't make herself say it. She rested her forehead on her knees. I said she could take all the time she needed to get ready. She said that she would never be. Like a snail shrinking its head into the shell, she wouldn't come out. I begged. I said I had closet-thoughts too. She said that's different. Hers was a monster. I poked apart her knees and lifted her chin with my fingers. I looked at her and said I could almost tell what that might be. She said I wouldn't be right. I said, If I am right, do you promise to tell me everything? She nodded.

A man, I said, looking straight into her eyes. She lost her calm.

His name was Leopard Lee. He was twenty-four and the head of Company Thirty-two. He was from the South, from a family of gardeners. He was a delicate man. She had met him at a head-quarters meeting two months ago and had secretly thought about him since. She told me that that was it. Her story was done.

I said, Did you two have private talks? She said, What do you mean? How could I do that? Well, how do you know he likes you? I asked. She said, Well I just feel that he does. She said she of course couldn't be sure, but anyway this was not what she wanted to tell me. I asked, What's the problem? She said, I just know I'm not supposed to have those thoughts at all. She said that the awful thing was that she couldn't get him out of her mind. She was disturbed and she didn't like that. I joked and said it sounded like a personal-life corruption and that she should bring the problem to the company meeting. She said it's not nice to make fun of other people's pain. I asked if it was really pain. She said it is supposed to be pain and it was. It dragged her, burned her. It made her mind pop up dirty thoughts, thoughts about men and teapots.

She looked helpless. I said I had exactly the same symptoms. She asked what had I done about it. I said I read a book. She asked if I had felt better after reading. I said that I did. She asked if she could learn the title of the book. I said, It's called *The Second-time Handshake*. It's a banned book, I got it from Little Green's suitcase. It was hand-copied, three hundred pages. She asked what the book was about. I said a story of a man and a woman. She said she supposed the book must have poisoned Little Green's head. I said that I had to agree. She said she did not want to be misguided by the book. I said of course but who knows what one's judgment may truly be. I said that I would not believe a strong-minded person like her would be poisoned by a book. It would be ridiculous. It would be a joke. She said that made sense. She told me to drop the book in her rain-boot at night. I then said that I would not be responsible for whatever happened in her head in the future. She said she would take responsibility for herself.

She devoured the book. Yan, the commander, the Party secretary, devoured the handwritten book in three nights with a flashlight in the mosquito net. When she returned the copy, she looked different. She told me, I want to write to him. But then her face fell. She said, I can't. It's not safe. We went to the Brick Factory. I asked her to explain to me why it was not safe. She said that the bookish man's letter to Little Green was opened by Lu – that's how the company knew where to catch them that night. The Party bosses could look into anyone's letters and suitcases at any time. There was no rule against this.

I told Yan that I had hated her for exposing Little Green. She said that I should. She lowered her head. She listened to my accusation quietly. I said, You are a murderer. I cried. She said she hated herself but it was what she was made to do. She had known for a long time that Lu had been spying on Little Green. As the Party secretary and commander, she had no choice when the case was reported.

Yan took my hands in hers and rubbed them. Her hands were rough, like those of an old peasant. She said that only now had she understood how unforgivable her act was. She herself now was in Little Green's position – involved with a man. How unforgivable it was, what she did. She said she was a frog who had lived at the bottom of a well – her knowledge of the universe was only as big as the opening of the well. Her naïveté and ignorance made her a murderer. She was fooled by Party propaganda, by *Red Flag* magazine and the *People's Daily*. She was trained to be a murderer. Who was not? She didn't understand the world around her, the world where the murderers go on living while the innocent died like weeds.

I remembered her snake-catching in the reeds. I asked her about it. Gazing at the sunset she said that it was for Little Green, to make her come back to her senses one day. She had collected sixty-nine water snakes in a jar which she stored under our bed. She had to reach the perfect number of one hundred. She said it was the first time in her life she had put faith in superstitions. Her grandmother once collected snakes to cure her disabled sister. When she had one hundred, her sister stood up and walked. She had been paralysed for six years.

You know the snakes are poisonous, don't you? I said. She nodded. Her smile was calm and that touched me deeply. I asked if she would allow me to join her. I said I would not be afraid of the snakes. She nodded, grabbing my shoulders.

We went out to hunt for the snakes separately. I never caught one. I was scared of these creatures, their shape horrified me. The grease on their tails made me paranoid. I had nightmares, my body wrapped in snakes. I didn't tell Yan about my dreams. I couldn't believe that she was not scared of them. When she brought more snakes back I imagined the horror she had gone through. She was my heroine again.

We talked more about men, in particular Leopard Lee. I suggested that, if she wanted, I could be her personal messenger. She shook her head and said if it was wrong for Little Green, it should be wrong for her too. I'm a Party member, I can't do things I have forbidden others to do. She looked sad but determined. She was being ridiculous, yet her dignity caught my heart. I was drawn to her as I looked at her. I couldn't have enough of her that evening. She was my Venus.

It's only superficial, isn't it? I said on our way back to the barracks. She said suddenly, I bet you can fight with Lu now because you've developed sharp teeth. She laughed. She made a hat of reeds for me as we discussed how the letter should be written and how to find an official excuse for me to deliver it to Leopard Lee.

I felt joy. The joy of being with Yan. The joy of having her depend on me. Two weeks passed. Still Yan had not given me anything to deliver. When she saw me, she avoided the subject. I could tell that she was happy, yet a little nervous. I saw her hang red-coloured underwear to dry. Bright red. She hummed songs, spending more time looking at herself in front of a palm-sized mirror by the door. She stopped swearing. I teased her. I swore the words she used to swear. She knew my intention. She just smiled, called me a brat. I grew anxious. I asked her about the letter to Leopard. She kept on equivocating. She said that she had no time to write. I said Leopard might have forgotten her. That night, when I was lying in bed, she opened my curtain and threw in a folded letter.

> Comrade Leopard Lee: How are you? I was
> wondering how the agricultural initiative is
> progressing in your company. Here we are
> making good progress. I have thought of our
> meeting often. It was meaningful as well as
> politically fruitful.

In the margin Yan had written, 'Will you please help?' I took a piece of paper and replied that I would do whatever the Party required of me.

The next day I rewrote her letter. I did not know what Leopard Lee looked like so I described Yan's face instead. I tried to imagine what they would do when they were together, how they would touch each other; just thinking of it made my heart beat fast. I wanted to describe Yan's body but I had never seen it. I described my own instead, touching myself and imagining my body was hers and my fingers his.

When Yan returned, I whispered that I had finished. She was excited and said that she could not wait for bedtime to read it. I told her that I wanted to see her reading it. Yan said then we should make an excuse to get in bed together. We made a plan, and waited for the dark to fall.

After dinner, Yan and I sat by the door. She started to repair her rain-shoes while I took out my rifle to clean. We said nothing to each other and pretended that we were concentrating on our hands. I took apart the gun and cleaned it. I was absentminded. I stole a couple of moments to glance at Yan. She sanded the cracked shoe, applied glue and let it sit. She didn't look at me but I knew that she knew I was looking at her. Her face flushed. She smiled shyly. Lightly she gave a few blows to the shoes. I adored her shyness because no one else would think that she could be shy. Her intimacy belonged to me.

Lu was reading Mao's work aloud. Other roommates had been going in and out of the room hanging their clothes on a string, splashing dirty water outside. The male soldiers in the opposite building were tapping their bowls with chopsticks. They sang, 'When the sun rises, oh-yo, oh-yo, oh-yo, yo, yo, yo, oh, oh . . .' Their song had no end. The soldiers splashed water on the muddy ground as well and walked into their rooms barefoot. The doors were closed. The song dashed on.

When darkness fell I was already in bed. I waited for everybody else to get into their beds. I looked around the room through the net. I looked at Lu from the top down. Her concentration amazed me. She really read the Little Red Book every day. I was sure she had memorized every comma and full stop. Did she enjoy this?

Or was she just putting on a show? Or both? Did she ever feel restless? She was not a machine, although she acted like one. Having seen her go through the death of 409 I knew she did not have an icy heart. What did she think of her friendlessness? I knew she needed friendship although she pretended she did not need anything but Mao's book. She was young, her body was full. She liked to watch her own feet, I noticed. She often took a long time washing her feet. They were tanned dark brown, and her toenails were as clean as peanuts. They were not like ours, dyed orangeish with fungicide. She used vinegar to rub off the dye on her toenails each night as the rest of us slept. Once the strong smell of her vinegar woke me up at midnight and I saw through the net that she had dozed off while applying it. Her feet rested on a stool, like two big rice cakes. It was a pair of young feet, elegantly shaped. I asked myself the reason Lu spent so much time taking care of her feet. And I understood. Her feet were her intimacy. She needed that intimacy to survive just as I needed Yan's.

I began to say that I did not have enough blankets and was afraid of catching cold. Yan sneezed and said that she felt cold too. Lu, as usual, was still studying. Annoyed by our noises, she said impatiently, Why can't you help each other, comrades? Why can't you think of something to solve the problem such as to share the blankets together? She fell right into our trap. I jumped down with my blankets, rushed into Yan's mosquito net. We closed the curtain tightly. I couldn't help giggling. Yan covered my mouth with her hands. I gave her the letter. She pulled the blankets up over our heads, and turned on her flashlight.

Her face flushed. She read and re-read the letter. She whispered that it was the best thing she had ever read. She said that she did not know I was so talented. She pressed her cheek against mine. She whispered the same words again and again, that I was talented. After she read the letter two more times, she wanted me to imagine how Leopard Lee would react after reading this letter.

I told her that he would fall in love with her. She told me to repeat what I had just said and I did. She whispered, How can you be sure? I whispered back, If I were a man I would. She asked if I ever tasted pellet fruit. I asked what pellet fruit was. She said it was a type of fruit that grew in the south. When it ripened it cracked itself open making pang-pang-pang sounds like fire-crackers. She said this was how her heart was beating now. I said I was glad I had talent. She said I should be because I made her spellbound and she was at the mercy of my hands.

Turning off the flashlight, we came out of the blankets for air. I asked if pellet fruit was edible. She said, Yes, it's sweet, but the fruit has an ugly shell like a porcupine. I said, I couldn't tell that you had such a mellow heart when I first saw you. I told her that her mellowness made me question whether she was a real Party hard-liner or just an armchair revolutionary. She said, Grind and level your teeth now.

Through the mosquito net I saw Lu finish off vinegaring her feet. She capped the bottle, stood up, turned off the light and climbed into her bed. Yan and I lay awake in the dark, too excited to sleep. Soon we heard Lu's snoring. The moon's pale lilac rays scattered through the curtains. I heard the sound of our room-mates' even breathing. The snakes were beating against the sides of the jar under the bed.

The restlessness came back. It stirred me deeply. I felt my mind and body separating themselves. My mind wanted to force sleep while my body wanted to rebel. Somehow I did not want to figure out why my body wanted to rebel. I was enraptured by a sense of danger, a heat, a spell.

Yan turned away from me, sighing. I wanted to flip her over but was afraid suddenly. A strange foreignness arose. My body stiffened. She murmured, I whispered, Did you say anything? I heard my own echo in the dark. She sighed and said, Too bad. I waited for her to complete the sentence. She went silent as if she were afraid as well. I said, I'm waiting. She said, Too bad you are

95

not a man. She sighed again. It was a deep and frustrated sigh. I felt dejected. My youth rose bravely. What would you do if I were? I asked. She turned back to face me and said she would do exactly what I had described in the letter. Her breath was hot. Her eyelashes touched my cheek. A warm stream gushed from my feet to my head.

We lay in silence. In fever. One of her legs was between mine. Our arms were around each other. Then almost at the same time, we pulled away. To make light of the uneasiness, I said that I would like to recite a paragraph from the Little Red Book. Go ahead, you armchair revolutionary, she said. 'Chairman Mao teaches us,' I began. 'Taking a stone he hit his own toe instead of another's; that's the result that all the reactionaries are going to get as they try to resist the revolutionary force.' Right, she followed, only when we are following the Chairman's teaching can we be invincible. Let's do a self-criticism, I said. She said, After you. What's on your mind? Confess. Make a clean breast of your guilt.

My guilt or your guilt, Comrade Party Secretary?

紅 杜 鵑

An old saying goes, 'When a good thing comes, it comes in a pair.' That autumn was a magic season.

When the beets in the fields was sweet enough to eat, we had to draft reports on how local peasants had been stealing our beets. We would deliver the reports to headquarters so the company would not be blamed for a decrease in output. Yan had been following a 'one eye open, one eye closed' policy which meant that she was not too strict on the correctness of the reports. In fact she knew exactly who the thieves were. It was not the local peasants, not the field rats. It was the soldiers themselves. I was one of them. The salary I received was not enough to cover my food expenses, so in late evening, I became a thief. I dug into the mud for beets, radishes and sweet potatoes.

Yan pretended not to see us. In fact, she was busy doing her own thing. She was driven by her belief in acupuncture treatment. She had been taking Little Green to our neighbouring farm hospital – Red Star Farm Hospital – to see a group of doctors from the People's Liberation Army who were there teaching the local doctors the techniques of acupuncture. Yan took Little Green there twice a day, at dawn and late in the evening. She got up at four-thirty in the morning, packed Little Green on the tractor and bounced all the way to the hospital for a session of needles and then took Little Green back, leaving her with the cafeteria people for breakfast as she herself rushed to the fields without eating anything to catch up with us.

I always brought an extra steamed-bread with me. I gave it to Yan when she came to the field. It took her three bites to finish a hand-sized steamed-bread. One day she came back soaking wet, mud pasted on her clothes. She said that she had fallen into a canal with her tractor. Yan was screaming happily. She said she was too excited to speak. She said, Magic has happened – Little Green is coming back to her senses. Yan shouted, A long long life to Chairman Mao! She asked us to shout with her. We did. When the soldiers encircled her for more information she said that she had left Little Green in the hospital for more observation. She said that Little Green had sung a phrase of 'My Motherland' this morning. Yan broke two poles that day carrying one-hundred-pound hods of manure to the field.

That evening Yan conducted as we sang opera at the study meeting. Yan's fever affected the company. No one paid attention to Lu who was standing in the corner shaking her head. Everybody sang 'Nothing in the world can put off a Communist' – an aria from *The Legend of Red Lantern*. After that, Yan for the first

97

time offered to perform her Erhu for everybody. She was admired and worshipped.

I sat back enjoying Yan's happiness. In her happiness I experienced again her heart-rending pain for Little Green. I suggested that we sing 'My Motherland' to keep Little Green blessed. Yan played a note on her Erhu. But she broke a string because she struck it too hard. She apologized to the crowd. Instead of adding a new string to the Erhu, she placed it aside and sang the tone. The sound was the same – her voice was exactly like Erhu. We could not help laughing. Yan did not mind. She sang in a high pitch:

> This is my great country
> It is the place where I was born and raised.
> It is a beautiful land where
> The sun shines everywhere,
> The spring breezes everywhere.

Yan's happiness did not last. Not a week. When Little Green got back she looked the same, like a vegetable. The acupuncture worked for a moment and then the nerves reverted to idleness. Yan refused to give up. She kept sending Little Green back to the hospital. One day the tractor broke down. She carried Little Green on her back and walked two hours to the hospital. The next day Yan did not wake up on time. She was too tired. I offered to take Little Green to the hospital. Yan insisted on going there herself. We ended up going together. We took turns in carrying Little Green. Little Green slept like a dead pig on our backs. She looked hopeless. Yan said she still had her last bet, the bet on the snakes. I did not say I didn't believe in that for a second. She had so much hope in her voice. She was insane.

I hitched a ride on a tractor to Company Thirty-two to meet with Leopard Lee. Yan sent me there as our company's representative to 'exchange revolutionary experiences' with his company. I was as excited when called for the mission as if I were going to meet my own lover. The letter, folded carefully, was in my inner pocket. I buttoned the pocket up in case my jumping on the tractor might shake it out. I checked to see whether it was still there every now and then. I had rewritten the letter the night before. Yan drowned in reading it. She was up at dawn. She told me that I had made her another person. True, I thought. She had become much softer. She was nice to everyone, including Lu. The soldiers were flattered, and Lu puzzled.

Yan gave a holiday to the company when it was not raining. She herself went to cut heaps of reeds the whole day. When she saw me, she smiled shyly as if I were Leopard Lee. To my own surprise, I spent more time thinking of her. I could not help it. I watched her eating dinner. She ate absentmindedly, shovelling food into her mouth. She would stare into distant fields or watch a bug chewing the heart of a cotton flower. She told the cafeteria to add more sugar to the dishes. She wore red, bright-red under-wear at night. She smiled at the mirror when she thought no one was around. She told me to buy her a bottle of vinegar when I went to the shop. She sat with Lu before bedtime to clean the chemical dye off her toenails. She sometimes sang operas with me and Lu. She sang like her Erhu, her voice made string-like sounds. The roommates said they could not tell the difference. She yelled, What's wrong with that? The roommates went to hide in their mosquito nets, covering their mouths with their hands and laughing hard.

When I saw Leopard Lee I was surprised by Yan's choice. He was a male version of Yan: with big and intense eyes, knife-like eyebrows and bristly oily hair. He was not as tall and strong as I had imagined. He reminded me of a monkey, with long arms, quick actions. I could tell by the way he was admired by his soldiers that he was a successful leader. They all called him Leo-pard. He responded to them affectionately. He joked with them and told them not to damage the sprouts when hoeing. He looked awkward after I had announced that I was from Company Seven. He looked at me from the corner of his eye.

I said, I have a letter for you. It's from . . . He flushed before I spelled out Yan's name. He smiled unnaturally and looked around. His hands trembled slightly when he took the letter I held out. He put the letter in his pocket, looked around again and then guided me through the fields to his office. His company seemed more established than ours. He had more barracks. The soldiers were older, the males were thinner and the females were fatter. They all wore straw hats. They were having their work break. The flies hovered over the smell of manure. The soldiers were lying by the field path like potatoes, hats covering their faces. The earth was as hot as a stove.

While pouring me a cup of water, Leopard called in his assistant, a short woman. He told the woman to begin as he walked out of the room. The short woman introduced herself as Old Wong. She began to lecture me on how the Cultural Revolution was progressing in this company. She kept pausing to look at me. She reminded me that I wasn't taking any notes. She rolled her eyes to show her dissatisfaction. I didn't pay much attention to her. I anxiously waited for Leopard to come back. I tried hard not to look out of the window. Finally Leopard came back. With no particular expression on his face, he asked if we were done. Oh, yes, I said, hoping he would get rid of Old Wong. But he showed no such intention. He asked if there was anything else I would like to know. I didn't understand why he had to ask this question: he knew exactly what I wanted. I sat there staring at him. Leopard played with a rubber band. He was nervous. The rubber band broke and it bounced off Old Wong's face. She screamed, hands on her cheeks. He said sorry and took a cigarette from the drawer. He lit it and began flicking it before there were any ashes. Old Wong asked if she should call up a tractor to send me back. Leopard nodded. I couldn't believe he was doing this, but I didn't know what to do.

I got on the tractor. The tractor driver started the engine. I looked at Leopard. I found him to be not good-looking at all. He looked away. He was too afraid of being caught. He was a coward. I began to dislike him, for Yan was facing the same risk, and was not afraid, and he, as a man, had no guts.

That night, in the mosquito net, Yan asked me how the visit went. I was afraid that I would wound her if I told her the truth. I said, Oh, he looked very excited. Yan asked whether he would write back. I nodded and answered with a yes in a sure tone. Yan was satisfied. She asked me to write another letter for her.

I delivered four letters to Leopard in two months. He never wrote back. I became hostile when I visited him. I wished that I could whip him the way I would whip a cow to make him fall for Yan. A couple of times it seemed that he wanted to talk to me, but he always managed to switch the button off just before the current got connected. I thought about why he acted withdrawn. He knew Yan well enough to know that she cared about nothing but to be with him. She would not be able to hide her feelings. They would be caught like Little Green and her bookish lover. They would lose their positions in the Party. If they declared their love, the farm headquarters would give them a certain day to get married and then assign them a little room in the barracks as their permanent home. The legends would end, and the chance to go back to Shanghai would be forever lost. They would be titled as local peasants the moment they settled down. Would this be what Leopard wanted for his life? I seriously doubted it.

I felt sorry for Yan, for she was so lovesick. Every night I listened to her murmuring and comforted her by making up stories about the miracles of love. I spent all my sugar coupons on her because she was a sugar addict. She ate up corncobs just because they were sweet. In order to keep sharing the bed with her, I continued to make excuses about the cold weather. I told her not to wash the mosquito net because the dirt made it less transparent. When the light was on, we could see everything in the room, but no one was able to see us.

101

Despite her lovesickness, in front of the ranks Yan was as tough as a rock. She took the company to a labour competition with our neighbouring Red Star Farm. We were to dig a canal. Yan's performance was admired by thousands. At night she was softer than fermented bread. I enjoyed seeing her flush when she read my letters. I asked her to imagine herself being a lover, insisting she tell me the details that I would use the next time I wrote. She would grin and say, Do you know how the local peasants buy persimmons? – They pick the softest. This is what you are doing to me. I said I had to know the details, or how was I supposed to depict it. She said, Where's your imagination? I replied that one could not imagine anything one had no sense of. She pressed her forefinger to my lips and told me to be quiet. She whispered that she had the sensations but could not put what she felt into words. She was too embarrassed about it. She grabbed my hand and pressed it to her chest. She asked me to feel her heart.

I wished I was the blood in that chamber. In the hammering of her heartbeat, the rising and falling of her chest, I saw a city of chaos. A mythical force drew me towards her. I felt the blazing of a fire rise inside me. Yan was wearing a thin shirt with a bra under it. The shirt was the colour of roots. The bra was plain white. Her bright red underwear added fuel to the fire. As she lazily stretched her body, my heart raged.

Closing her eyes she moved my hands to her cheeks. Slowly opening her eyes, she stared at me. Lips slightly parted. I could not bear it, the way she looked at me, like water penetrating rocks. Passion overflowed in her eyes.

I made an effort to look away, staring at the ceiling of the net. I heard Lu's cough. She was sitting three feet away at the table, concentrating on Mao. She turned a page.

Under the blankets, Yan's arms were around my neck. She held me closer. Her breasts pressed against my shoulder. She turned me towards her. She untied one of her braids, then moved my hands up to untie the other. I smoothed her loosened hair with my fingers.

I heard Lu brushing her teeth. She spat outside, then closed the door and turned off the light. The bedframe shook as she climbed in. I waited for her snoring. Yan began to whisper in my ear, reciting some of the phrases I had used in the letters. She was a rice-shoot in a summer of drought.

I continued to drop Leopard letters every two weeks. He said, Thanks for the letters, and nothing more. I went back to Yan empty-handed. One night when I was writing another letter Yan lay next to me in tears. She said that she knew all I had been telling her about Leopard was lies. She said, Your hands are too small to cover the sky. You made me into a fool. She said it quietly. A pitiful fool, she added. I tore the letter up in guilt. I said I did that because I didn't know what else to do. I said I was sorry for trying to gloss things over. She said, You don't have to apologize. I said he might just be afraid, and he might need more time. She shook her head and smiled sadly. She said she wasn't pretty enough for him, wasn't intelligent enough, wasn't feminine enough. She was a cheap fool. She was stupid and that was that. She picked up a mirror and turned it towards herself. After a long time staring into it, she said she saw an old, weather-beaten face. She said she was twenty-five, she had nothing but the useless Party position titles. That was what she deserved because one gains what one plants. She deserved the decoration.

I could not bear her sadness. It haunted me when she said that she had nothing except the Party titles. She had me. I went up to her and took the mirror away from her face. I was unable to say anything. I wanted to say: You are very, very beautiful. I adore everything in you. If I were a man, I would die for your love.

By four o'clock I was able to dismiss my platoon. We were repairing a bridge. My policy – when the assignment was completed, they were allowed to take the rest of the day off. The soldiers liked me. In many cases, those who finished the work would stay to help the others, in response to my call 'to carry forward the Communist collaborative spirit'. Lu didn't like my policy; she called it 'capitalist contract bullshit'. She asked me to change it and I had no choice but to acquiesce. But when she wasn't inspecting, I did things my way.

When the work was done I walked across the bridge. Along the canal side there was a huge slogan painted on canvas and mounted on thick bamboo sticks which said 'Do not fear death or hard work'. We had created the canal ourselves during my first winter at the farm nearly a year ago. I felt proud every time I walked by it.

This particular day, as I passed by the bridge I heard a local boatman calling me from his boat. He told me to come quickly; he had discovered a drowned body. I ran down to the boat. It was a female body. The boatman slowly flipped her over like an egg roll on a skillet. Before me was Little Green. I lost my breath. Her face was puffed. Her whole head had swelled like a pumpkin. There were traces of cuts on her arms and legs. The boatman said, It looks like she had a fit. You see these cuts? She struggled, but got tangled in the weeds. I stood motionless.

Someone brought the news to Yan. She came running down from the bridge like a mad horse with her hair standing back on its roots. Her face was blue and red as if it had been beaten. She wouldn't listen when the boatman told her that it was useless to attempt mouth-to-mouth life-saving. She's been dead for hours, the boatman said. Yan kept pumping and pumping at Little Green's chest. Heavy sweat ran down her hair in tiny streams. Her shirt soon was soaked. She didn't stop until she completely exhausted herself.

The Red Fire Farm headquarters held a special memorial service for Little Green. She was honoured as an Outstanding Comrade and was admitted posthumously into the Youth League of the Communist Party. Little Green's grandmother attended the service. She was beautiful like her granddaughter. She had an opera singer's elegance. She hugged Little Green. She had no tears in her eyes, her face was paler than the dead. Lu, representing the farm's Party committee, issued her a cheque for 500 yuan as a condolence. Little Green's grandmother took the cheque and stared at it.

Yan left suddenly. She did not come back for dinner. I went to look for her, searching everywhere before I finally found her sitting under the bridge. The jar in which she used to collect the snakes was beside her. A few days ago she told me in great delight that she had just reached the perfect number – one hundred snakes – and was expecting Little Green to come back to her senses magically.

I stepped closer to Yan and saw that she was pulling each snake's head off its neck. The dark brown blood of the snakes spattered all over her face and uniform. When all the snakes were torn, she took up the jar and smashed it.

I went up to her. She crouched at my knees. I held her as she began to cry.

紅 杜 鵑

After Little Green's death, Yan was no longer the Party secretary and the commander that I knew. She changed me along with her. We discussed the reasons why we were losing sight of the 'brilliant future' the Party had drawn. We asked ourselves why we were getting poorer and poorer when we had been working so hard on the land. Our monthly salary of twenty-four yuan barely covered food, fuel oil and toilet paper. I had never been able to buy any new clothes for myself. Were we going to spend the rest of our lives this way? The irony was bitter: the Red Fire Farm was a model Communist collective, the wave of the future. It was one of ten farms in the East China Sea. But none of these farms – Red Star, Red Spark, May Fourth, May Seventh, Vanguard, East Sea, Long March, Sea Wind and Sea Harvest – with a total of over 200,000 city youth sent to work and live in them, could even grow enough food to feed themselves. The farm had been getting food supplements from the government every year. And the government had made it clear to the headquarters that we would not get any help next year. We asked ourselves what it really meant when we shouted, 'Sweating hard, growing more crops to support the world's revolution'.

Yan lost interest in conducting political study meetings. She became vulnerable, weak and sad. We had fights. She said she wanted to quit her position. She said she was no longer the right person for the job. Lu fit it much better. I said I did not like seeing her become decadent. Dispiritedness would not save us. She said quitting was her way. I asked, What would happen after you quit and Lu took power? Would we be sleeping together? She said, I didn't know you liked my power better than you liked me. I said, It's not the power you have in hand, it is our lives. You can't make it better but you can make it worse. She said her life was a waste, it was a jail here. I said, Where could we go? How could we escape? There were nets above and snares below. We run, we die. Mao and the Party had set our fate. We must drag on.

Yan left for seven days' intensive political training at the farm headquarters. I slept alone. And I became upset. I was afraid of losing her when she and Leopard met again. It was a strange feeling, a feeling of continuous distraction. I dreamt of Yan at night. I looked forward to the sunset when the day announced its end. She became my lover in her absence. At sunset a new feeling was born, for her. Its colour crossed out my heart's darkness.

*

I wrote to my parents in Shanghai. I told them about the Party secretary, Commander Yan. I said we were very good friends. She was a fair boss. She was like a big tree with crowded branches and lush foliage, and I enjoyed the cool air sitting under her. This was as far as I could go in explaining myself. I told my mother the farm was fine and I was fine. I mentioned that some of my roommates' parents had made visits although the farm was not worth the trip.

My mother came instead of writing back. I was in the middle of spraying chemicals. Orchid told me that my mother had arrived. I did not believe her. She pointed to a lady coated in dust standing on the path. Now tell me I was lying, she said. I took off the chemical container and walked towards my mother. Mother, I said, who told you to come? Mother smiled and said, A mother can always find her child. I kneeled down to take off her shoes. Her feet were swollen. I poured her a bowl of water. She asked how heavy the fungicide container was. Sixty pounds, I said. Mother said, Your back is soaked. I said, I know. Mother said, It's good that you work hard. I told her that I was the platoon leader.

Mother said she was proud. I said I was glad. She said she did not bring anything because Blooming had just graduated from the middle school and was assigned to a professional boarding school. Her Shanghai-resident number was also taken away. We have no money to buy her a new blanket, she still uses the one you left. It's good to be frugal, don't you think? Mother said. What about Coral? I asked. Will she be assigned to a factory? Mother nodded and said she had been praying for that to happen. But it's hard to say, Mother shook her head. Coral is afraid of leaving. The school people said that if she shows a physical disability, her chances of staying in Shanghai would be much better. Coral did not go to see a doctor while she was having serious dysentery. She was trying to destroy her intestines to claim disability. That was stupid, but we were not able to stop her. A lot of youths in the neighbourhood are doing the same thing, they are scared of being assigned to the farms. Coral is very unhappy. She said she had never asked to be born, she said that to my face. My child said that to my face.

I placed Mother in Yan's bed that night. I wanted to talk to my mother but instead fell asleep the minute my head hit the pillow. The next morning Mother said she'd better leave. She said that I should not feel sorry for myself. It shows weakness. And her presence might have increased my weakness and that was not her intention in being here. She should not be here making my soldiers' homesickness worse. I could not say that I was not feeling weak. I could not say my behaviour would not influence the others. I wanted to cry in my mother's arms, but I had been an adult since the age of five. I was the model for my mother's other children. She must see me be strong. Or she would not survive. She depended on me. I asked if she would like me to give her a tour of the farm. She said she had seen enough. The salty bare land was enough. She said it was time for her to go back. She asked me to take care of Orchid's foot. Her foot had been pierced by a reed and become infected.

Mother did not ask about Yan, about whose bed she had slept in the previous night. I wished she had. I wished I could tell her some of my real life. But Mother did not ask. I knew Yan's title of a Party secretary was the reason. Mother was afraid of Party secretaries. She was a victim of every one of them. She ran away before I introduced Yan.

Mother refused to allow me to accompany her to the farm's bus station. She was insistent. She walked away by herself in the dust. Despite Lu's objection to a few hours' absence, I went to follow my mother through the cotton fields. For three miles she didn't take a rest. She was walking away from what she had seen, the land, the daughters of Shanghai, the prison. She ran away like a child. I watched her while she waited for the bus. She looked older than her age: my mother was forty-three, but looked sixty or older.

When the bus carried Mother away, I ran into the cotton fields.

I exhausted myself and lay down flat on my back. I cried and called Yan's name.

The day she was expected back, I walked miles to greet her. When her tractor appeared at a crossroads my heart was about to jump out of my mouth. She jumped off and ran towards me. Her scarf blew off. The tractor drove on. Standing before me, she was so handsome in her uniform.

Did you see him? I asked, picking up her scarf and giving it back to her. Leopard? she smiled, taking the scarf. And? I said. She asked me not to mention Leopard's name any more in our conversation. It's all over and it never happened. I asked what happened. She said, Nothing. We didn't know each other. We were strangers as before. Was he there? I was persistent. Yes, he was. Did you talk? Yes, we said hello. What else? What else? We read our companies' reports, and that was all.

She did not look hurt. Her lovesickness was gone. She said, Our great leader Chairman Mao teaches us, 'A proletarian must liberate himself first to liberate the world'. She scraped my nose. I said, You smell of soap. She said she had a bath at the head-quarters. It was their special treat to branch Party secretaries. She had something important to tell me. She said she would be leaving the company soon.

I closed my eyes and relaxed in her arms. We lay quietly for a long time. Now I wish you were a man, I said. She said she knew that. She held me tighter. I listened to the sound of her heart pounding. We pretended that we were not sad. We were brave.

She told me that she had been assigned to a remote company, Company Thirty. They need a Party secretary and commander to lead eight hundred youths. Why you? Why not Lu? It's an order, she said to me. I don't belong to myself. I asked whether the new company was very far. She said she was afraid so. I asked about the land condition there. She said it was horrible, the same as here, in fact worse, because it was closer to the sea. I asked if she wanted to go there. She said she had no confidence in conquering that land. She said she did not know how she had become so afraid. She said she did not want to leave me. She smiled sadly and recited a saying, 'When the guest leaves, the tea will soon get cold.' I said my cup of tea would never get cold.

Lu turned the light off early. The company had had a long day reaping the rice. The snoring in the room was rising and falling. I was watching the moonlight when Yan's hands tenderly touched my face. Her hands soothed my neck and shoulders. She said she must bear the pain of leaving me. Tears welled up in my eyes. I thought of Little Green and the bookish man. Their joy and the price they paid. I wept. Yan held me in. She said she could not stop herself. Her thirst was dreadful.

She covered us with blankets. We breathed each other's breath. She pulled my hands to touch her chest. She caressed me, trembling herself. She murmured that she wished she could tell me how happy I made her feel. I asked if to her I was Leopard. She enveloped me in her arms. She said there never was a Leopard. It was I who created Leopard. I said it was an assignment given by her. She said, You did a very good job. I asked if we knew what we were doing. She said she knew nothing but the Little Red Book. I asked how the quotation applied to the situation. She recited, 'One learns to fight the war by fighting the war'.

I said I could not see her because my tears kept welling up. She whispered, Forget about my departure for now. I said I could not. She said, I want you to obey me. You always did well when you obeyed me. She licked my tears and said this was how she was going to remember us.

I moved my hands slowly through her shirt. She pulled my fingers to unbutton her bra. The buttons were tight, five of them. Finally, the last one came off. The moment I touched her breasts, I felt a sweet shock. My heart beat disorderedly. A wild horse broke off its reins. She whispered something I could not hear. She was melting snow. I did not know what role I was playing any more: her imagined man or myself. I was drawn to her. The horse kept running wild. I went where the sun rose. Her lips were the colour of a tomato. There was a gale mixed with thunder inside me. I was spellbound by desire. I wanted to be touched. Her hands skimmed my breasts. My mind maddened. My senses cheered frantically in a raging fire. I begged her to hold me tight. I heard a little voice rising in the back of my head demanding me to stop. As I hesitated, she caught my lips and kissed me fervently. The little voice disappeared, I lost myself in the caresses.

Yan did not go to Company Thirty. The order was cancelled because headquarters was unable to connect the drinking-water pipe there. We shouted, 'A long long life to Chairman Mao', when we got the news. Lu was unhappy. She would have taken Yan's position if Yan had gone. She said it was the rain. It rained too much and it spoiled her luck.

It was May. The crops were shooting up. For the past five months, headquarters had ordered the company leaders to pay attention to their soldiers' political awareness. Only when the minds have politically advanced, will the quantity and quality of the products be advanced. This is the key to our economic success. Lu read the instruction loudly to the company. She said that every soldier was required to give a speech at the nightly self-criticism meeting. Lu became angry during these meetings when, as usual, two thirds of the people dozed off. Lu said that there must be a class enemy hiding in the ranks. We must stretch tight the string of the class struggle in our minds to stay invincible, she said.

To push us to work harder, Lu also passed down an order: one would be allowed to pee or shit only two times a day during working hours and could stay in the restroom no longer than five minutes. Anyone who broke this rule would be seriously criticized. Only the lazy donkeys shit more than that, Lu said. And lazy donkeys deserve to be ruthlessly beaten!

When Lu asked Yan to give mobilization talks to the masses,

Yan stepped in front of the ranks and said, Please repeat after me: Chairman Mao teaches us, 'Trust the people'. She dismissed the meeting in less than one minute. Lu said, We can't expect the studs to be straight if the beams are not. Yan said, What's your problem? Tapping her pen on her notebook, Lu said, Comrade Secretary, I think you've got spiritual termites in the house of your mind. Yeah? Yan looked at Lu sideways. You know where I got those termites? From you. You've got termites fully packed in your head. You have no clean beams or studs in the house of your mind. They were eaten up a long time ago. And now your termites are hungry, they are climbing out from your eyes, ear holes, nose hole and asshole to eat up other people's houses. Yan walked away, leaving Lu purple.

Although my excuses about the cold weather were becoming less convincing, I still slept with Yan, pretending it was out of habit. Lu became uncomfortable. She said it was not healthy for two people to dissociate themselves from everyone else. She pointed out at a Party members' meeting that Yan had slackened her self-discipline and was developing a dangerous tendency towards revisionism. She criticized her for divorcing herself from the masses and forming a political faction. Yan told me to ignore Lu, she called her a political bug.

One afternoon I found my bed had been checked. Later that night I also noticed that Lu's snoring had stopped; I wondered if she had been listening to us. The next day Lu came and said that she would like to have a talk with me. She asked me what I did with Yan at the Brick Factory. I said we practised Erhu. She said, Is that all? Her eyes told me she did not believe a word of it. You know I've been receiving reports from the masses on you two. She always used 'the masses' to state what she wanted to say. I said, I'm sorry, I don't understand you. She said, I'm sure you understand me perfectly. She smiled, I've noticed you two have been wearing each other's clothes. It was true Yan and I had been paying attention to looking our best. It was true that we wore

112

each other's clothes and I had worn her three-inch-wide belt. I asked Lu if it was a problem. Lu did not answer me. She walked away with a we-will-see smile. The same night a new slogan appeared on the cafeteria wall. It said 'Be aware of the new patterns of the class struggle'. Lu gave a speech at the night's meeting calling for attention to 'hiding corrupters in the proletarian rank'. She emphasized that the company should not allow a tiny mouse shit to spoil a jar of porridge.

The same night, on our way back from the hot-water station, Yan and I talked about Lu's suspicions. Yan suggested that we stop sleeping together. She told me that Lu was secretly calling for approval from the upper Party committee for a midnight search in every mosquito net. You must obey me, Yan said seriously. I said, All right, but after tonight.

Yan held me in her arms. I felt as if her arms were about to break my ribs.

The next dawn, I was awakened by an unfamiliar breath on my face. I cracked open my eyes. I saw a blurred head swaying in front of me. I was horrified: it was Lu. She was in our net watching us.

My heart screamed. I tried to stay in control. I closed my eyes, pretending that I was still sleeping. I began to tremble. If Lu lifted the blankets, Yan and I would be exposed naked. Lu could have us arrested immediately. I felt Lu's breath harden. My fingers underneath the blankets were taking a firm hold on the sheet. I prayed, to what, I didn't know. Just prayed. I felt Lu's head getting closer and closer to my face. Her hand reached my neck and touched the end of the sheet.

Yan turned to the wall in sleep. Lu's shadow ducked off. I was paralysed. When I reopened my eyes, Lu was gone.

Lu stopped asking me questions. And I noticed that I was followed either by her or by some of her trusted followers wherever I went. I had become Lu's target to attack Yan.

It was hard not being able to be close to Yan. The day became senseless. Yan acted tougher than before. She worked hard and showed no emotion. She dragged Lu to be her partner in carrying stones. To exhaust Lu, she took a full hod and walked as fast as she could. Although Lu curled like a shrimp when she was working with Yan, she never complained. As if she knew one day she would win, she bore the pain almost gracefully. A couple of times I saw her wiping off tears at night while taking her study notes.

You know I really don't mind having my body hung upside down or my buttocks pricked by a needle, Lu said to me raising her head from her notebook with a ghastly smile. Faith is all that I need.

Three weeks later, one evening after work, when there was no one in the room, I begged Yan to stop torturing Lu. I asked her to think about the consequences. I said, Don't forget that a dog will jump over a wall if it is forced into a corner. Yan pulled me against the door and said, Lu wants the power, she wants to push me off my position. It doesn't matter whether I'm nice to her or not, she's decided to be my enemy. She knows very well that by breaking you, she can break me. Yan then told me that two weeks ago, when she nominated me to be a member of the Communist Party to the farm's headquarters, Lu voted an objection. She won't allow a tiger to grow a pair of wings, Yan said to me. Do you understand? You are my wings!

I said I did not really care to join the Party anyway. But you need the Party membership, said Yan. It's a weapon for your future. I said, What could you do about Lu's objection? 'If someone takes the initiative to hurt me, I will hurt him back.' Yan recited Mao's quotation and continued, I went to headquarters this afternoon. The Chief wanted to talk about Lu's promotion with me. I did the same thing to her that she had done to you. I picked some bones out of her fucking egg. It was successful. The Chief dropped the proposal.

I asked what she was going to do with Lu's hatred. She said she could not care less as she herself was a dog pushed into the corner. We walked on a foggy path, stepping on the dew. I said

114

I was tired of life and I hated being a bullet lying in a rifle chamber. Yan said she felt the same way. But it's better to fight than be torn alive, she said. It must be fate that we were born at this time. If you can't go back to your mother's womb, you'd better learn to be a good fighter.

Spring Festival came. To set ourselves up as good examples for the soldiers, Yan and I volunteered to guard the company's property over the holidays, so that we could spend time together. After the last soldier was gone, at dawn, Yan and I went to the fields to dig radishes and cauliflowers. We cooked delicious soup that night.

After dinner, late in the evening, Yan and I went for a long walk in the frosted field. I felt that I was completely at peace, both in mind and body. I looked at Yan, her rigid features against the black sky. She was an iron goddess. I once again felt my worship of her and it made me fall speechless. I walked shoulder to shoulder with her. She stared into the far distance, buried in thought. The cold air was brisk. I took deep breaths. Yan was thinking about her future and mine, I was sure. It depressed me to follow her thoughts. What control did we have over our own future? None. The life we were living was our assigned future, just like our parents: one job for a lifetime – a cog fixed on the revolutionary running machine, not until broken down does it pass.

Yan took my hand and held it tight. We sat in the dark reeds, depressed and pleased at the same time.

When we got back to our room, Lu appeared unexpectedly. She said that she wanted to replace either Yan or me, so that one of us could have a break. We were greatly disappointed, but neither of us said a word.

The invisible battle between Lu and us was as tough as the frozen salty brown mud. Lu never stopped watching us. She became addicted to watching us. Yan and I lived around her traps. During the day, we rearranged the grain storage and selected the cotton. Yan and I remained silent most of the time. At night, we each slept in our own nets and thought about each other. One afternoon, I found Lu's shadow hiding behind the door, listening to our conversation. After I signalled to Yan where Lu was hiding, Yan picked up a wooden stick. Pretending she was chasing a rat, she knocked open the door and exposed Lu. Lu smiled awkwardly, she said she was looking for some mosquitoes to clap. Yan was annoyed. One day when Lu was out in the fields, she took Lu's skull and threw it into a manure pit. Lu turned purple when she got back and could not find the skull. Yan did not admit to the act. Lu did not say anything more about the skull but carved the date on the door. When I looked at the dull but determined carving strokes, I could feel Lu's choking strength. Strap it tight! Yes, tighter! Tighter! One night I heard Lu crying out in her sleep.

红 杜 鹃

After the Spring Festival, we went every day to hoe the cotton fields. The wind from the East China Sea mixed with sand and felt needle-sharp. It pricked our skin and cracked our lips. Frost damaged the buds. The soldiers were resentful. They swore when the water pipes were frozen in the morning. They picked fights over tiny things like who had more space on clothes lines. It was useless when Lu called for a united and harmonious family. Yan was busy looking for Lu's faults. She wanted to kick Lu out of the company. Lu knew it and was doing the same thing to Yan.

Yan and I had long stopped meeting at the Brick Factory because we could not tell where Lu would send her human watchdogs. Yan's face was long. She started swearing again. There were executions of all types on the farm. Headquarters was frustrated at the soldiers' faithlessness. Posters of people being sentenced to death were often seen on the walls. It was called 'killing a chicken to shock the monkeys'.

Yan one day came to me and told me that Orchid had become Lu's watchdog. She had been following us secretly. I disagreed. I said Orchid was a good human being. Yan said no one in this company was human any more. We were dogs. We fought for others' meat. Weren't we willing to do anything to buy comfort? Lu's been assigning light jobs to Orchid, and that was suspicious. I said to Yan, You see an enemy behind every tree. She said she did perhaps. It's a mad house. The Red Fire Farm.

One morning, while I was hoeing in the cotton field with my platoon, a white van drove by and stopped on the path. It was unusual to see a van. A group of well-dressed people in green army coats got out and walked towards us. As they passed, they looked at us from head to foot with critical eyes. You, a man suddenly pointed his finger at me. I wiped the sweat off my face and said, Me? Yes, you. The man came closer and asked, How old are you? He was about forty years old. He spoke in standard dialect, like a broadcast announcer's Mandarin. I told him I was twenty. He asked me if I could give directions to the headquarters. A woman in the group was taking notes of our conversation. As I was giving them instructions, they encircled me, observing my profile, squatting on their heels, narrowing their eyes to measure my body length and features. The man asked me if I had blisters on my hands. I showed them the blisters, on each of my hands, my shoulders and my knees. They studied the blisters and took a close look at my nails which were all dark brown because of working with the fungicide. I heard the man whisper to a woman. The woman wrote something down in her notebook. A few minutes later, they went back to their van. They did not follow the directions I had given them.

That night, during the study meeting, instead of dozing off, the

117

soldiers were gossiping about who those people were and why they had come. Finally a girl whose aunt was working in the government's cultural bureau explained the cause: Comrade Jiang Ching, Madam Mao, was reforming the movie industry and had sent a group of her associates to find correct-looking young men and women to train as China's future film actors. The type of look which could convince the masses that if there were a pair of enemy bayonets set across their neck they would not renounce their Communist beliefs in exchange for life. The chosen few would be taught to play the leading roles in movies. As a political requirement, the candidates had to be outstanding workers, peasants or soldiers.

I told the news to Yan and she thought it was fantasy-talking. Our faces were in no way close to beauty. We were brown potatoes. The chance of being chosen was like a needle being found in an ocean.

Someone in my room hung a broken mirror next to the door the following day. Everyone began bending sideways to take a look at herself before leaving the room. At noon I saw Lu making faces at herself when I opened the door. After a few embarrassing moments, Lu told me to take the mirror down. I said it was not my mirror. She said, Do as I say. She added that she would hold a meeting tonight on what we needed to do to stand clear of bourgeois influence. I took the mirror down and gave it to Lu. Lu hung the mirror in front of the company bulletin board and painted a large slogan behind it as a reminder, 'The collapse of a dam begins with an ant hole.' That night Lu lectured for two hours on how important it was to fight the invisible ideological enemies.

Lu's lecture did not stop people's filmstar fantasies. They wore their best clothes and made all kinds of excuses to go to headquarters to pass by the windows of these unusual guests. Orchid and I were assigned to go to the headquarters' shops to buy preserved vegetables. We saw that headquarters was full of people. Everyone was discussing where the Film Studio people would be and I heard someone say they would take the Red Heart Drive to come back.

Orchid asked me whether we should get on the Red Heart Driveway when she saw others moving that way. I hesitated. You never know, Orchid encouraged. She then told me that the day before a girl was picked when she was brushing her teeth in Company Thirteen. They asked her to put on more toothpaste and to continue brushing while they did the interview with her.

Orchid and I went to Red Heart Driveway. We waited, like many other people, pretending that we were just taking a walk. After half an hour, we saw the white van appear. Everyone suddenly became animated and began to smile at the van. I smiled as it passed.

Orchid and I were using the restroom when we heard someone practising a Mao poem loudly while having a bowel movement in the men's room. 'Four seas stir float cloud water angry,' the man recited, then he stopped. I heard his shit drop. 'Five continents shake flutter wind thunder fighting.' Again the sound of shit dropping.

'The Communists are like the seeds,' a girl was singing Mao's quotation song behind me. 'The people are like the earth. We must integrate ourselves with the people wherever we go . . .' Orchid yelled, Don't get too excited. You're going to fall and integrate with the manure. 'Bloom and grow roots in the people . . .' the girl continued.

A week later, Yan and Lu were called to headquarters by the farm's chief Party secretary for an important meeting. They came back with an announcement: two women and one man had been selected from the entire Red Fire Farm to go to the Film Studio for the first regional contest. I was one of them.

I looked at myself again and again in the tiny mirror. Imagining the mirror a huge screen. I practised all kinds of expressions I thought would look good to the millions in the audience.

Yan told me that I was given the choice of either dancing or reciting one of Mao's poems during the contest. I decided to recite

Mao's poem, 'Praising the Winter Plum'. The Winter Plum was Mao's symbol of the Communist Party and the Red Army. Yan watched me as I prepared the recitation. She sat there like a Buddha statue. When I asked her how I did, she said she saw a golden phoenix soaring out of a chicken coop.

Three days later, Yan was assigned by headquarters to take me to Shanghai for the contest. The night before we took off, Yan did not come back until midnight. Without saying a word, she took off her shoes, got into the net and closed the curtain tightly. I knew what was on her mind but could do nothing to help.

Shut the fucking light off, will you, Comrade Lu? Yan yelled from the net. I haven't done my study yet. Lu sat on her stool firmly. It's bedtime! Yan shouted. Lu stood up and said, I am studying Marxism! Yan interrupted her, I don't care if you're studying capitalism! I just want the light off! Lu sat down, turned her pages and said, Stop acting like Hitler! Yan jumped off the bed, switched off the light and got back into her net. Lu went to switch the light back on. You whore! Yan shouted furiously, opening the net curtain. She picked up her Erhu from underneath the bed and threw it at the light. The light bulb broke along with one of the Erhu's strings. I'll report everything to headquarters tomorrow, Lu said in the dark.

I kept quiet. What could I say? It was the possibility of my departure that upset Yan. Regardless of how much she wanted me to leave this place, my taking off would mean that she would have nothing else to rely on. Since her belief in Communism had begun to collapse, she was no longer emotionally strong. I had no idea where I would be taken if I won the contest.

The next morning, Yan appeared calm. She poured all her saved sugar into my porridge. Lu watched us as Yan went to pull out the tractor and hurried me on. The soldiers watched in silence. Yan took me to headquarters to get a stamp to leave the farm. We transferred to the truck to Shanghai.

*

120

We sat closely together on the farm's open truck. It began to rain after we crossed the country border approaching the city. I tried not to think too much about what was going to happen: whether Yan and I would be apart for ever. Yan took out a plastic sheet from her bag to cover me from the rain. I tried to pull the sheet to cover her. Don't bother, she said impatiently. I held her arm and said, Maybe I won't even pass the regional contest. Don't you dare to shit on my face, she said.

Its gate was more solemn than I had imagined, the Shanghai Film Studio. In front of me was a big flowerbed with two dark reddish buildings standing imposingly on each side. Yan and I walked through the studios where we saw painted ocean backgrounds and wood and ceramic naval vessels. We lost our way and ended up in a place where we saw burnt houses and a collapsed bridge. We explored underground tunnels, artificial trees, plastic human body parts dressed in Communist Army uniforms and Japanese army uniforms and a burnt Japanese flag.

A security guard came yelling after us. We showed him our official letter. He directed us to the performance hall where I saw many young people gathered. We were guided to our seats. I looked around. A red slogan hung above the stage: 'Devote all our energy to the Party's cultural business!' There were two other slogans hanging vertically: 'Follow Comrade Jiang Ching!' and 'Long live the victory of Mao's revolutionary line!' In front of the stage was a long narrow table covered with a white cloth. About fifteen judges were seated behind the table.

A girl who sat next to me was the most beautiful girl I had ever seen in my life. She told me that she was from my neighbour-ing farm, the Red Star Farm. She had a cherry-like mouth. Compared to hers, my mouth was as big as a frog's. She had hips that curved out from the waist. Mine were a straight column. When her name was called, she went on stage calmly and performed without rushing. Her piece was a combination of dancing and story-telling. As she performed, she laughed and cried like real

121

life. I began to feel short of breath. The sounds around me were like layers of echoes. My rivals sitting beside me became blurry figures and heads. I knew nothing about professional acting, there was no way I could compete with them. I kept thinking that I couldn't even speak Mandarin properly. When my name was called, I panicked. Instead of standing up and walking to the stage, I bent over the chair in front and covered my head with my arms.

Yan shook my arms and shoulders, but I could not make myself move. I was shaking hard. The announcer repeated my name and said that it was the last call. I felt that I was going to faint. I had double vision. My legs were strengthless. Yan yelled ferociously in my ear, Get your ass moving, you pig-shit-head! For our ancestors' sake it's your only chance to escape from hell! She cried, You pig-shit-head, you louse-won't-touch corpse, you have disappointed and dishonoured me.

I jumped up. I wiped the sweat off my face. My army coat fell from my shoulders. I strode to the stage.

I stood in front of the judges. I saw no expression on their faces. They looked me up and down. The one in the centre with the bald head took his glasses off. I opened my mouth but I was voiceless. My mind went blank – I forgot the lines. Yan rose up from the audience. Her face was purple.

The words spilled out from my mouth by themselves. Chairman Mao's poem. I was almost shouting, Praising the Winter Plum! The sound was resonant and clear like a bugle call. Yan smiled, her mouth was motioning with me:

> The wind and the rain sent the spring away
> But the snow has brought it back.
> There are ice columns a hundred feet long
> Hanging dangerously down from cliffs.
> There is a little plum flower blooming.
> The flower has no intention
> To compete with the spring.

She is here only to announce
The coming of the spring.
By the time the flowers bloom
All over the mountains,
She will be hiding among the flowers
And she will smile with great delight.

Yan looked at me with gentleness. She held my hands throughout the trip back to the Red Fire Farm.

As I awaited the results of the contest, the soldiers in the company began to distance themselves from me. I could sense their envy and bitterness. After two months, when I started to believe that I must have been eliminated, Yan brought back an announcement from headquarters saying that I had been selected for the second regional contest.

My parents in Shanghai were glad to have the chance to reunite with me for the weekend. My father warned me not to believe anything. My father was older than his age. So was my mother. They had no more courage left. Their drive was greatly weakened by their experiences. My father was no longer the ambitious astronomer who named his son Space Conqueror. He was crushed under the unit Party secretary's feet, trampled upon. He was as timid as a mouse in shock.

I was sent back to the farm and was called back for three other regional contests. I forced myself not to think about the event after every contest.

Yan buried herself in hard work. A few times, I found her looking at me from a distance with the saddest expression on her face. She rarely spoke, and when she did her voice sounded tired. I did not know what to say. I tried to keep myself busy in weaving my new future. I did not want to deal with my feelings. I could not. I could not face Yan. It was too hard. I tried to forget before time separated us.

*

In the early spring of 1976, after the final contest, I was sent to the Shanghai Film Studio for a special class to test my ability to learn. Many of the people I had met and had thought were excellent, such as the girl with the cherry-like mouth from the Red Star Farm, had been eliminated. People who had showed a lack of performing skills were kept on. Later I was told that one of Jiang Ching's principles was that she would rather have 'socialist grass' than 'capitalist sprouts'. The judges thought of me as having less talent but politically reliable.

In the class, I was instructed to carry a plastic bag, pretending it was a heavy stone. I was described as having a plain background – that is, no one in my family had been an actor – but being quick in responding to instructions.

In another acting exercise, I was asked to drink a cup of water. The instructor stopped me and said, No, no, no. You are not drinking the water right. He said I had two problems. He said that a person from the proletarian class would never hold a cup in such a superficial manner – using three fingers on the handle. He instructed me to grab the cup with my hand. He pointed out that a proletarian person would never drink water sip by sip like a Miss Bourgeois with tons of spare time. He showed me how to drink down the water fast in one gulp and wipe my mouth with my sleeve.

The studio checked my family background and my political record and then sent me back to the farm. I was told that I had been accepted.

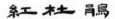

124

When I got back and told the exciting news to Orchid, she shocked me with a rumour: headquarters was conducting an investigation into me and Yan. Lu was the investigation-team head.

I went to Yan to confirm the rumour. Yan looked like a desperado. She told me Lu had made secret reports on us to headquarters. The locust had begun its chewing. It had begun its destruction. Yan was ordered by headquarters to 'put her cards on the table', on her own initiative, before the masses' force would be used.

I denied it, Yan whispered to me. I denied everything. I have mastered the Party's tricks. I told the chief Party secretary that I couldn't have had a more revolutionary relationship with you than with any of my comrades. I gave many examples of your achievement as an outstanding platoon leader under my leadership. I expressed our loyalty to the Party. I was shameless when I did that. In a mad house I suppose one could say anything, couldn't one? The chief discharged the case because Lu was holding no concrete evidence. The bastard Lu went to file a report to the Film Studio Party committee. The bastard was fantastically insane. I had to admire her.

The Film Studio sent a team down to check out the case. They had talks with Lu. They did not speak to me or Yan. The chief seemed to be changing his mind about me. He set up a two-man investigation team and conducted a chain-talk with everyone, one after the other, in the company. Yan worried. She said, They will seek out some spider's webs and horse's tracks because, fortunately and unfortunately, the masses do have 'brighter eyes', I suppose.

I asked Yan what to do. She fell into silence for a long moment, then said, citing a saying, 'If the tactics of a devil are a foot high, the tactics of Taoism will be ten times higher.' I asked how she interpreted it. She told me to do two things: first, deny everything if interrogated: second, do as she told me. Do not ask any

125

questions. When I asked why she could not discuss her plan with me, she replied that that was part of her plan.

Lu used the full scope of her power as if Yan was already out of the picture. She stopped her Mao work-study routine, saying that she had mastered the essence of Mao thoughts. She smiled her way in and out of the room and hummed songs at work. She ordered pork chops at lunch and dinner. She gained weight. A week after I was back, one clear morning, Lu gathered the company in front of the storage bins for a meeting. She ordered everyone to recite Mao's poem with her and pay attention to its latent meaning. The ranks followed her:

> Around the little globe
> There are few flies bouncing the wall.
> The noises they make
> Sound shrill and mournful –
> An ant trying to topple a tree –
> How ridiculous the way they over-rate their strength.

Everyone in the ranks knew what Lu was insinuating. They shot secret glances at Yan. Yan stood among the ranks like Mount Everest towering in a storm. I was surprised that she recited the poem loudly showing no anger. I've warned all of you before, said Lu, and I'm warning you again. She paced back and forth, giving big arm gestures. A fly only parks on a cracked egg. She turned to Yan. Am I not right? Yan nodded humbly.

Lu smiled arrogantly. She took a piece of paper out of her pocket and announced a decision from headquarters: Until the investigation team reaches its conclusion, there will be no candidate sent from our company to the Film Studio.

I looked at Yan. I could not hide my disappointment and shock. Yan was chewing down a corncob. Her features twisted, she looked like a wounded fighting bull. After staring at Yan for a moment, Lu asked whether Yan needed some aspirin for she did not look well.

Slowly turning towards the ranks, Yan questioned, How should a lamb respond when a wolf asks to pay her a New Year's eve visit? The soldiers did not dare answer. They all turned to stare at Lu. Lu clenched her fist, then ordered the ranks to cite a paragraph of Mao's teaching. 'If the broom doesn't arrive, dust won't go away by itself. Same goes for wiping out the reactionaries.'

Yan said to the ranks before closing, Learn from me, comrades, learn from my stupidity. I took a fish eyeball as a pearl. She started to laugh. The soldiers watched her.

Lu smiled insidiously. Folding her arms in front of her chest, she said, The winner will not be the one who laughs the loudest, but the longest.

Helplessness enveloped me. Yan had stopped talking to me for days. I began to feel sick inside. How much would denying everything help? What could be more normal in this country than to be made a reactionary because the Party decided to call you a reactionary? Although I had never doubted Yan's fighting style, I was frustrated this time for she was not doing much except having lips-and-teeth combat with Lu. I asked myself again what could possibly be done. I was at the end of my wits.

I worked by a threshing machine the whole day. The noise was threshing my thoughts. My disappointment was so great that I could not stop thinking about my misery. The ears of grain were thin, thinner than mice shit, heaped around my feet, heaped up, burying me. I yelled at Orchid when she came to shovel the grain. She yelled back, It's late autumn, you cricket. How many days can you keep jumping?

I began to have an intense headache. After midnight, it grew worse. As I kept tossing, I suddenly heard a whisper. The voice was from underneath. Are you awake? It was Yan. She prodded my straw mattress with her fingers. I said, What are you doing? Her whisper was loud enough for Lu to hear. Yan said she wanted to meet me at the Brick Factory. I did not say anything. I kept quiet because I was thinking she might have gone mad like Little Green. I lay on my face. I wanted to cry. She prodded more. I whispered, Go back to sleep, please, people are going to hear you. She said she did not care. She said she wanted me. She said, It's midnight, it's safe. She said, It's been too long.

I noticed Lu's bed shook a little. Are you going to come? Yan continued. I'm going to take the tractor and I expect you to be there with me. She opened the net curtain and sneaked out of the room.

Darkness jumped on my face as I stepped out of the room. I felt the end of my world as I followed Yan out of the room and got on her tractor. I was sure that Lu had heard everything.

I held the tractor bar. Yan drove like a water snake moving through the reeds. She arched over the steering wheel like a jockey. Although the driveway was big enough for two tractors, when a heavily loaded tractor from the opposite direction passed by her, she jumped like a kangaroo rat.

The night was stiflingly dark. The tractor's headlights and engine noises horrified me. Yan kept up high speed. The tractor kept jumping. I screamed at Yan. I said, I don't want to go crazy with you. I shouted, You go to hell, you go and die alone. I don't want to be jailed. I don't want to be Little Green. Yan shouted back at me. She shouted clichés, clichés like 'winners don't quit, quitters never win'. I shouted that we would never win. Red Fire Farm was where we would be slaughtered. Lu would be slaughtering us. She said, Yes, Lu would be very happy to slaughter us.

The tractor zipped through reeds. My face was whipped by the leaves. I screamed. She said that I was stupid and I dreamt too much. She shouted, I am teaching you to be a killer. Be a killer to win. Stupid, do you hear me?

She made a sharp turn next to the irrigation channel. I almost fell off the tractor into the river. She encircled my waist with her right arm and controlled the tractor with the left. After she completed the turn, she slowed down. I heard another tractor coming from behind. She told me to jump off as she loosened her grip on my waist. I did not move. I thought I heard her wrong. She repeated it. I heard her say, Jump off the tractor, go back and order your platoon to make an emergency search at the Brick Factory. I said, What do you want to do? She yelled, Was my order clear? Before I answered yes, she pushed me off the tractor.

I fell into the reeds. When I rose, I saw that the other tractor had passed in front of me like a tiger sweeping over the bushes. Without seeing clearly, I knew the driver was Lu.

I was shaking. I could not think. I ran as fast as I could back to the barracks and gathered my platoon on three tractors. I kept saying, Brick Factory, Brick Factory. I did not say anything else. I did not know anything else to say. I took my rifle and loaded it.

In half an hour the platoon reached the Brick Factory. My squad head came and reported that two tractors were found parked ten yards away from each other in the reeds. As I ordered the search, I started to realize Yan's plan. I was wrapped in fear. The shadows of the soldiers moved between the brick lanes.

A memory emerged of Yan playing the Erhu for me. The touch of the music. I kept walking and a strange feeling rose slowly in me telling me that I was going mad. I cried out nervously. I said, Stop. The word came out of my mouth and caught me off-guard. The soldiers took the word as an order. They all stopped and got down on their knees. Before I gathered up my mind, I heard a noise in the distance. I began to believe that I had really gone mad because I thought I was hearing Little Green's murmuring and the sound of bodies thrusting.

The squad head asked me if we should move forward. I heard myself say, Load!, in Yan's voice. We followed the sound. Noises increased. I began to lose my sense of reality. I let the soldiers pass me. I heard the sound of something, like a bag of potatoes being tossed. I heard odd steps mixed with animal-like sounds. My fear deepened.

It was at the moment when I heard my squad head shout *Freeze!* that my heart was paralysed. The squad head reported to me that he had caught the evil-doers. Flashlights and rifles were raised in the air. The spot was brightened as if the moon had dropped. I adjusted my eyes from the dark to the light and the image that faded into my sight split my heart in half.

Yan and Lu were locked together, half naked, like a pair of grotesque mating silkworms. The strong flashlights whitened their bodies. Shadowing her eyes with a hand, Yan got up. She made a move pretending to run. The soldiers tightened their circle, and she was made to give up.

A petrol tractor came, the chief Party secretary stepped down. The soldiers made a path for him. I stood in amazement. I was amazed by Yan's plan. I understood that Yan would always be my ruler.

Yan put her shirt back on slowly. She looked around and picked up Lu's shirt. She went to cover Lu with it. She performed elegantly. Lu lay motionless, in shock. It has nothing to do with her, Yan said calmly pointing at Lu. I seduced her and I'll take the punishment for my crime.

Lu screamed, No! She screamed, It is not what you see. Not at all! I am Yan's victim. Yan kept silent and then said, I am sorry. She kept saying, I am sorry, as if she had lost control of her nerves. Lu cried and said, It's not that. It's a trap. A trap in which two reactionaries had planned to murder a revolutionary. She pointed at me. She said I was the ally.

The soldiers looked confused. Anybody in the company who had a brain could not have believed for a minute that Yan would have a relationship with Lu. The two were as incompatible as fire and water. Yet the chief would not notice the subtlety. He fell right into Yan's trap. Yan moved forward. She was taking advantage of everyone's shock. She fell down on her knees and covered her face with her palms as if deeply embarrassed. She convinced the crowd that what they had caught was an unbelievable truth. The truth that seemed so much like a bad puppet show.

I took Yan's hint and rode on the confusion. I pointed at Lu's nose, I said, Lu, you will double your crime by making unfounded and scurrilous attacks on an innocent. I said to the chief, The real reactionary has begun her attack. The chief nodded and said, Let her perform. Lu yelled, Chief, I am asking for justice. Yan said, Chief, it's not Lu, it's me. Lu said, Chief, you can't let them get away with it. We can't be soft on treating the reactionaries.

The chief locked his hands behind his back and began to walk back to his tractor. A robber cries stop the thief! he sneered. Lu crawled to his feet. I swear I've never cheated on the Party. You must trust me. The chief got on the tractor and signalled the driver to start the engine. You two, the chief pointed at Lu and Yan. My best officers in the entire farm have shamed me. He stopped as if it hurt him to go on. Lu begged for a chance to explain. The chief said, How do you explain when I have seen all this with my own eyes? The tractor began to pull away as the chief pronounced his sentence: 'To make a clean field, one must pull up weeds by the root.'

As a comrade with a good record, my case was dropped. I was to be sent to the Shanghai Film Studio to be trained as an actress.

The headquarters held a farewell party for me. Everyone made a toast to congratulate me. The chief awarded me a red flag with golden embroidered characters. I was the Honoured Soldier. Our Red Fire Farm is proud of you being chosen, said the chief. You must live up to the people's earnest expectations.

Not for a minute could I stop thinking of Yan. She was detained and shut in a dark room in a water-tower with Lu. I could not imagine leaving the farm when Yan was not safe. But I knew by giving up my chance I would not help Yan's situation. It could only reveal more evidence of the truth that Yan and I were the real evil-doers. I realized that for Yan's sake I had to go.

I began packing. I had taken Yan's life. What would be left

for her at the farm? I could just imagine her lying in the cold net alone at night with nothing to look forward to the next day.

I got up in the early dawn when it was still dark. I climbed down into Yan's empty net and sobbed while embracing her things. I took her Mao button collection with me as I left the net for good.

It was still dark as I waited for the first truck to Shanghai at the crossroads. The wind was strong. The churned-up sand and dust felt like thousands of tiny whips hitting my face, drilling through my collar down to the spine. In saying goodbye to the fields, all the experiences I had had with Yan rushed up to me, beginning with the day I arrived at the farm and saw her appear on the horizon.

The truck came. I got on. As it pulled away, I felt the world surrounding me begin to spin like a wheel. When the truck passed by the water-tower, I saw in my blurred vision a figure standing on top of the water-tower with a red flag fluttering behind her.

PART
THREE

紅
杜
鵑

The dust and dampness had gelled my hair. I had been sitting on an open truck for four hours now. The cold wind cooled my burning insides. The cow-hair-rain quietly came down, mixed with the descending fog. It wet my scarf. The loose threads of the scarf touched my chin, reminding me of Yan's wet braids. Fields of green rice paddies flew past my eyes. My mind kept going back to Yan. I was a shell with its pearl missing. I swallowed a mouthful of cold air. My red scarf was blown away. I failed to catch it. The truck kept running. The scarf carried my sorrow. It descended on a wet field. A cow had been ploughing not far from it. An old peasant held a whip high. The whip made a crisp roaring sound above the cow's head.

I called my mother at work from a public phone. I told her that I was in Shanghai. Mother went speechless. She was too excited. She met me at the bus station. She ran towards me and almost fell. When she regained her balance she looked me up and down. Mother took my hands in hers and said I had grown. Through the bus station window, spring was flourishing. Leaves were dripping dew. Mother said that the fresh green leaves always brought her hope. Taking my hand she looked at my fungicide-dyed nails and tried to scratch the brown colour off. I told her not to bother. Mother put down my hand and said, You have gained quite a bit of weight. I said that I weighed a hundred and fifty pounds. Your face is the shape of a pea now, Mother laughed. She was so happy. I said, Do I look like a real peasant? Yes, you do, very much.

We transferred on to another bus heading home. Mother told me that Blooming was assigned to a design school where she was being trained to paint propaganda posters. Coral was in the process of graduating from middle school. If nothing goes wrong she should be assigned to be a factory worker, Mother said. Let's hope that she's the luckiest person in the family. I asked about Space Conqueror. Mother said he had become a young man now. He was quick in maths, but that still did not promise him a good future. He had to go with the policy. He would be assigned either as a peasant or, if he was lucky enough, a worker in a factory outside the city. I asked Mother what happened to those youths who did not go with the policy. Mother reported that none of these people met a good end. They were shamed in the neighbourhood. Their families were bothered every day until the appointed youth moved to the countryside. Mother said to me, You are a good child. You went as you were supposed to. You have been behaving properly as a big sister. You have never caused any trouble since you were born. I did not tell my mother that being a big sister wore me out.

The moment I showed up in the neighbourhood, the neighbours acted strangely. They stared at me as if they had never seen me before. She's going to be a movie star, they murmured. The Old Tailor, Little Coffin, Big Bread, Witch Chao, the women downstairs all commented behind my back. I heard them say, She's really not that good looking at all.

The neighbours visited me, group after group. The most frequent question they asked was whether I had now received my permanent city residency. My father had to explain that there was no such thing yet, that I was just picked up and had to go through more tests.

We had dinner. I had not had one like this for a long time. We had sweet and sour pork, green vegetables and tofu. Blooming took leave from the boarding school to be with me at dinner. I did not have much to say, nor did my sisters and brother. They had their future to worry about, especially Coral. If I were to be granted a permanent residence in the city, Coral would lose her chance to become a worker. She would be sent to a farm because

136

our family needed to have one peasant to pass the policy.

Mother talked about the dishes. She tried to celebrate the moment. She never showed her despair. That's my mother. Father was proud of me being chosen but was not optimistic about my soaring stardom. He said to me, One is crushed harder when one climbs high. The neighbourhood kids called my name at the window during dinner. They all wanted to take a look at the movie star. But I could not forget Yan. Her face was in front of me all night.

The Film Studio was a palace of displayed slogans. It was surrounded by dark-red maple trees. The leaves were like joined hands. They blocked my view. The leaves branched in and out of the building windows. The studio walls were painted white with red slogans written on them. 'Long live Chairman Mao's revolutionary arts' policy!' 'Salute to our greatest standard-bearer, Comrade Jiang Ching!'

I presented a sealed official letter to the studio security guard. He told me to wait as he went inside. A few minutes later a man and a woman appeared in the hallway. They threw themselves at me enthusiastically. The man introduced himself as Sound Of Rain, the head of the studio acting department, the woman as Soviet Wong, his assistant. They picked up my luggage and asked me to follow them into the studio.

We passed through a series of gates. The sun was shining through the maple leaves. The leaves were spreading their pinkish rays on to the dustless pavement. The workers walking underneath the maple trees were covered in reddish light. They greeted us with flattery.

Sound Of Rain had a pumpkin head with fat cheeks sagging on the sides. Soviet Wong had the face of an ancient beauty. She had slanting eyes, a long nose, a cherry-shaped mouth and extremely fine skin. She was about forty. It was the way she moved, her elegance drew me in. She spoke perfect Mandarin. She had a silky voice. Sound Of Rain spoke of Soviet Wong. He said that she was a graduate from the Shanghai Film Acting School in the fifties and was an extremely talented actress. Sound Of Rain said that I should be proud that Soviet Wong would be one of my four instructors. I asked how it was that I would have more than one instructor. Sound Of Rain said it was Madam Mao Comrade Jiang Ching's order. Soviet Wong said that she was very happy to receive the assignment of being in charge of teaching me. I asked what I would be learning. She said I would be taking intensive classes in politics and acting. I asked if she would do any acting with us. She went silent. Her lips tightened and her head lowered. A lump of hair fell on her face. Her steps slowed down. The Revolution's needs are my needs, she said stiffly. Her resentment spat out between her teeth. She looked clearly un-happy. Flinging back her hair, she quickly sped up to catch Sound Of Rain. Her graceful back bent slightly to the right side. She pretended to be very happy. She must be as durable as bamboo — capable of bending in all directions in the wind. I walked carefully, watching my own steps.

Soviet Wong walked half a step behind Sound Of Rain, never overtaking him or lagging behind him one step. They both wore blue Mao jackets with collars buttoned tightly to the neck. They nodded, Sound Of Rain first, then Soviet Wong, at the workers who passed by. They paid the workers full-scale smiles. The smile made me nervous although it was the most admired smile in the country. It was the smile that Mao had been promoting with the slogan, 'One must treat one's comrades with the warmth of spring.' Lu at Red Fire Farm was an expert at that type of smile.

Finally, we arrived at an abandoned studio set. It was the size of a stadium engulfed by foot-high weeds. As we made a sharp turn, a single little house appeared in front of me. It was an old house with a cement sink on the ground. Wild plants climbed around the sink. This is where you girls stay, said Soviet Wong. This used to be an old film set, Sound Of Rain explained. There are more living quarters behind the house. It was built as a horse shed for films. We had it converted into a living space for the boys chosen. Twenty-five of you are assigned to live and work in this area. You will be guarded. No visits to or from families except the second Sunday morning of the month. Anyone who breaks the rules will be eliminated. We want no outside influence. Absolutely none, Soviet Wong echoed. My thoughts went to Yan.

What about letters? I asked. What's so urgent about writing letters? Soviet Wong suddenly turned to me, suspicion rising in her voice. Her long thin eyebrows twisted into a knot in the middle. I reacted quickly to this sign of danger. I said, Oh, nothing, I was just asking.

She did not believe me. I could tell that she went on with her own thinking. You have dark circles under your eyes, which shows that you don't sleep well. What's your problem? We hope your promise to the Party was not a fake one. She turned to Sound Of Rain and said, We must take preventative measures against possible calamities.

I was offended but I knew I must not show my feelings. The engine of my brain sped up to its limit. Nothing is more urgent than the assignment I have been given, I said, trying hard to sound sincere. It might be my late Mao study habit that causes the dark circles around my eyes. She asked, Why don't you tell us the name of the person you would like to write to so we can check to make sure that it is good for you to keep the correspondence?

Although I couldn't see her motive, I sensed that Soviet Wong's offer was insincere. I have no one to write to, really, I slacked off my tune to make the words carry no eagerness. Soviet Wong stared at me, eye to eye we wrestled. Sound Of Rain looked at his watch and said to Soviet Wong, We should not worry. He went to whisper to her. I heard a phrase. A virus-free egg, he said to her.

Pushing open the door of the little house, Sound Of Rain and Soviet Wong called, Come out, girls, let's meet a new comrade. Four young women stepped out, one after another like snow

139

flakes dancing in the air. I blinked my eyes. Their beauty astonished me. They looked terribly alike, like sisters. I said hello. Sound Of Rain and Soviet Wong stopped me and said, Speak in standard Mandarin. No local dialects. I introduced myself in an awkward Mandarin. I said I was from Red Fire Farm.

The young women gave their names shyly. The first one said that her name was Firewood. She was a worker in a steel factory, and was the daughter of three generations of workers. Her head was the shape of an egg. Features spread out from the nose. She had a small thin mouth. So small that it looked like the anus of my hen Big Beard. Her double-lidded big slanting eyes were pleasant, though they were drawn very close together and reminded me of the eyes of a fox. She was in a bright vermilion shirt. Two long pigtails swung on her back. Her enthusiasm was like her name.

The second woman introduced herself as Cheering Spear. I could never describe her beauty fully. It was a gripping power that her look held. One would submit oneself in front of her beauty without wanting to. She stood there and just shined. She was about my age. She had a low voice, cool eyes which sent out a message that she knew what she wanted. She was confident. Her hair was combed up like the horns of a sheep and tied up with brown rubber bands. She had thick eyelashes. She spoke to me but did not look at me. I stared at her moving mouth. I did not understand why she did not look at me. Her Mandarin was more than correct. She articulated each syllable making sure the 'er' sound found its way into all the sentences. She spoke 'dee-fang' (place) as 'dee-er'. She said she was a journalist from the *Beijing Daily*. She said she was from the people. Finally she turned and looked at me. She looked at me but showed that she was not interested. It was a pair of rival's eyes. There was an unfriendliness behind the friendly face. She wanted to roll me over I sensed. I used to be a horse-rider, she said. I dealt with the toughest horses. I worked three years in Inner Mongolia raising horses for military usage. I could do acrobatics on horseback. I play accordion. She went and picked up an accordion from her bag and played out a string of notes. She sang:

> Riding towards the sun I sing and raise my whip high.
> I raise horses to support the world's revolution,
> Fearless I ride the horse,
> Towards the red capital Beijing,
> Towards where the sun rises,
> Towards where Chairman Mao lives.

She stopped, raised her head, looked at me. She said that it was difficult to describe herself. She gave a fabulous smile at Soviet Wong and asked her to help with the words. She said to Soviet Wong, You are the one who knows me best. Soviet Wong looked pleased. She said Cheering Spear was a modest youth that everyone should learn from. Learn enthusiasm, learn healthy thinking, learn honesty from her.

Of course, I said. I moved to the third one in the rank. She was thin, wearing a golden-yellowish cotton shirt. She introduced herself as Little Bell. She said her father was a soldier who was an orphan before the Liberation. He was sold to a public bath station to work for the rich as a foot-massager, she said. It was in his miserable memory of the past that I grew up. I don't think I am beautiful, she said. I really don't. Good looks don't make a person beautiful. She made a shy smile toward Sound Of Rain who was staring at her. Please forgive my shyness, she said. Little Bell lowered her head, smoothing her hair down with her fingers.

Very well expressed, Little Bell, Sound Of Rain said in a low muffled voice that sounded as if it came from a jar. Good looks don't make a person beautiful. The matter is not about how you look, it is about how your looks can serve the proletarian purpose. This is said by our Supervisor from Beijing. I asked who was the Supervisor. Sound Of Rain replied that he was the one who was solely responsible to Comrade Jiang Ching. A great genius of arts, he said.

141

When Sound Of Rain mentioned the word 'Supervisor', everyone's expression all of a sudden filled with deep respect. I immediately sensed the man's importance. When someone in this country was called by his title instead of his name, he was beyond general importance. For example, Mao was called the Chairman, and Chou, the Premier. The omission of the last name displayed the power of the persona.

The fourth woman spoke. Her name was Bee OhYang. I did not see threat on this face. It was a face of innocence, a face lacking knowledge, a face of purity. She said she wished she were like her name. By that she meant a bee had a sharp sting, but she did not. I lack a fighting spirit, she said. I'd like to learn to correct my spirit. She said she was from an old village in the south. All the villagers have one surname, OhYang. The village is poor. It produces nothing but babies. I am the glory of the village. But I say that I belong to the Party. My mind, my heart and soul. As she spoke tears welled up. She was moved by her own words. Bee was a dark-skinned beauty. She had a sculptural look, a full mouth, melon-seed-shaped face, shining short hair cut to the ear lobe. Her heavy southern accent made her Mandarin hard to comprehend.

The room was sunny. It smelled of wood mould. There were five beds all hung with mosquito nets. My thoughts went to Yan and our mosquito net.

It is very nice, I said. I wish I had arrived earlier to help with the cleaning. That is fine, said Soviet Wong. You will have plenty of opportunities to make up for it. Ha, ha. Everyone in the room cheered. From tomorrow on, Sound Of Rain said, you will have to learn everything from scratch, including walking, talking, eating and expressing, because, he made a long pause, because only one of you will be finally chosen for China's new screen. It is the last competition you have to go through. You will have a year to perform at your best. The Supervisor will make his decision after that.

*

142

We were taken to a hospital for a medical check-up. The doctors acted secretively. I was put in a room and I undressed. The lower part of my body was being checked by three women doctors. A big woman doctor put on rubber gloves and carefully inspected my private parts. A few minutes later, the big woman took off her rubber gloves and recorded something in her notebook. The other two women let their grip loosen and allowed me off the bed. No word was said as they shuffled out. When I was taken out of the room I saw Little Bell weeping. I was about to go up to her but was signalled back by Firewood. Firewood said in my ear that they had doubts about whether she was a virgin.

The whole afternoon we read Mao's talks on the arts. I was bored but feigned interest. We sat in a circle. Read and read. At dinner I ordered two bowls of noodles. Soviet Wong showed me the correct way to hold chopsticks. A discussion was held after dinner in our room. The girls talked about how important Mao's work was as our guide to the future. Little Bell was happy again. She was considered still a virgin after a serious record-check. Sound Of Rain and Soviet Wong yawned but did not leave until crickets sang loudly in the yard. The door slammed behind them. The smell of mould grew stronger.

We washed ourselves by the sink and poured the water into the grass. A cricket followed me as I came back into the room. Cheering Spear went to turn off the light. The cricket began to sing excitedly in the room. Cheering Spear got up holding a flashlight to search for it. I heard her foot slap five times. She shut the cricket up. The room became deadly quiet. In the dark, I realized that it was a lion's den I had entered. The darkness silenced a roaring cry. The coldness of thoughts froze me. I could hear the sound of my dream's spine breaking. I knew that I had to succeed so I would be able to help Yan one way or another in the future. With that thought I drifted into sleep.

I was awakened by the noise of someone exercising her voice outside the window. It was six in the morning. I got up and stepped outside. The dog-tail-grass swayed in the rising sunshine.

With one hand behind her ear, Firewood pushed her voice until it cracked. We said good morning to each other and I heard her voice crack again. Firewood told me that she was frustrated by her voice. She asked me if I could show her my voice. I said, We are not going to be trained to serve the opera troupes, are we? Firewood slid down into a split. She did not answer me as her facial muscles twisted in pain. Do you know Comrade Jiang Ching? Firewood asked. I looked at her, I looked at that proud face. I knew the question need not be answered. Firewood swung her torso left and right. I know a little thing about her, she said, bending towards me. She likes to watch Western movies, especially American Hollywood movies. What are Hollywood movies? I asked. Firewood gave me a secret smile then went back to her exercises.

I leaned my head backwards and stretched my arms towards the wall. It surprised me to see three figures standing behind me. My other roommates – Cheering Spear, Little Bell and Bee OhYang – had been listening to the conversation. I made a friendly smile at them. They spread out and started stretching their limbs.

A guard stopped sweeping leaves by the gate with a broom made of bamboo and walked over to our little house. He was a middle-aged man with a dark beard. His name was One Ounce. Sound Of Rain sent me to tell you to get ready, he said. You are going to be inspected by the Supervisor, the greatest master of our time.

We put on outfits that would make a good first impression. Firewood put on another vermilion shirt and sea-blue navy trousers. Cheering Spear dug out a garment printed with square patterns. Bee OhYang took out two slightly differently coloured white shirts and tried to make up her mind. I decided to wear my old uniform, the one given to me by Yan.

We sat in the room by our beds, all dressed up, waiting. The temperature in the room rose with the sun. I saw a lump of muddy stuff in the corner under Cheering Spear's bed. It was the body of the cricket that had followed me into the room last night. It was motionless on the floor.

Cheering Spear was standing by the door where a little mirror hung. Looking at herself in the mirror she played with her hair-pins. She tried to curl her fringe. Her face displayed her ambition. She took a cotton ball and rubbed a pimple underneath her nose. She rubbed back and forth, moving her features up and down.

Observing Cheering Spear, I suddenly felt short. Her beauty discouraged me. I tried to ignore my fear.

I took a pen and made some scratches on the paper. Dear Yan, I wrote and then scratched it out. Dear Yan, I wrote and scratched it out again. Selected works of Mao Tse-tung, I wrote. Criticism on Revisionists. Yan, how are you? I tore up the paper. The Supervisor did not come.

I had a nightmare that night. Yan had become a faceless figure who wandered the fields of the farm. A sleepless night followed. It rained at dawn. The dropping sound of the rain took me back to Red Fire Farm into Yan's mosquito net.

After lunch, a whistle blew. At the gate we saw Soviet Wong. Behind her were about twenty young men. They marched past the gate. These are the chosen boys, Soviet Wong introduced them. You will be working together in the future. The men had one similar face – big double-lid eyes, thick eyebrows, Buddha-like nose and mouth. They looked so similar, as if made from the same mould. No one said hello. We stood. One man suddenly flushed. Soviet Wong asked him to tell the reason why his face flushed. The young man tried to tackle the question. He scratched the back of his neck. He said it was because he was not used to looking at women. Soviet Wong said, Is your mother a woman? Don't you dare say that you have never looked her in the eyes before. The man went speechless. Soviet Wong continued, If one has no guilty thoughts, one's face should not flush. The man who had flushed lowered his head. The redness went down to his neck. The others who were standing next to him paid him pitiful looks. You may weigh my words later, said Soviet Wong.

These young men had been brought to Shanghai to play supporting roles in Red Azalea and in all the time I was at the studio we never spoke, except to read lines to each other.

Soviet Wong took us to an old building covered with ivy. From behind the huge rusted iron door a heavy smell of mould rushed out. I covered my nose with my hand. Soviet Wong immediately showed irritation. I cannot believe someone who used to be a peasant is afraid of bad smells, Soviet Wong's voice rang high. Is the smell worse than pig shit in rice paddies? I put down my hand quietly.

One Ounce turned up a dim light. We were in an unused studio with a stage set like a cave and a few rows of benches. Soviet Wong sat us down. We began to read Mao's talks on the arts again.

I had a hard time concentrating on Mao. My mind kept flying away. For three weeks we had classes in politics, Mandarin, acting technique and Wu Shu – various kinds of Chinese traditional boxing and fencing. Comrade Jiang Ching was trying to develop something new in China, trying to combine film and opera, although no one knew much about how to make films work. The result was films with a strong flavour of opera – the make-up and lighting, the stylized voice and pose. And now it was the proletariat, and the women, who were the heroes. People all over China had to watch the films, or be labelled reactionaries. With all the lessons, life seemed full every day. But secretly, we had been waiting, waiting to be inspected by the Supervisor. The waiting seemed endless. Sound Of Rain showed up once in a while, always delivering a report on the new achievements in the arts: Mao and his central political bureau members had just watched and praised Comrade Jiang Ching's new model opera. Sound Of Rain would drop us a stack of newspapers and a copy of the opera's manuscript, asking us to read them and write study

146

reports. We read and wrote. We discussed Mao's idea of the proletarian arts.

One day we were told that we now had become special material. We were ready to compete for Comrade Jiang Ching's big assignment.

It was the title role of Red Azalea. Red Azalea was Comrade Jiang Ching's ideal, her creation, her movie, her dream and her life. If any of us grabbed it we grabbed the dream of stardom. The story of Red Azalea was a story of passion in the midst of gunfire. It was about how a woman should live, about a proletarian love unto death. To me it was not only about the past wartime, about history, but it was also about the essence of a true heroine, the essence of Yan, the essence of how I must continue to live my life.

Soviet Wong read through the screenplay. Her tears spattered down on the script. At first I thought that she was moved by the story, then I sensed it was something else. Her sadness did not come from the story, but from despair, the despair that she could never be allowed to play the role she desired. She had to teach us to play the role she wanted to play. Her youth and beauty would be wasted on teaching us. She was assigned to teach people she wished to stab. She was tormented and murdered by our growth.

We took turns reading the parts. I saw the other three, Firewood, Little Bell, Bee OhYang, falling out of the race. They were not in touch with the role. They were not feeling the pulse of Red Azalea. Cheering Spear was different. Cheering Spear was approaching the role. She was getting closer, even closer than I was. Too close. She put me in danger. She was taking away my hope.

Cheering Spear had been in touch with everything. There was never a moment when she had nothing to say; everyone else had their mouths shut and sat nervously. She always had something to say. Things that were useful to advance her future. She said

147

that she admired Soviet Wong, that just being near her made her happy. She did not say this in Soviet Wong's presence, she said this at meetings, meetings at which the secretary on duty would take notes, which Soviet Wong would get to read later on. Cheering Spear said that she was not even close to being as good looking and talented as Soviet Wong. Then she would contradict herself and say that she resembled Soviet Wong a great deal while in fact their looks were as different as an elephant and a pig – Cheering Spear looked like a true proletarian heroine while Soviet Wong had the porcelain features now completely out of favour with Comrade Jiang Ching. Cheering Spear was never ashamed of her flattery.

Soviet Wong did not talk more to her than to the others. But things moved for Cheering Spear. She was put on stage to lead the crowd in the reading of Mao's new instructions. Cheering Spear became the centre of attention. The newspaper and magazine reporters and photographers spoke with Cheering Spear. They interviewed her. They asked who she was and where she was from. Cheering Spear never changed her words. She said, I am Soviet Wong's student. I am what she made of me. I am the soil and she is the cow who cultivates me. I am her harvest. Cheering Spear did not say anything else, she only said what was useful. The newspaper praised Soviet Wong as an example of the Party's loyalty.

The race for Red Azalea came down to Cheering Spear and me. Soviet Wong said we must practise hard because the Supervisor from Beijing would soon come to take his pick for Comrade Jiang Ching. Nothing was said about the others. No one told them that their chances were thinner than a thread. Soviet Wong decided to call Cheering Spear candidate A and me candidate B. It was becoming obvious that Soviet Wong preferred her over me. But she had to leave me in the race at least for a while because it would have been too blatant if she did not. She could not put me aside when it was always Cheering Spear and me who gave the right answers to the questions in class. Our scores had always been close. In Mandarin class we were the only two who were able to get the one-hundred-syllable pronunciation table right. Soviet Wong had to show her fairness, because she represented the Party.

Always in our classes Soviet Wong would be very abstract in what she asked me to do so that I would find it difficult to follow her. Then she told me that I reacted to her teaching too quickly. You have not been really listening to me, she said. You refuse to listen. But I do, I said. She was teaching us how to improvise in the character of Red Azalea. What are you wearing? she asked, suddenly pointing at my feet. A pair of self-made straw shoes, I replied, satisfied with my own sharp wit. She smiled almost bitterly. What do the shoes look like? They look like the ones Chairman Mao wore in a photo taken by our foreign friend Anna Louise in Yanan cave, I said.

Soviet Wong looked even more bitter. She told me to watch Cheering Spear practise. Watch each other, she ordered. Watch carefully. I did watch carefully. Even when I closed my eyes I could see how Cheering Spear played Red Azalea. Cheering Spear was an ardent performer, an energetic spirit. She exhausted herself. She gave all of herself. She was lavish with her emotions. She had no use for subtlety in performance. She loved to be melodramatic. Soviet Wong asked me to watch, so I watched. I learned what was not working and I knew I would not perform the same way. When Soviet Wong asked me what I had learned for the day, I answered honestly. And I ruined myself. When I realized that I had ruined myself it was too late.

The air in the studio became chilly. The chilliness penetrated my bones. Soviet Wong suddenly pointed at me and asked me to explain the concept of the proletarian dictatorship over revisionism in art. It did not take me too long to form an answer. In order to discard revisionism, I said, we must exercise the dictatorship over the enemy in our own head first. My voice was clear. The content was from *Red Flag* magazine. Soviet Wong commented, We must be careful of those who are giants in language, but midgets in practice.

Soviet Wong picked on me. She picked on me whenever she could, over the smallest things. One day she misplaced a prop – a tea mug – and pointed me out to the class as the one who must have lost it. I told her I had seen her place the mug in her drawer. I went to point at the particular drawer backstage. She came and pulled the drawer out. In it was the missing mug. Soviet Wong was furious. She recited Mao's teaching: 'The one who thinks she is smarter than the masses is the one who will be abandoned by the masses.' I was confused and angry.

Soviet Wong never regarded us as a teacher did her students, but as an old concubine to newcomers. She did not know how to confront the danger we represented. Comrade Jiang Ching's desire to change the image of the movie screen and her affection for working-class-looking youngsters killed Soviet Wong's future as an actress. Her ancient beauty was considered out of date. She never truly liked Cheering Spear. In fact she hated her. But Cheering Spear's flattery made her feel less hurt.

Cheering Spear had a smoother look than I did. The harsh lines of my features irritated Soviet Wong. She was at a loss to understand Comrade Jiang Ching's new aesthetic of beauty when it came to my rough skin. Every morning when she saw me she stared at me with an expression of having just swallowed a fly. Have you washed your face? she would ask disgustedly.

Soviet Wong would shake her head before I delivered my lines. Nothing I did looked right to her. Many times her deep resentment turned to a hatred that would express itself on impulse. Your irises are not big enough, she said gazing at me. They won't appear as bright as a heroine's should on screen. Comrade Jiang Ching's requirement of a leading actress is that she have a pair of bright flaming eyes. Those eyes symbolize proletarian righteousness. I do not see that you have them. It's a terrible pity. Really, maybe you should not have been picked up in the first place. It was definitely a misjudgment. Sloppiness will certainly spoil things.

Soviet Wong asked me to tell her whether I was near-sighted. I said I was not. She took me to the studio's medical centre and had a doctor check my vision. I had perfect sight. On our way out, Soviet Wong said to me, But you do look near-sighted, believe me.

I looked at myself in the mirror that night. After half an hour of studying the size of my irises I started to believe Soviet Wong. It was true that my irises were not as big as they were supposed to be. From then on, I could not forget that I looked near-sighted. In my performance, I became more and more conscious of my looks. My self-confidence was disappearing. Soviet Wong yelled stop! before I even started my lines. She said, The way you stand is wrong. You forget that your feet should form a forty-five-degree angle. Day after day I felt more and more like I was too crippled for Red Azalea. Soviet Wong weakened my nerves. But I refused to quit. I knew exactly what she wanted and I just could not give it to her, at least not so easily.

There was noise of someone talking outside the window. It was Cheering Spear. She was expressing her appreciation to Soviet Wong for the whole afternoon's lesson. The two had become more and more close these days. They ate together at every meal. Soviet Wong helped Cheering Spear learn her lines into the night. They made a good image of the teacher–student relationship. But to me they were two tacticians.

I forced myself to hang on.

No one was giving up, not Firewood, Little Bell, nor Bee OhYang. Firewood had hurt her vocal cords through her excessive voice exercises every day. She believed that if she could blow a pip on the wall she would gain a silky voice. She believed that her problem was her voice. Karl Marx became Karl Marx because he read so many books that his feet rubbed a pair of footprints into a library floor, Firewood told me. Success belongs to the strong-willed. Firewood took this story from *Red Flag* magazine as her inspiration. Her practice was encouraged by Soviet Wong, who would sometimes offer to accompany her on the piano. Firewood's singing was like a rooster under a blunt knife. Soviet Wong played piano with her eyes closed as if Firewood's howling massaged her sour nerves.

Firewood ended up developing a knot on her vocal cords. I secretly felt good that her chances to win the role now were zero. My other classmates must have felt the same way, but we hid our feelings. We all brought Tiger Balm for Firewood. We care for you greatly, we all said and smiled melodramatically.

A gale of wind had blown down two maple trees that day. I went to the bushes to brush my teeth and found the trees lying flat with their roots out. Before I finished brushing, the gale started howling again. I rushed back and found One Ounce sitting in the centre of the room. Ten o'clock, he said, erecting all his fingers slowly. You will be brought to see him, the arm-in-arm comrade of the greatest standard-bearer, the Supervisor.

Bee OhYang sat down on her bed and began to sob. Little Bell made a strange sound in her throat. Firewood went out and came back with a bowl of water. Cheering Spear dripped some hair oil into the water and recombed her horn-like hair with oil-water. Both Firewood and Bee OhYang rebraided their braids. They looked shining and new from head to toe.

The gale continued. It lifted dust and leaves from the ground. It tore the old Mao posters from the wall. We walked carefully on our way to the cafeteria, making sure that we did not step on Mao's face. An hour later, Sound Of Rain and Soviet Wong showed up with a van. The windows of the van were covered by black cotton curtains. Soviet Wong conducted us into the van. I coughed as I got in. The smoke in the van was heavy. It was a Party high-ranker's personal van. In astonishment we sat down quietly. The driver was a young man in a People's Liberation

Army soldier's uniform. He wore white gloves. Sound Of Rain waved at Soviet Wong to shut the door. The van took off smoothly. Firewood, Cheering Spear, Little Bell, Bee OhYang and I sat in the dark with all kinds of thoughts running through our heads.

How would my fate be decided? Soviet Wong had gradually dropped my lessons. She arranged for me to work in the cafeteria peeling peas. It was more than clear that she wanted to get rid of me. She made me wait at the bottom of the list to receive acting lessons. Most of the time I was neglected. Sound Of Rain did not seem to object to what Soviet Wong had been doing to me. He seemed to trust her judgment. They both began to say that they did not want ever to produce capitalist sprouts. It all started after my argument with Soviet Wong about the missing mug. I knew what was happening, as did everyone else in the studio. But no one said anything. No one dared to oppose Soviet Wong.

I kept myself composed. I stopped pretending to be who I was not, because there was no way to please Soviet Wong anyway. She had convinced Sound Of Rain and now everyone around me to dislike me, and they did. They all wanted to please Soviet Wong. They began to say that Cheering Spear seemed to be the only qualified candidate, because she acted with passion. By passion they meant how many tears an actor could shed. I had to admit that it was something Cheering Spear was capable of while I was not. I had to admire her talent in reciting dry, slogan-like lines with such passion. Cheering Spear was a big tear-machine. Shedding tears was the only thing she pursued when acting. Not only did she shed tears, she could make the right amount of tears pour out at the right moment, without dragging out the snot. Getting the tear to drop was Cheering Spear's concept of acting.

Cheering Spear looked down on me because I was not able to do what she did. I was jealous of Cheering Spear's talent. Soviet Wong said to me, You see, it is not a matter of acting technique.

153

It is a matter of who has more feelings for Chairman Mao. We definitely need a real Communist to play a Communist.

I was in the van with my rivals. We all carried our own thoughts, thoughts of how to kill one another. I missed Yan so much. After we had waited for hours in a carpeted meeting room, a secretary-like young man came to the room and made the announcement. The Supervisor had just left for an important call in the capital. The meeting was cancelled.

红 杜 鹃

I broke the rules. I lied to Soviet Wong. I asked for a three-day leave. I said my mother was sick and needed me to take care of her. Soviet Wong said no at first. I tried again. I said there were no peas for me to peel today. The cafeteria people had gone to a rally. Soviet Wong then said yes.

I went back to Red Fire Farm. I went to visit Yan. I saw her working in the middle of the rice field among the others. The soldiers looked me up and down. I saw envy and distance in their eyes. I waited by the edge of the field as Yan walked over. She washed her hands in the irrigation channel and then dipped in her bare feet. She looked at me. She did not smile. She took up my bag and we walked towards the barracks.

Yan was no longer the company commander. Her case with Lu ended without anything definitive. No one believed that she could possibly have Lu as a lover. Yan later admitted to head-quarters that it was her way to get even with Lu. What she had put on was a show. The Chief was displeased with the nasty way she took revenge but did not want to carry the case further. Lu

154

insisted on pursuing the case, she insisted on having me rein-
vestigated. But the Chief would not reconsider my case. I was
gone and he was the one who had personally granted me the
title of Honoured Soldier. To denounce me would have meant
exposing his poor judgment. The case vanished as if it had never
happened. Yan had resigned and now was a squad head. Lu was
transferred to another company and became a commander.

Yan was the eldest in the squad. The new soldiers looked the
way I used to look. They sang 'My Motherland'. They worshipped
Yan. She had her food on the table at mealtimes. They brought
it to her. Her bowl was full. The young soldiers served her. They
said, Here is your hot-water container, I just filled it up for you.
Yan lived alone, in the same room we used to live. All the other
beds were gone. She set her bed in the middle of the empty room.
With the white rectangular mosquito net, the room looked like
a funeral home.

I sat opposite her by the door. I looked at her face. Her skin
was deep brown. She almost looked like an African. She had
aged. Wrinkles had deepened. A thread of white hair in her braid.
She used to have thick braids but now they were thin like mouse-
tails. She took out a package of flour, poured the flour into a pot,
added water and lit a kerosene stove. She cooked the flour with
sugar. She was offering me the best food she had. The taste was
awful but I tried not to show it. She sensed it. She asked me how
good the food was at the Film Studio. I did not answer. I did not
know how to answer her. She said it must be beyond comparison.
She pulled over my bowl, pushed the door open and poured the
flour paste outside. Shutting the door she said, I am sorry. Can't
help it. She went to wash the bowl in a water jar. She washed
the chopsticks and dropped them twice. She put the bowl and
the chopsticks into a cotton bag and hung it on a bamboo stick.
When she did that her back bent sadly. She mopped her face
with a muddy towel. Sadness attacked me. She turned around
and said, Thanks for coming. She smiled and my tears welled up.
She said, What do you want me to do?

155

She sat back down. She tried to get the conversation going. She said, Say something. I said, Say what? Anything. I said, Where is your Erhu? She said she had given it away. I could not say more. She clapped a mosquito on her leg and rubbed and cracked the mud off her feet. She said the soldiers were new, but they were smartasses. The minute they were assigned to the farm they started to work their way back to the city. They made excuses to take leave shamelessly. Some of them took leave without asking for permission. They pretended to be sick all the time. They were a bunch of hypocrites. Their hearts were never in the farm, not for a second. They served her meals to flatter her. They know how to use me, she said. They make me sick.

I wanted to say forget about them, let's talk about you. But I could not. What could I say? She was trapped. No way out. She was twenty-five, a squad head at twenty-five would have no future. This was her future. I wanted to embrace her and comfort her but felt ashamed to do so.

She said, Tell me about the Film Studio, tell me about the new people you met. I said there was not much to tell. She said, I want to know. I told her about Cheering Spear, Firewood, Little Bell, Bee OhYang, Sound Of Rain and Soviet Wong. I told her about what we do. She listened, pacing back and forth in the room. She stopped, staring outside into the fields. Before I finished, she suddenly said, We should forget about each other. It did not shock me. I understood why she had said that.

I said, You know I can't disobey you. She said, Then take off now. I said, I made the trip to see you, it wasn't easy for me. I lied to them. I am risking my future. If they find out, I will be eliminated. She put on her muddy rain-shoes and said, Not easy? You must think my life is easier. I said, I have never thought that way. She interrupted me. She said she did not want to start an argument when she was feeling down. I said, I didn't come for this. She said, I didn't ask you to come. I said, I'm going. She stepped out.

I emptied my bag. I lay biscuits I brought for her in her net.

Her net was washed clean. I remembered the time when we did not wash the net so no one would see what we were doing inside. I remembered her passion. I touched her pillow and found there was hair, her hair, scattered all over the bed. Her hair had been falling out and I was not doing anything about it. I wanted to run, to run away from my shame.

The wind blew the door open. Yan's towel dropped from the towel holder by itself. I picked up the towel and saw her rifle leaning against the wall. I suddenly missed Little Green. I missed her singing 'My Motherland'.

Yan's rifle was rusty. I looked out of the window. The field was lifeless. The sun was drying up the earth. The earth looked like a bald-headed man. The crops bent with the salty wind. I realized that I did not belong here any more.

I stepped out of the room. Some young women saw me and whispered to each other. They walked by me, carrying hoes. I asked them about Orchid. One of the women said she was at the Brick Factory.

I walked through the reeds. I felt fortunate that I was free of this hardship. The more fortunate I felt the more the guilt grew in me. Yan is left behind, I kept thinking. How could I leave her behind? I came to eat a cake in front of a starving child. How shameful. I reminded her of her misery. I am a hypocrite. I came to comfort her. It did not cost me anything to speak kindnesses.

The Brick Factory was the same as when Yan played Erhu here for me. I walked through the brick lanes and saw Orchid and a team laying the unbaked bricks down in patterned walls. I asked a young man if I could help him push the cart. He said the work needed a man's strength. I said I knew that. I had worked here before. I knew the way around. I took up the loaded cart. It contained a hundred pieces of bricks. The man watched me. I pushed the cart on to an iron track and made a turn down a lane. The man yelled, Where are you from?

Orchid saw me. She did not come to greet me. She stood where she was, holding a stack of bricks, mouth half open. I said, Hello,

Orchid. She did not say hello back. She said, What are you here for? I said I came to visit. She went back to laying the bricks. Her sweat soaked her from back to waist. We worked side by side. After she finished laying a cart of bricks, she straightened her back, wiped the sweat off her cheeks and said, Yan is not here. I said that I knew. She said, I know you did not intend to visit me. I said, I missed the farm. She gave a sarcastic smile and pushed the empty cart along the track. I noticed that she was crippled. I followed her. We stopped at the loading zone. Fresh bricks were pushed out of a slicer like cakes. I helped Orchid load. We loaded the bricks carefully. We pushed the cart down a lane and began to lay the bricks. I asked, What happened to your foot? She said, A reed pricked through it. She said, You were there, weren't you? I said, Yes, I remember, I was there. Hadn't it healed? Orchid said, Yes. This is how it healed.

I straightened my back. I saw the kiln chimney exhaling white smoke. It fell last summer, the kiln, said Orchid. Three people died, two were injured. I don't know how long the Brick Factory will stand. Why did you come? Before I could explain she said to my face, I don't like seeing you. I really don't. She said she wanted to be honest with me. She said nobody wanted to see me. A movie star. An old-time acquaintance who took a ladder to the clouds. Nobody wanted to be reminded of how bad life was for them.

I did not say anything until we emptied the cart. Before Orchid pushed the cart back to the loading zone she said, Do you know Leopard and Yan? They have been seeing each other. She made a gesture meaning 'underground'.

I was feeling better as I waited for the bus to go back to Shanghai. Yan was seeing Leopard. I knew she had always thought of him. I felt a little bit relieved. I wished she had been in love with Leopard, yet immediately I thought myself nasty, because I knew she was not in love with him. She was miserable. I remembered how gay, open and forgiving she could be. I knew how she behaved when she was in love.

The sky darkened and no bus came. My stomach began to shrink inside. I had not eaten a thing since morning. I went to a roadside stand and sat down by it. I heard the crickets singing. I thought of how I lied to Soviet Wong and hoped nothing went wrong. I could cover my lie if I made it back to the studio dormitory tomorrow morning before dawn. I knew a secret path behind the sheds that led to the room.

I sat breathing the dark air. The countryside had a quietness that seemed sacred. I looked into the night. I heard the whistle of a steam engine from far in the distance. The darkness smelled wet. I then saw a light dot. At first I thought it was a lightning bug. But it was moving closer, and then I found that the light did not go off as a lightning bug would. It was a flashlight. Someone was walking in the dark. I stared at the dot of light. It came towards the bus station. I sensed something. I kept staring for a few minutes. I saw the figure of the light-holder. A familiar figure. A horn blew, the bus was arriving. The light dot began to jump, up and down. I heard her breath. It was Yan.

The bus entered the station. She was steps away. I waited until our hands touched. We did not have time to say anything to each other. She had walked miles. She took out a wrapped bag from her inner pocket and passed it to me. The bag smelled of biscuits. She was gasping hard. The bus took off.

When I got back to my parents' house they told me that Soviet Wong and Sound Of Rain had just left. They had received reports from my roommates that I was missing. They came to check on me. They came to find me. Did you tell them where I had gone? I asked my mother. I did not know where you were and I told them so, she said. They said your mother was lying, said my father. They said harbouring a wrong-doer was a crime. Father turned to Mother, You stubborn woman, you shouldn't have argued with them! I must argue because they were being unreasonable, said Mother. What did they say? I asked Mother. Mother looked at me and said angrily, They said you had been a bourgeois individualist, they said you always acted alone, you had no sense of groupism. You're selfish so you should be eliminated, yes, that's what they were trying to say. They said they had come for my opinion, for the parents' opinion of their child. They came to nail you down, they came to accuse, to lock the dunce cap on your head.

My father waved at my mother. He sighed and sighed. Where have you been? To the farm, I said. What's the matter with you? Didn't you sense that they were after you? Why can't you know your place and behave yourself? Can't you see we have enough trouble in the family? He pointed at the porch and raised three fingers meaning Coral, his third child. She was on the porch and was mad at me. I asked what happened. Before my mother said anything, my father dragged me to the kitchen and shut the door. He told me that Coral was assigned to Red Fire Farm because I had left it. My father's voice was hoarse. It is very unfair to Coral, he said. But she was assigned and she had to go. My father said that he and Mother wished they could go for Coral, to save their child.

I was frustrated. I said to my father, What do you want me to do? To change places with her? It would be a lie if I told you that I would do that. I was at Red Fire Farm. I served my term. I made it out by myself. If she had guts she should . . . I stopped, realizing that I talked selfishly. It was timing and politics that decided my fate. It did not have much to do with any personal effort. I knew nothing of acting but I was made an actress.

I don't want to hear your reasons, said my father. It doesn't help Coral if either of us wins the argument. I just want you to be aware of the fact, and the fact is that you're no longer a peasant and the family needs to have a peasant to fulfil the government's quota, and Coral, your little sister, is assigned to that role.

I said, What can I do? How can I help? Accept your lot and stay in your place, said Father. Your mother and I can't afford to have more losses. If you get kicked out of the studio, we will have two peasants at Red Fire Farm.

I wished I could have said it out loud, that I am not doing well at the Film Studio, but I could not let them down. I said, You just saw how my teachers dislike me. How can I stop them? My parents went silent. They were hurt.

I should have gone downstairs to see them off personally, my father murmured. Soviet Wong and Sound Of Rain must be upset about my impoliteness. You are an idiot if you think that would have made any difference, said Mother. They did not deserve to be treated as guests. Not in my house. One should at least pay attention to the master when hitting his dog. I will never put on a smiling face when someone comes to spit on my daughter's face. Hold back your bad temper now, yelled Father. Don't you have to put up with enough bad treatment by behaving this way at work? I don't regret it a bit, yelled back my mother. Live honourably or die, that's my principle, and I want my children to behave according to it.

But see what you have caused them? When they behave according to your principle, this idealistic nonsense, see what happens to them? They get crushed by society! Mother said, I can't believe it. You, the man I am married to, the father of my four children, disgrace my principles.

My father beat his chest, kicked his feet, swore that he did not mean that.

Coral did not speak to me. She was packing for Red Fire Farm. It hurt me to see her leaving for the hardship I had gone through. I did not know how she would ever make it out. I did not know what to say to her. Guilt filled me. I gave my salary to Mother and asked her to buy Coral some necessities. Mother told me that Coral had said that she did not want anything from me. I knew I could never pay the price for her suffering.

I did not come home the day Coral was supposed to leave for the farm.

*

161

I expected Soviet Wong to question me. But she did not. She had conversations with everyone else in the room but me. I thought she would openly criticize me but she did not. She talked to my classmates about Red Azalea, about the exciting energy the movie was about to generate. She gave out part of the script, but did not tell me when and what to play. I was left out. No one was in charge of me. I was not told what was wrong with me. All of a sudden I had nothing to do. I was assigned to watch everyone else rehearsing. I heard loud voices reciting the lines. I heard Cheering Spear reciting lines in her sleep. My pain felt like water penetrating into sand, soundless, into the core of my being. I did not seem to exist any more.

I was not the only one who was unhappy. Bee OhYang had been warned because she was playing too much table tennis with a male student. It was reported that they were flirting with each other as they hit the balls. Bee OhYang cried and denied that there was anything going on between her and the man. Soviet Wong had spoken to them separately. She called all of us to a meeting. She started that she had discovered that the couple had not gone too far. She advised us. She said, A healthy mind is the most important thing in life. As I listened I watched her face. Every nerve on it expressed righteousness. Her skin was very white. Her handkerchief smelled of Tiger Balm. She told us a story, a story she had witnessed. It was about how a former young actress corrupted and destroyed her own future by having an affair with an older man. Soviet Wong pointed out that the actress had read too much *Jane Eyre*. *Jane Eyre* destroyed her.

I immediately wanted to read the book *Jane Eyre* although this was the first time I had ever heard of it. According to Soviet Wong, the couple was caught on Chow Family Pond Road. While they were hiding in the bushes late one evening, the woman was recognized by a passing comrade. As the saying goes, there is no such thing as a windproof wall. Their deed was brought out into the light. It was useless when the woman confessed that she regretted what she had done. Soviet Wong had heard her say it at a mass rally. But it was too late. She was considered a criminal for the rest of her life. She now worked as a restroom cleaner in the studio.

Soviet Wong said, I sincerely hope you do not follow her catastrophic road. She rested her sight on me and nodded lightly. I wanted to avoid her stare but forced myself to face her. My mind was picturing how the young actress was touched by the older man in the bushes. I now knew who Soviet Wong was talking about. She was a young actress, a rare beauty with a pair of flowery eyes. The whole studio called her a prostitute. Anyone could joke about her. The male workers made dirty jokes about how they had had her. She became the joke. Strangely, I did not see a sad expression on her face. She had the face of a rogue. She did not care any more. She joked back with the workers. She told the wives who had scorned her that she had slept with their men. She told the workers that she had slept with their bosses. She became a real whore.

Sunday morning I went back home to spend the day with my parents. Our yard was a mess. The Wu-Lee Hardware Workshop was assigned a new ambitious leader who, on his first day on the job, declared he would expand his shop into our yard to make a bicycle shed. He had his workers cut out all the greens and erect the frames of a shed. We protested, fighting for the yard, shouting the whole day. But he had more men than we did. They were desperate men, the new employees. We lost. The cement was poured over the grass. My parents said to the leader, You can't do this to us. We have been putting up with your machine noise and the chemical smell for years. You can't have an inch and then take a foot. You can't take away our only yard, our greens. My parents almost begged. The leader was unmoved. He said, I am doing this to open positions for the unemployed, people who desperately need rice in their bowls. You think I want them? The hopeless, the society-walkers? Where is your conscience? Don't you have any feelings for the proletarians?

163

The day at home was depressing. Blooming was in boarding school, Coral at Red Fire Farm. Space Conqueror was sent by his middle school to a tractor factory to learn to be a worker. Father leaned on the table all day working on his project, a pop-up book, *Fly to the Moon*. He made maps of Mars and the Moon. My mother said he should be a member of the solar system instead of this family. I watched Father painting the black hole. He was patient, glasses hanging on his nose-tip. He said, Let me tell you what makes the moon shine, would you like to hear it? I said, So what whether the moon shines or not.

After lunch Mother sat down with *Dream of the Red Mansion*. She called me, recommended the book to me. She thought I was now mature enough to read it. She said that it was all right to read it because Mao had said that the book did not have to be read as an ancient back-garden love story; it could be studied as educational material. The book revealed a vivid picture of China's feudalistic society, the ugly nature of the oppressor class. This was Mao's newest instruction. Mao recommended everyone read it from his perspective. I said to Mother, Maybe some other time.

I did not tell my mother that I had stolen and read the book a long time ago when she hid it in a closet. It was what I used for Yan's love letter to Leopard. I took the poems and phrases from the book. It was a story I told Yan. Yan never got to read the book but she knew all the details of the story.

I asked my mother to explain love. Mother said that I had embarrassed her. She said that there was no lesson to learn regarding this matter because all one had to do was to follow the guide of nature.

The guide of nature. Had I ever not followed it? Yan and I learned from nature and did the best we knew how about our needs. The river of her youth overflowed its bank when she was not allowed to have a man to love. I had to pretend to be a man for her. But I gave her my full love.

*

Back at the studio there was a big meeting. Afterwards every unit was given a document to read criticizing 'Chou' – Confucius. The government wanted the workers to read between the lines and begin gossiping about Chou the Premier, his illness, his conflict with Comrade Jiang Ching. We were led to wonder about his loyalty to Mao. When it was my turn to read the lines, I read without interest. I did not care about the Chous. It bored me. People were asked to comment. People gave comments. The comments of nonsense. We must keep China red for ever, this was every speaker's opening line.

红 杜 鹃

I saw a net full of dead turtles and snake-like brown-green fish in the yard. It was Monday morning and I was assigned to pick up some study materials at a bookshop near my parents' home. I decided to stop at the house. Since I was no longer in favour, the studio people would not notice my absence. When I got down from the bicycle, I wondered who had brought those turtles and fish. The lady who was my neighbour said to me, Your friend has been waiting for you by the staircase for hours.

I made guesses of who it might be. I found I was unable to park the bicycle when my guesses came into focus. The turtle and fish brought me the smell of Red Fire Farm. I leaned the bicycle against the wall and rushed in. I saw her rise from the staircase. Yan, my commander, looked like a bride. New haircut, to the ears. She wore a brand-new indigo jacket with red shirt with the collar showing, deep-blue pants and a pair of brand-new square-toed black shoes. She looked determined and calm.

Though still pale, she was no longer sad. She looked at me and tried to compose herself. She then said hello to me. By her trembling voice, I knew she wanted me badly. I went up and took her hands in mine. Now she knew that I wanted her just as badly.

I didn't expect you, I said. She said, Just finished the harvest. I cleaned the turtles and fish for you this morning. I caught them yesterday.

I stared at her. I tried to see how much she had changed from the last time I saw her. I tried to learn if she was doing all right. She turned away from me and said, Look, only dead fish and turtles stare.

I guided Yan to my family's apartment. I opened the door and took her to sit down on the porch. I poured her a cup of tea. I looked at her. I didn't know how to start the conversation. I said, You look good. She said, I don't know. I guess I was born a cheap thing. I feel like a pig, nothing matters to me. She stopped and there was a silence. She then looked around and pointed at a painting of Mao on the wall. She said, It's good, who did it? Blooming, I said. It was her homework. Yan sighed and said that she always wished she could paint but she gave it up because she could not get Mao's nose straight.

She pointed at the big wooden bed and said, It's big. I said, Yes, Blooming and I slept here, but she only comes home on Sundays. Yan asked about my mother's health and I said, Still the same. She wasn't given any day off. She has to go to work everyday, I said. She goes, gets sick, and when her heartbeat goes over one hundred and ten she gets a letter from the doctor and a day off. She comes home. Rests. Has to be at work the next day. And the bad circle starts again. Yan said, Doctors are assholes these days. It's all about power. Everyone wants to show off their power. I asked if she saw my sister Coral at the farm. Once, said Yan. She was carrying bricks with the team. She was slow, the last one dragging behind the ranks. She is not as strong as you. I said, I know, I remember Mother once told me that Coral was weak, she could not stand up until she was two years old. The nanny Mother hired secretly stole all Coral's food coupons and sent them to her village to feed her own children. I asked Yan how I could help my sister. Yan said, Oh, come on. Coral is not the only one in prison.

Yan said, Look at me, I am old. She was looking at herself in a mirror. I looked at her in the mirror for a while. Rebuttoning her collar she said, Life goes on, it really does.

I said, How is Leopard? Yan glanced at me then said, His father has just passed away. He came back to Shanghai to attend the funeral. Did you come with him? I asked. Who do you think I am? His daughter-in-law? Anyway, Leopard left the farm first and I just got in today. You are dating him, aren't you? I looked at her. She went silent. She sipped the tea and bent to look at the wood patterns on the table, then she looked at the newspaper. After a while she said, You know I never started with him. It's an old meal already, I mean our relationship. My best years were not with him. He missed it. Am I sounding like a pig? Well, of course I wrote him letters. How can I say that I never started with him? You delivered *my* letters to him, didn't you . . . ? Then you left for good, and he came to me. I mean he sent a letter to me. He asked me to meet him in the Brick Factory. He said he had always wanted me. He was just afraid of political pressure. His secretary was after him. Do you remember that short heavy girl you always described to me? The one who showed up every time you passed the letters to Leopard? Yes, I do, I said. I remember Old Wong. Anyway his company now is doing poorly, Yan continued. Their fields are closer to the sea. They're saltier than ours. He even lost his seeds. He let the soldiers eat them. They had nothing to plant. He is more desperate than I am. So we, you know, talked about this stuff. He said he always loved my letters. My letters! For Buddha's sake, my letters. Then of course I confessed I never wrote those letters. You know he forced me out of the closet. I told him about you. Oh well, nothing shocking, you know, something to the effect that you were a better writer than me. That's all. Are you embarrassed?

167

Does he love you? I asked. He says he does. But I don't know how much I can count on that, Yan said. And you? I asked. She said, Well, you know, I am not good at it. She sipped the tea and began to chew the leaves. I hope you like him enough, she said, swallowing the leaves slowly.

Have you had . . . Before I started the phrase Yan lowered her head shyly as if she knew what I was going to ask. Well . . . she said. The farm was too dangerous to . . . You know one gets caught easily. She looked at me, cheeks reddening. I said, How can I help? She said, He is coming.

I jumped up and looked out the window. What? Who? When? She said, I invited him to meet me here in the afternoon.

How bold! I said. She said, I guess so. But you know, I'm just going to meet him and we'll have a cup of tea together. What's so shocking about that? Just to sit and have tea? I laughed at her poor lie. It would be like scratching the foot over a boot, I said. It will make you feel quite itchy afterwards. She said, Well, you know me, unless . . . I said, Yes, maybe I can do something. Her face flushed. Do it for me please, she said. I nodded. I said, I know you want him. She said, Well . . . I said, Do you want him? Would you like to have a space alone, with him, for a while? She turned to the window and nodded lightly. Will you be my guard? she asked, slowly, without looking at me. I will, I said. I will be your guard. I'll always be your guard. You know I used to be your guard. I want to. She said, Would you? She turned to look at me. She looked into my eyes, then said, Would you? I stood up and went to the kitchen. I could not bear her burning eyes.

As I was making jasmine tea for her and myself, the feel of her touch went through me. I felt the warmth of her body, I was possessive of that body. My hands shook. The hot water streamed out of the mugs on to the floor and wet my feet. I grabbed a mop and began to wipe the floor. My mind went on seeing things. I could see the joy on her face, the joy of being taken, being deeply penetrated. I could feel her wetness. I could hear her animal-like groan. I knew the way she moved when she was aroused and could not help herself from pulling me closer and closer to her, pressing me, pasting me to her skin, leaving teeth marks on my shoulders. I wanted to be an observer, to observe Leopard doing what I have and have not done.

Yan stood by the kitchen entrance, looking at me.

It was ten in the morning. We had a few hours before Leopard arrived. Yan asked me if I would have any problems with my working unit. I said I would lie again. Yan asked how I would lie. I thought for a while and said I would break my bicycle then tell Soviet Wong that I had a traffic accident. Yan said, Would it do? I said, To lie or not to lie – the result will be the same because they will not believe me anyway.

Yan suggested that we go and take a shower in the public bath-house on Salty Road. I agreed.

We were hand in hand like schoolgirls. Her braids were sun beaten, yellowish. A neighbour saw us as we passed by; he nodded at me, looking at Yan, and said, A relative from the countryside? Then he asked Yan, How do you like Shanghai? Ma-ma-hoo-hoo, Yan said in the Shanghai dialect. So so. The neighbour was surprised. He said, Her Shanghainese is pretty good. I am a Shanghainese, can't you tell? Yan said. The man shook his head. You look Tibetan.

Yan said, Let's go to the department store. I want to buy something I've wanted to have for a long time. We moved through the crowd and stepped into Shanghai Second Department Store. We went to the fabric counter. Yan said she was too old for the colours she liked. She said, Maybe I could make them into underwear. What do you think? I said they cost too much to be worn as underwear. We moved on to the clothing counter. Yan saw bright red underwear. She immediately asked a clerk to show her some. Without consulting me she bought a set, the bright red underwear. Stop it, she said to me when she saw me smiling. I said, Can you ever get over the colour red? I started laughing. She said, What's so funny? I said it had just popped into my mind how we used

169

to use red cloth to make bags for the Little Red Book. She said, Well, to me red is a passionate colour, and one is what one wears. I said, Is this what you have been wanting? She said, As always, you know me better than the worms in my intestines.

I said I was afraid of being seen by any unit colleague. She said, What's all that shit about? I said, You don't understand the studio people. They are starving wolves. They don't like me. Yan said, But you made it through their competition. Shouldn't they respect you? I said, Lu is everywhere. All right, she said, now I understand.

The exit was mobbed with people who spoke northern and southern dialects. Although there was not much to buy and choose from in the store, Shanghai was always the nation's fashion centre. People from outside the province came once every few years to buy clothes that would last for generations. They sat on the pavement and smoked tobacco, showing their rotten teeth.

We passed a street where there was a window display of opera performances. Yan looked at each picture slowly and said suddenly, I dreamed about you being in these. She turned to me and said, In my dream, you didn't look like yourself any more. You were someone else, someone like Lu. I guess that was my fear. But, see, you have not changed much. I said, I would have had a better chance if I had changed.

We stopped talking but kept walking. I found that I could not think about Yan's leaving. I could not think about her life back at Red Fire Farm.

A young girl was walking towards us. She was as fresh as a peach picked from a tree. She was wearing a sea-blue diagonal-striped skirt and a pair of green plastic sandals. Yan stared at her and her feet. I said, You don't have to envy her pretty toenails. Yan said, My toenails are ruined by fungicide. I would love to wear sandals but I can't.

She was not confident walking among the city girls. The people who stared at her weather-beaten face annoyed her. We went to a soup shop where it was steamily hot. Yan went to sit at a table

170

facing the wall. I went with her. We sat facing the wall. A waitress with a long face came to mop up the dirty table. We ordered two red-bean soups. The soup arrived. The edges of the soup bowls were like dog teeth. We ate carefully with spoons. Yan ordered steamed bread. She ate four pieces and I ate two. The shop was wallpapered with Mao portraits and Mao quotations. There were smeared red-bean fingerprints on the wall. The Mao portraits were fading yellow-brown. The smell of tobacco was heavy. Yan and I sat and said nothing to each other.

The waitress came. Her face grew longer. Shit or get off the pot, she said. Yan gave her a sidelong look. The waitress said, What's wrong with you, villager? Yan kept quiet. I asked, Why can't you be a little friendly? She shot back, Why should I be friendly with you? Who are you, you villagers? Yan looked her up and down. I knew she was thinking about a way to attack. The waitress was in a heavy sweat. She mopped the table and swore. Let's go, Yan said. As we walked out on to the street Yan said she could have made a fool of that waitress but thought she was pitiful. Unhappy people are dangerous, she said.

We bought tickets for a shower-bath, three yuan per person. Our numbers were 220 and 221. The bath-house was located behind a rice shop. Hundreds of bicycles were parked in rows on the pavement. Men and women fished in and out of the bath-house, their wooden sandles making ding-ding-ding sounds on the cement.

We waited in the ladies' line to get in. A crooked-faced man was guarding the entrance. He was loud voiced. Number one-eight-five, tub-bathing, he yelled as he let one in. Ten minutes went by, no one came out. The woman in front of us began to chat with the guard. She complained about the slowness of the bathers. The man said, People are all the same. They come to shower three times a year, they pay so much, they have to wait for so long, so of course they want to get their money's worth. They have to spend as much time as possible in the bath. It's not

171

unusual that we have people fainting in the tub. The man laughed as he shook his head. I won't, said the woman. It's stupid. I can't imagine being carried out naked. The guard said, Who knows? One thing I can guarantee everybody here is that you will come out a couple of pounds lighter. The crowd laughed with the guard. A woman came out. One-eight-six, tub-bathing. The guard let in another. What about shower-bathing? I asked the guard. No shower-bathing space available yet. As I've told you, people are taking their time.

Yan said, We should have paid a little more to have the tub-bathing for two. I said I doubted the cleanliness of the tubs. I motioned her to take a look at a woman a few yards behind us who obviously had some type of skin problem. Yan scratched her head and said, Oh no. The woman in front of us asked the guard if he knew anything about the incident which took place a few months ago. The guard said, How could I not know it? The woman asked, What happened to that nasty man? The guard said, He was arrested of course, and sent to jail. It was not his first time doing this type of thing. He was good at it. He had a fine face and had no trouble dressing up like a woman. How did you let him pass? the woman asked. The guard was a little embarrassed. He said, How was I supposed to know? A few hundred women pass through every day. How could I tell he was a man? If he was normal, he wouldn't have joined the ladies' line. How did you finally catch him? the woman asked. The guard said, Well, there was an old lady. She was so old, about seventy years old, and very demanding. She never cared about her body being seen, she ran around the whole bath-house naked complaining that the water temperature was too hot. She would faint if the air got too steamy. And you know, when there isn't much steam in the air, things get clear. She happened to notice his you-know-what. And then she fainted. We took her out and cooled her down. When she woke, she told us what she saw. The man was just getting dressed. He tried to make an escape, but I'm vegetarian, and my strength never fails me. The woman turned to

172

us and sighed, Isn't it bizarre? The guard said, What's so bizarre about it? A few hundred men are arrested each year for peeking through the women's shower window.

The guard told the woman that the year before he caught a woman in the men's big tub. She looked boyish, tall and slim. She had a flat chest. She had thick, thick hair on her thing. As a matter of fact, she came to bathe all the time. She said she worked as a porter. I couldn't tell from her voice. It's natural for a young boy to have a girlish voice, right? I let her in every time. I never doubted that she was a man. She was friendly and bought me cigarettes. She was nice.

But how was she discovered? We couldn't wait to hear the story. The guard lit a cigarette, inhaled, and said slowly, You cannot slurp up hot porridge in a hurry, can you? He went on. A strange thing happened. Our men's tub tickets all sold out and still there were people waiting. It got me suspicious. Why had our customers become so enthusiastic about bathing all of a sudden? Well, word got out. The men said they were hooked on the tub. With all the steam in the air, it was like walking in a big fog. Strange hands would massage their sun instrument. It blew their minds. They became seekers. The sound of bathing covered their moaning. The woman was actually . . . Well, do you have to make me say it? She was a beast!

Tell me how you caught her, said the woman to the guard. Well, the guard said, I caught the tiger by visiting the cave, you see. The woman widened her eyes. You mean . . . you did . . . that? The guard nodded. But it was for the purpose of getting rid of her! The woman stared at him. You can't say you didn't have any fun with her, can you? He raised his hand to his mouth and whispered to her. She was such a hot bitch. It was hard to let her go. When I sent her to the State Security Department, to tell you the truth, I did feel quite sad. Her body, it was . . . she sat on my . . . Such a beast. Damn. I suppose I can never forget her.

Finally, the guard yelled out our numbers. We gave him the

tickets and stepped into the bath-house. The lobby was narrow and had a high ceiling. The men's showers were to the left, the women's to the right. A blue cotton curtain hung by the entrance. The steaming air came out when the curtain swung open. We went in. It was crowded. The air was steamy. There was a rough-faced lady sitting by the entrance with a red band on her arm, a string of locker keys in one hand and a bell in the other. She rang the bell and yelled, Be careful with your purse and bags. Stealing will be punished. Don't forget to return your locker key. No clothes-washing inside.

We could not find a locker. People were busy changing. We saw an old lady was finished with her locker and took it over. I told Yan that I was still thinking about the guard's stories. I couldn't believe such things happened here in this house. Yan said, I suppose they could happen. Look, we can't really get to see much in such steamy air. I looked around. Indeed, we could not see far.

Yan looked at me as she took off her clothes. As if she was showing me that her body was the only thing that stayed unchanged when time had withered her face and mind. Farming kept her muscles strong, her body ripe, her breasts firm. Even though I was no longer familiar with her thoughts, her body brought me back to the time when we sang 'My Motherland' together, with Little Green. In Yan's nakedness, my desire resumed.

The rough-faced lady with the bell was staring at Yan. She yelled, she rang the bell, but her eyes were on Yan's body. Among the little sagging bodies in the room, Yan's was like a pine tree standing among bushes. Her lotus-bud-like breasts stuck out proudly. She was having a hard time stuffing our clothes in one locker. I put a towel around her shoulders. The rough-faced lady took her eyes away. I thought of how the guard would watch Yan if he were around. I told Yan my thoughts. Yan joked, You are no different. She finally locked up our clothes. We walked towards the showers. Yan said, I enjoy you watching me. I said,

Maybe we should have got a two-people tub and forgotten about the skin disease. She said, The shower will still be good. Let's go inside, the air seems thick.

The shower room had many shower heads. All occupied. Everyone was busy washing. The hot water was running constantly. We could only find one shower head so I told Yan to take it while I went out and told the rough-faced lady that I couldn't find a shower head. The lady said, Well, then you will have to wait till the next shower head is available, or you can share one with your friend. I asked how long I would have to wait. She said, Maybe five minutes, maybe fifty minutes.

I went in and told Yan what Rough-faced Lady had said. Yan said, I feel as if we were in our mosquito net again. Would you wash my back for me? I took a piece of soap, rubbed it on a towel and began washing her back. I applied the soap again and smoothed her back. I had not touched this body for so long and now I knew how much I missed it. She stood under the running water and said to me, Rub me harder. As I kept rubbing, her breasts became full. My hands became hot. I stopped. Yan began to rub me. I looked around. One bather on my right side was rinsing. She glanced at Yan, admiring her robustness. I motioned to Yan. Yan noticed the bather and stared back. The bather lowered her head in embarrassment. That woman's body reminded me of a piece of furniture — a door-thin back, flat breasts, nipples like drawer-knobs, table-leg legs and the face of a cooked aubergine. The woman took up her soap box and clothes, wrapped herself in a towel and got out. I took over the shower head. We washed until we were tired.

We were in the steamy changing room. I dressed more quickly than Yan. I watched her getting dressed. She noticed and smiled at me. She knew that I liked to watch her. She slowed down, rubbed her shoulders with the towel. I adored her long neck and broad shoulders. Their elegance. It was the body I used to devour every night. Her breasts, their fullness. I wished I could caress them again. My heart swung when my eyes drew on them. Yan bent over to pick up her bra behind me. Her breasts brushed over my face. I love you, I whispered to her. She smiled and said, I know. She put on her bra and buttoned it up. I stuffed the towel into the bag. She tied up her shoes. As we walked out of the bath-house she said to me that she had become more corrupt than I could imagine.

紅 杜 鵑

It was noon. We each had a bowl of noodles on the way back. There was an old lady standing on the corner. She carried a basket covered with a wet towel. She was secretly selling jasmine. We paid fifty cents and bought a string. We brought the jasmine to our nose and smelled it all the way back. Yan had one petal in her mouth. She ate it when we reached our street.

Yan lay on my bed lazily playing with the jasmine. I took the jasmine from her hand and spread the petals on her hair. I smelled her. I smelled her hidden sadness. She unbuckled her belt and took off her jacket. She said she wished to die on this bed. I began to kiss her, and she came to tears. She turned away from me. She was attacked by sadness. I went to protect her. My kisses told her how much I had missed her. But the only thing we could not talk about was Leopard. No matter how badly we wanted each other, our situation pulled us apart. Hopelessly apart. Without warning, without pushing. All of a sudden we were no longer familiar. Yan was desperate. I was desperate. We did not want to realize that we had been holding on to something, a dead past, that could no longer prosper. We were rice-shoots that had been pulled out of the mud. We lay, roots exposed, but we did not want to submit. We would never submit. We were heroines. We just tried to bridge the gap. We were trying our best. The rice-shoots were trying to grow without mud. Trying to survive the impossible. We had been resisting the brutality of the beating-weather. The hopelessness had sunk into the cores of our flesh. I would not let her see me cry. But she saw my tears in the kisses. She said, Let it be a dream. I said, Leopard is on his way, shouldn't we get ready?

The sound of steps in the stairwell. It's my father, I said. What do we do? Yan put her jacket back on quickly and buckled her belt. I took out one yuan and said to her, Go and buy two tickets at East Wind Theatre. Why? To get my father out of our way. Which show? she asked. *Lenin in 1918* and *Lenin in October*, I replied. Remember – buy two connected shows. I wanted to have my father stay away for at least four hours. Yan said, No, we can't do that to him. I said, Leave the matter to me. I took Yan to the back window and told her to slide down by the roof. When I saw her do so and cross the fence, I shut the window.

I asked my father what made him come home early. Father did not ask why I was there. He said there was good news. The Shanghai Natural History Museum was about to reopen. The museum people had come to the printing shop and talked with the head to 'borrow' my father to direct a sky show. This is the news I have been waiting for, Father said excitedly. It's my dream to work with the stars. I'm tired of translating technical manu-scripts for Albania. My rotten Russian will never get better. Cook me some fried rice, Daughter.

As my father dug around in a drawer, I began to cook him a meal. I hoped Yan got the tickets with no problem. Usually those films had no audience because they were the only two foreign films and had been running for years. Almost everyone knew the story, and teenagers would recite Lenin's lines around the neighbourhood: 'We will have bread; we will have milk; the revolution will succeed. Long live the Soviet Union!'

Yan got back when my father was eating. I introduced them. Yan was shy. She would not raise her head. My father said, Do

177

you see the man-made earth satellite hanging from the ceiling? Yan raised her head to look at the ceiling. My father laughed, then said, Forgive me, girls, I just wanted to see my daughter's best friend's face. I hope you don't mind my joking. Yan tried to look composed. My father said, All my daughter's friends are shy. My daughter is a naughty monkey, isn't she? Yan lowered her head, her face flushed. Disagree? asked my father. Then you don't really know her. He seemed happy. He was rarely in such a good mood. I took my chance. I said, Papa, I've bought you two movie tickets. How nice, said Father. Which movie? *Lenin in October* and *Lenin in 1918*. No, he said, I've seen those movies a hundred times. I really have better things to do. Do you have to disappoint me? I said, putting the tickets on the table. I thought you always liked Russian things. I sat down on the chair and pouted. I waited. And my father said exactly what I expected. Well, I suppose I have to please my daughter, he said, picking up the tickets from the table. Oh, my! It starts in ten minutes. Take off now, I said. I am sure you will enjoy it. I pushed him out. My father walked downstairs shaking his head.

I feel guilty, said Yan. I said, Believe me, he will have fun. Whenever Papa watches a movie, he is like a child. He surrenders completely to it. I know my father. We are safe now.

Yan asked how safe the room was. It was a small porch with big glass windows and glass doors covered by flowery green draperies. Will you be guarding me from behind the draperies? Yan asked. I nodded. No one will come at this time of day, I said. Outside the windows are big trees that block the neighbours' view. Above the leaves is the sky. You won't mind the birds watching, will you? You can watch the clouds changing shape. I do that often.

Yan sat on the bed as I arranged the curtains, folded blankets and placed the pillows. Yan looked at me. I turned away because I could not bear her looking at me. I could not bear looking into myself. Yan's eyes were speaking the unspoken. I saw hesitation in her sureness. I leaned out of the window. Yan asked me what

I was doing. I said, Expecting Leopard. Yan became nervous. She came and sat by my side. She placed her head against my thigh. She held my waist. She said she must overcome her nervousness. I said, Why don't you kiss me? I felt her lips, her embrace. I said, The leaves are so green, the reeds must have grown full size at the farm. There is a cloud passing by. Don't you think it looks like a giant cotton-ball? She did not answer me. She kept on doing what she was doing. I stared into the yard. I watched peach blossoms rain down, petals on top of petals. I let Yan's warmth go through me. I kept composed. I could no longer see the yard. It was a green ocean I saw. I was floating with Yan in the tides.

Leopard appeared at the entrance of the lane on a bicycle. He parked the bicycle under a tree. He carried a black plastic bag on his back. He had a new haircut too, combed with gel. His eyes looked unsettled, his steps uncertain. He looked like a first-time thief. His face was red with guilt. He was in a navy-blue outfit. He saw me. He waved at me, embarrassed. His smile was funny. I waved at him and said that I would be down to open the door for him. I turned away from the window. Yan was on her knees. She raised her chin, looking at me, eyes burning. I tried to help. I kneeled down in front of her. I said, Leopard is downstairs, should I get him?

I went down and opened the door for Leopard. He ducked in. He was too nervous to say hello. I closed the door and sprang up the stairs. Leopard followed me up the staircase and on to the porch. Yan was sipping tea by the table. Leopard took off his bag, placed it right next to his feet as he sat down on the other side of the table. He said, Well, cleared his throat, then gave a dry laugh. Yan did not look at him. There was silence. A long awkward moment. We tried to avoid each other's eyes. Leopard had a hard time placing his hands. He began to speak. He said he got stuck in traffic. He said he borrowed the bicycle from his uncle who was a retired doorman. The bicycle had a rusted chain and a flat tyre. He said that he was sorry to keep us waiting. Yan, still not looking at him, asked how the funeral went. Leopard said it was fine. Yan asked about his mother. He said she was fine. She had gone to spend some time in the countryside with his ninth aunt. The ninth aunt was living alone. Her son, Leopard's cousin, was recently arrested and sentenced to jail. Yan asked why. Leopard said he did not know. The reason was obscure. The ninth aunt never made it clear to the family. His cousin was twenty-seven and was a violinist and had written a song called 'To Her'. Was he involved with any female? asked Yan. Leopard nodded and said her name was Moon. Silence. Three minds drifted away to their own realms. Leopard looked at his watch. The watch was new, a big Shanghai-made watch. Yan took another sip of tea. The birds outside the window sang loudly.

Yan did not ask Leopard about anything else. Leopard did not bring up any subject. They sat like two company leaders in a headquarters' meeting guarding their tongues. I said the weatherman on the radio said that there would be cow-hair-rain this afternoon. Leopard said, Oh, yes? Yan said, Oh, the cow-hair-rain, yes. I always like the cow-hair-rain, I said. Me too, said Leopard. Me too, said Yan. They looked at each other.

I went to the kitchen and poured a mug of jasmine tea. I went back to the porch and placed the tea in front of Leopard. I refilled Yan's mug, then sat down. The smell of jasmine perfumed the porch. The sunshine in the room moved slowly to the west. The clock in the living room sounded like a slow heartbeat. I stood up and pulled the curtains down. The room was shaded green.

Before I stepped out on to the porch, Leopard looked at me pleadingly. It reminded me of the day I went to Company Thirty-two to deliver Yan's letter. How I wished he would give me this look. I remembered my disappointment. Yan's disappointment. Her lovesickness. I could not forgive Leopard. Yet, I forgave him. For he once was the reason Yan needed me, for he had made us two one.

I locked the glass door behind me. I went to the kitchen. I pulled out a chair, sat on it and looked out of the window. I watched a woman neighbour with a new shining mushroom

180

hairdo, passing through the lane carrying a basket of spinach. I watched a group of kids playing with rocks. I watched as cooking smoke came out of the opposite window and a housewife poured a jar of water on the ground. I watched. But my mind was not with me. My mind was with Yan and Leopard.

The Old Tailor entered the lane. He looked like dried corn. He took out his sewing board and set it up in the yard by the wall. He did this every day. He was never in a hurry. He placed a half-done jacket on the board and picked out a needle from a rusted little can. He put on glasses and tried to put a strand of thread through the needle. He could not do it. He tore the thread with his teeth and tried again, then again. I watched him, my mind still on the porch. The sound of the clock became louder. I paced back and forth in the kitchen. I heard no sounds on the porch.

I tried to stop my desire. The desire to watch them. The desire to watch my other self – Yan. I felt as if I had never left the porch. I was in Yan. It was three instead of two people on the porch. My curiosity swelled. My lust was irresistible. Yan knew I was guarding her. She knew I was behind the draperies. She wanted me to participate in this, didn't she? I could not help but want to see the way her lips would crack open and her breath heat up. I could feel arms around my shoulders. The snake-like arms that wrapped me up. I could not tell whether they were Yan's or Leopard's or both. I wanted to feel Leopard's body. I wanted to have the three of us connected like electrical wires.

As my fingers touched the draperies, I trembled. I was sure this was not the right thing to do. I hated spies. And I would be spying. What if Leopard found out? What would happen? Would Yan hate me for ruining her pleasure? Would Leopard be angry?

I forced myself back to the kitchen. As I looked out of the window again, I saw the Old Tailor ironing the jacket. He ironed the collar then the sleeves. He put the iron on a stove. He waited for the iron to heat up. He fanned the stove. The flames rose. The Old Tailor turned my way suddenly. It was too late for me to hide. He smiled at me. His smile made me suspicious. It was a mysterious smile. Did he guess what we were doing? Should I be prepared? Should I warn Yan about him? Would he come up? How fast could he come up? What should I do if he did?

The Old Tailor was a respected neighbourhood activist. He had reported thieves and adulterers. He was honoured for his 'revolutionary sense of smell'. His greatest interest was not in the making of clothes but in searching for back-door news. He was involved in many families' troubles. He was often praised on the district blackboard. Now he kept smiling at me. I smiled back. I reached for a string outside the window. I pretended that I was checking the dryness of the hanging clothes. The Old Tailor went back to his ironing. He took a big sip of water, picked up the heated iron, sprayed the water on the jacket with his mouth, then hit the sleeves with the iron. White steam poured out.

I backed myself into the living room. I was tortured by what I could not participate in. My mind was drawing the pictures for me. Wild pictures. I paced carefully, taking care I made no noise. My steps stopped at the draperies. I stood still, listened very hard. My breath became short. I could hear nothing. Nothing at all.

My desire overtook me. I carefully, carefully opened the slit of the green draperies. I looked in and saw an overwhelming red colour first, and figured it was Yan's red underwear. My hand dropped. The slit closed. I could feel my skin being scorched. My heart was breaking. I did not understand my feelings. I did not understand why I was hurt by what I saw. I forgot what I was supposed to do.

He was possessing her. Leopard was possessing Yan. The way he caressed her showed that he was in love with her. I could tell. I knew what he looked like when he was not in love with her; he was arrogant, polite and only pretended that he was interested. But now he was utterly absorbed. He was the slave of his love. He was in tears. The way he was caressing her made me hate him. He murmured to her. He was telling her about his pain in not being able to love her enough. I hated his truthfulness. I felt invaded. My jealousy was irreconcilable. It refused to share the same sky with Leopard. I was furious at his love.

Yan was in a thin white shirt. Her eyes were closed. Her beauty was extraordinary. It melted me. Leopard was unbuttoning her bra, then his hands went into her underwear. She responded to him and encouraged him. She arched her chest to invite him. My tears came uncontrollably. He held her in his arms and then buried his head between her breasts. He raised himself slowly. He stared into her eyes. He could not take his eyes off her face as he slowly penetrated her. He kissed her eyes. His tears wet her cheeks. She brushed his hair with her fingers and rounded her arms on his back. He cried out in pleasure, then she followed. I lost my thoughts. My senses went on while my mind stopped functioning. I saw two bodies making love again and again. I smelled the jasmine. I remembered the taste of Yan, I heard the hardening breath, and I felt, felt betrayed. I was terrified by this feeling and forgot I was secretly watching the couple.

Before I realized what I was doing Yan saw me. She saw me in tears behind the glass. The draperies were pulled aside. She stopped Leopard and sat up. She stared at me. Leopard was confused, then he saw me. He was shocked. He put on his clothes. Yan sat naked, sat still, like a statue. She realized what this had done to me. She had planned this. She sensed my rage. She looked away. She put her head in her palms. She said, Come in, please.

I opened the porch door, and stepped in. I could not say a word. Is someone coming? asked Leopard. Should we leave? I wanted to say I am sorry, but my tears got in the way. I remembered that I had to pretend. I had to pretend that nothing had happened between Yan and me. She was my commander. I was her soldier and her guard, as always. Yan slowly put on her clothes. She looked outside the window for a while. By then I was able to say to Leopard, Would you like to have more tea? Leopard looked at Yan and then asked me if he could use the bathroom. I guided him to the bathroom and came back to the porch. Yan was buttoning up her clothes and I went to kneel in front of her. She embraced me and said, I am sorry to do this, but I just have to. I think we are now ready to go on with our own lives. You are done with Red Fire Farm.

I went to the kitchen, looked out of the window. I allowed my tears to pour out silently. I will always love you no matter what you do to push me away from you, I kept saying in my heart. The Old Tailor was still sewing. The lane was as quiet as a deep well. I put some water into a wok and set it on the stove. I lit the stove and waited by the wok for the water to boil. I heard heavy breathing rise again inside the porch. Leopard was groaning. There was the sound of wrestling. Then Yan gave in.

As I looked through the green draperies again, Yan was sitting on Leopard's lap. Leopard was devouring her. Can he read the poetry of her body like I do? Can he understand the way her heart sings like I do? I tried to deny what I saw and I tried to convince myself that Yan did not love him. But Yan kept throwing me into reality. She knew I could not stop watching her. She wanted to put my heart to death. I watched her. I had no choice but to watch her. How every tip of her hair was soaked in sweat, as was Leopard's. Yan was facing me, her chin was up, her eyes were closed. She was trying to exhaust herself. She had him in her. His face was between her breasts. He murmured. He whispered her name again and again. His hands were pressing her hips. As her breath came harder, her arms circled him like two snakes strapping tight a squirrel. She kissed him deeply. She was showing this to me. She was doing it to me. I could feel my heart laid bare on the ground, being stepped on, like the hen Big Beard's egg. I did not close the draperies. I forced myself to face Yan, to experience the death of my love for her, to accept what was given to me by fate. I remembered she had said to me that she was more corrupted than I could imagine. She was doing this to let me hate her and forget her so that she could forget me, in order to stop the pain she had been having. She was always the ruler, the manipulator. She was always in control. She was destroying our love to preserve their love. She was murdering our love with her own hands. I hated her selfishness. I would not be manipulated this time. I felt sorry for Leopard, for he was brainlessly in love, for he did not know what he was getting into. Maybe I was wrong. Maybe Yan was not the person she used to be, a true heroine, a goddess with a ring shining around her head. Maybe she was changed by the farm, by her life, by my leaving her alone in the mosquito net. Maybe she was corrupt to a degree I could not imagine, where she no longer had a faith in love, or in anything. Maybe Leopard's lust made her forget what she wanted to remember. Maybe, after all, she was doing the right thing by coming to my house to seduce me.

Yan looked pale when she opened the porch door. She and Leopard were all dressed. My calm must have surprised her because she said, We would like to leave. She wanted to escape from me. Then I said, Congratulations. I did not know why but I just said it. I laughed. I said to Leopard, I enjoyed guarding you two. If you ever need me again, do not hesitate, just let me know. I said to Yan, Goodbye and take care. I tried to put my arm around her, but it was impossible. She disgusted me. She sensed it. She squatted down and pretended to tie her shoes. But she was trying to hold back her tears. She knew, just as I knew, that we would not meet again. She said to Leopard, Let's go. As if feeling he owed me something, Leopard said appreciatively, You have been a big help, how can I thank you enough? Take care of your woman, I said. He said, I am glad that you are not a man, otherwise you would have been the one to win her. Although Leopard said the words sincerely, they sounded to me like mocking. I said to both of them, It's been my pleasure. I found I could say no more and I went to open the door for them.

I heard the sound of footsteps on the staircase. It was Mother. I said to Yan and Leopard, Wait, just say hello to my mother, would you? They nodded. I rushed on to the porch and took a quick look inside. Everything was in order, the pillow, the chairs and the blankets. My mother stepped in. I said, Mama, these are my guests from the farm. This is Yan and this is Leopard. Mother said, Oh, Yan, how could I stop my daughter from talking about you? She went over to Yan and Leopard. They flushed and lowered their heads. I said, Mama, they would like to leave. Mother pulled me to the kitchen and said to me, How come you have served them nothing? I told her that I had served them tea. Mother said, Tea is nothing. Serve them some dumpling soup. The water on the stove is boiled. I could make dumplings in ten minutes. I said, No, there is no need. I let go of Yan. I had to let her go.

At six o'clock in the evening, my father returned from the two films. He was exhausted and had a headache. He told me that I could never make him go to the movies again. I did not talk to him or the rest of the family. I felt so lonely. That night the cow-hair-rain tapped on the window and streamed down on the glass like running tears.

紅 杜 鵑

No one in the studio said anything about my war with Soviet Wong. Everyone became more careful in their own daily presentation. They watched Soviet Wong's interest come and then disappear and figured out how to act according to what she liked. Nothing was verbally expressed. It was all in the eyes, in that very window of the heart. Every act was precisely performed.

Cheering Spear came to me one evening when I sat among wild grass looking at the setting sun. I was thinking about Yan. I was absorbed in my past. It was a way to escape from the present misery. Cheering Spear had a blade of dog-tail-grass in her mouth. She stopped in front of me. She blocked the sun. I looked at her. She was smiling. She took the dog-tail-grass out of her mouth and said, I don't mean to tell you what to do, but if I were you, I would withdraw now. I would propose to go back to where I came from. It is better to bend with the wind when it blows.

I was surprised at her boldness. My anger rose to the tip of my tongue. Mind your own business, I said. I looked at her as I continued, I know no one can be happier that I am falling out of the race. It's written all over your face. Go and take a look at that face now. Don't block my sun here.

I just wanted to show that I care about you, Cheering Spear said. I could never be wrong about what's on your mind, I said. I hate spies. You can go and report on me now, I told her. She looked at me and said, Yes, I will, if you would like me to. She put the dog-tail-grass back into her mouth and said, I am glad that you have a sense of where you'll end up. I said, You don't know anything about me. Then let me give you some advice, she said. You would feel better if you were more prepared. You know, you are such a bourgeois individualist. Everyone in the studio is convinced that you are the capitalist sprout.

Cheering Spear often reminded me of Lu. It seemed that I could never escape from Lu. There were Lus all over China. I was reminded of the old saying, 'Poverty gives birth to evil person-alities.'

Really, I don't have to mind your business since it has already been taken care of by our Party, Cheering Spear said as she lightly walked away. Her shadow on the ground was extremely long that evening. It remained in my sight for quite a while before it was dragged away. Strangely, I thought of those vultures, the eagles who wend their way up mountain paths and wheel in the sky looking for a chance to dive and pick up their meals.

The next day, a notice was sent to us by One Ounce. It said that the Supervisor had arrived in Shanghai and was scheduled to visit the studio sometime during the week to pick the final actress to play Red Azalea.

Meeting the Supervisor, impressing him, might reverse my fortunes. Soviet Wong told us to pick our own material and prepare ourselves for the competition. Before we began our practice, Cheering Spear came to me and said, I think you are going to be the one who wins. I did not answer her. I did not know how to trust her. She asked after a while, in a casual tone, what I was going to perform. Would it be 'Azalea visits the Red Army headquarters' or 'Azalea tells her story'? Sensing that I did not want to answer her, she smiled and said, I am going to perform 'Azalea in jail'.

I looked at Cheering Spear. I felt pity for her. It was hard to believe that she chose this part, the part in which Red Azalea is in jail, behind bars, in which not much gets shown. The scene had only two lines. I could not believe that she could throw away her chance like this. I looked at her, doubting whether I had heard her right. Cheering Spear convinced me. She convinced me that her stupidity was real. She was going to perform 'Azalea in jail'. It was her choice. I let out a breath. A secret pleasure filled me. I said, Are you sure? She said, Yes, this is what I am going to do. Then she asked, Which part are you going to do? I said, off-handedly, 'Azalea tells her story'. I said I chose the scene because it was material that allowed me to show different aspects of the character. She said, Let's wish each other success. She appeared unusually friendly as we practised together and gave comments on each other's performance. She constantly complimented me. I could see success lay at my feet.

The day arrived when my fate would be decided. It was morning, about nine o'clock. A cloudless day. The sunshine axed into the rehearsal room through the windows. The room was filled with people. Everyone was waiting for the Supervisor. Cheering Spear and I were busy going through our last rehearsal in our heads. We paid no attention to how Firewood, Little Bell and Bee

OhYang were feeling. They were assigned to play the supporting roles. Soviet Wong, Sound Of Rain, a group of studio heads and the newspaper reporters were already seated. They each had a mug of hot tea in their hands. They waited patiently.

I stood by the window. I was taking deep breaths. I wondered what the Supervisor looked like. What was his taste? Would he choose me? Would he not choose me? Would he choose Cheering Spear? Would he not choose Cheering Spear?

Cheering Spear did not look as nervous as I did. She came in late and sat by me. She was wearing a red shirt. The red colour reflected on her face. She was in good spirits. She asked me whether I was nervous. I said I was, a little. She said she was not. She shook hands with me as we saw a car drive in through the studio gate.

The man called the Supervisor was introduced to us. He was wearing a pair of big sunglasses. No one got to see his face much. He was in a green military uniform. He was a medium-sized man. His hair, combed back, was extremely black. He was not as old as I had imagined. He was about forty. He stepped out of the car and walked towards us with vigorous strides. Soviet Wong and Sound Of Rain went running up to greet him. They shook hands. He was guided into the room and seated in the middle seat. The performers, Cheering Spear, Firewood, Little Bell, Bee OhYang and I, gathered at the back corner of the room. Soviet Wong announced the programme. The programme of two candidates running for Red Azalea. She announced Cheering Spear's name then my name. When she went to sit down by the Supervisor, our competition began.

The Supervisor did not look at us. He crossed one leg over the other and lit a cigarette. He did not take off his sunglasses. Cheering Spear marched up to the platform in the centre of the room. She had changed into Red Azalea's costume – a side-buttoned cotton jacket printed with a pattern of red azaleas. She was confident. She began her lines. It shocked me, it knocked me down – she was performing 'Azalea tells her story'. She was performing

189

my material. But she did it better. She added good details. My mind went completely blank. I could hear nothing but a deafening tone in my head. Cheering Spear was doing my piece. I had nothing left to perform. If I performed what she did everyone would think that I'd imitated her.

I lost my chance to win before the battle. I could not believe that Cheering Spear had done this to me. I could not believe that she was reciting my lines. It was so sudden, so devastating. The Supervisor was looking intensely at Cheering Spear. Soviet Wong was smiling. She looked so pleased.

Cheering Spear ended her performance. She finished her last phrase like a first-class acrobat who landed on tiptoe on the seat of a running bicycle. There was much applause. Cheering Spear bowed to the audience, to the Supervisor. Soviet Wong went up the platform to congratulate her. The Supervisor looked impressed. He went to shake hands with Cheering Spear. He asked her whether she knew how to ride a horse. When Cheering Spear said yes, he asked whether he could see her perform on a horse in Shanghai Stadium. She said of course, when? She said that she had been longing for a horse ride for so long. The Supervisor invited Cheering Spear to sit by him. He talked about arranging a horse ride.

Then came my turn to perform. I had twenty minutes to fight back. I had twenty minutes to convince the Supervisor that I was better than Cheering Spear so he should pick me instead of her. But I was already beaten to the ground. I was bleeding inside. My time was slipping away. I went up to the platform. My legs were shaking. I gave the most stupid performance of my life. I performed 'Azalea tells her story'. I recited the lines thinking how I could convince people that I was not imitating Cheering Spear. The audience began to yawn. Then it was finished. I was finished before I began. My limbs were cold.

I was going back to my seat in the audience when I heard Cheering Spear saying to an interviewer that her success was due to Soviet Wong. Soviet Wong had mothered her excellence. The

190

next day the Party newspaper published a big picture of Cheering Spear on a horse led by Soviet Wong.

The revolutionary task needs you to be a set-clerk, One Ounce delivered the message to me flatly. I was in my room, idling. I had been idling for hours. If you do not like it, the studio will not mind your going back to Red Fire Farm. It took him thirty seconds to announce that order. No one in the room looked surprised. I realized that my good fortune had come to an end. I wanted to ask, Who made that decision? My tongue was so stiff that I could barely make a sound. Feeling a sudden weakness, I went out of the room. I held on to a maple trunk and sat down on the grass. The Party committee, of course, One Ounce volunteered. Who exactly are those people? I looked at him. I am sorry, I don't know, he said. I am just a guard delivering the message from the upstairs.

I packed my things and walked out of the room. I was on my way to becoming a set-clerk at the studio. It was early morning, around six-thirty. Cheering Spear, Firewood, Little Bell and Bee OhYang were already up doing their routine exercises. Their voices were clearer than usual. As I passed by, they stared at me. Behind the dead-pan expressions, I knew they were happy. I kept walking towards the gate. The maples were swaying and birds were flying up and down picking their food under my feet. One Ounce went to open the big wooden gate when he saw me coming out. It's all right, I can just go through the side door, I said. One Ounce insisted. The bolt was rusted after a few rains. One Ounce rotated the bolt hard. The rusty sound was hard on the ears. After he wrestled with the bolt, the door was pushed open. The birds flew away. One Ounce stretched out his right arm and made a humble gesture to let me pass.

I did not allow myself to feel. Firewood, Cheering Spear, Bee OhYang and Little Bell resumed their voice exercises behind me. They sang:

Who smashed the fetters for us?
Who saved us from the fiery pit?
Who led us to the golden road?
Oh, the sun above the sky,
Oh, the brightest beacon in the sea,
It is you,
The greatest Chairman Mao and the Party,
You are the saviour of our lives.

The next day a producer at the Shanghai Film Studio gave me a big mop, a script, a notebook and a box of chalk. He asked me to memorize the script which contained one thousand and forty-two shots. It was the shooting script of *Red Azalea*. My eyes hurt when I looked at the title. You see, said the producer, a set-clerk is the person who records the set, and this means everything. If there is an ant crawling through the set, a good set-clerk will record it. It is a big responsibility, because we shoot scenes in a disorderly fashion. For example, a man opens a gate and steps into the hallway. It may take two scenes to complete the action. We will shoot the outside scene in Hunan and then shoot the inside scene back in Shanghai in the studio two months later. You have to be able to remember exactly what clothes he is wearing, for example, and how he wears them at different locations. For example, was his collar open or closed? If you make a mistake, you will have a person enter with his collar open and all of a sudden it is closed. The scene would be wasted, of course. Only one foot of the film, which costs our peasants a season's grain, will be salvageable. The wasted film could be food for generations of our peasants. And you know what that means to the country.

I forced myself to listen hard to the producer. He asked me to make thirty copies of his notes to the crew. We have only three days left before shooting, he said. He asked me to put out the shooting board, draw up the shots, check the costumes, the props and the extras. The floor, the producer said, pointing his finger down as if reminding me of something important. You should begin by mopping the floor, he said seriously. When I took a mop he said, Listen, we don't need feeble labour. Each carrot has its own patch. Remember that or you will be sent back to Red Fire Farm.

I did not raise my head when I mopped the floor. I felt I had no face. There was a rehearsal going on in the recording studio. I heard someone yell repeatedly into a microphone. The voice had a strong Beijing accent. It was the Supervisor's voice. I remembered this voice.

I finished my job by six o'clock in the evening and went to a back room to smoke. I had started smoking the day I was dismissed from the actor-training class. I sat on a bench. The surroundings were dark and damp. I did not switch on the light. I needed darkness. I came every day and smoked cigarettes in the dark until my lips numbed.

After the break I had to finish mopping the rest of the stairways in the building. The mopping seemed endless. I suddenly remembered an old saying, 'It is difficult for a snake to go back to Hell once it has tasted Heaven.' I was that snake now. Each day I felt worse than the one before. Every morning, the moment I woke up, my body and my soul went in separate directions. The soulless body went to mop the floors and the bodiless soul went to the realm of vague hopes. A few times, the body and soul joined momentarily when I felt the mop become a machine gun. As I mopped with it, it fired.

I inhaled deeply. I forgot time. Suddenly a voice, a tender voice, rose from my back. Why do you like to sit in the dark? the voice asked.

I thought I had imagined it. I kept still. The voice repeated itself. The sound softer. A Beijing accent. I stood up and was about to switch on the light. I'd like to smoke in the dark too, the voice said. Can I have a light? I kept still in the dark. Thank you, the voice said. I heard the noise of a person standing up and moving towards me. Who are you? I asked.

I am like you, a set-helper, the voice said. How do you do? I saw a cigarette held out to me. I passed him my cigarette. The two cigarettes touched. The smoker inhaled. It was a gentle face that I saw. The face faded back into the dark. My mind went back to its own thinking.

I thought of my parents. I had stopped talking to them. You don't deserve those dunce caps, my mother said to me over and over. I told her that I was sick of her sense of justice, her fantasy. I told my mother not to interfere with me. I said, Why don't you ever learn? What's wrong with you? Is it because your own life hasn't been miserable enough? My mother said, said with her own logic, I don't regret a bit about my way of living because I have been truthful to myself. I could not stand her logic. I said, I don't want to inherit your life. It is a terrible, terrible and terrible life. I yelled at her. My mother went to take pills. I said, Don't you see? Can't you see it's not working? Your philosophy does not work for me. My mother refused to give up. She said she didn't believe that evil should rule. I said, It's ruling. She said, It's impossible. I said, I mop floors, don't you see? She said, What did you do wrong? I said, I wish I knew the answer. My mother started her repetition: That shouldn't have happened to you. I said, It's happening to me. She said she would like to have a talk with my instructor. I laughed.

The instructors came before my mother gathered her guts to go and confront them. Once again it was Soviet Wong and Sound Of Rain who came. They came to put a dunce cap on me. They wanted me to acknowledge a crime I did not commit. They wanted me to say, Yes, I deserve to be kicked out because I am bad. My mother asked, What did my daughter do wrong? You have shielded a wrong-doer, they replied. My mother refused to be confused. She fought to the end. She fought to the last step of the staircase. She said, Tell me what's wrong with my daughter. They said, Everything. Everything's wrong with your daughter.

She said, Give me an example. They said, We don't need to. My mother said, Comrade Soviet Wong, I would never ever want my daughter to call you teacher.

My mother followed them out of the lane. She yelled before falling on the cement. She yelled, You can't make a criminal out of my innocent daughter. My father dragged my mother back upstairs. He said, You are making things worse. Don't you know they represent the Party? My mother yelled, But I am not guilty. My father pushed her to sit on a chair. He told my mother the simplest things in the world. The simplest things to make my mother understand the world she was in. My father told her that he had just been fired from the Shanghai Museum of Natural Science because he disagreed with his Party secretary boss over a technical plan. He had been accused of using science to attack the Communist Party. My father told my mother that Coral was forced to become a peasant because I was out of Red Fire Farm. Coral had to become a peasant to meet the Party's policy. She was working at Red Fire Farm in Company Thirty, the company that had no drinking-water pipe of its own. The Party tells people what to do, not the other way around, my father said. My mother refused to understand the world. She refused to understand the things that did not make sense to her. She shut her senses up because she preferred to live in her own world. She lived with the god of justice. She broke three dishes one night while dish-washing. I woke up in the early morning and found Mother sitting in the kitchen staring at the sinkhole, alone.

Where is your interest? the voice in the dark interrupted my thoughts. I have no interest, I said. I need some comments on a costume I've just picked, would you care to give some? the voice said.

The light was switched on. Under the hazy gas light I saw a man in an ancient red-silk robe with an embroidered golden dragon on the chest and silver waves at the bottom. Under a hat decorated with diamonds shone a pair of bright almond-eyes. Long and thin eyebrows like the wings of a gliding sea goose. Smooth pale skin shaded mauve on the cheeks. A delicate nose and a tomato-red full mouth. He cited:

> Spring river the moon shines a flowery night,
> Autumn maple the sun hurries a dewy morning.

I stared at the man. I thought, It must be the make-up. The make-up made him look femininely handsome. Who are you? I heard myself say. I have told you, I am a set-helper like you. Where are you from? Beijing.

He stepped over to shake hands with me. Staring at his painted face, my mind was occupied by a strange thought: Was he a woman or a man? He seemed to be both. He was grotesquely beautiful. He lowered his head, then looked away, almost bashfully. Lifting his robe carefully, he walked towards the door like a swinging willow – he was wearing costume boots with four-inch-heels.

What are you doing here? I asked. Playing, he said. Don't you remember Chairman Mao's teaching, 'Make the past serve the present'? I am playing with that idea. I asked, What do you supervise here? Everything, he said. By the way, how do you like this costume? I told him that it looked unusual. I had the costume man send it to me, he continued. Isn't it gorgeous? He told me that he was collecting ideas to create good art for the people. He asked me to give opinions on the model operas. I said, How could anyone have any opinions? The Party's opinion is the people's opinion. How dare I have my own opinion? I was eliminated by Soviet Wong because I had opinions.

My words just gushed out of my mouth. My anger made me shake. When I spoke of Soviet Wong I became vicious. I expressed my hatred eagerly. I did not care who was listening at that moment. He waited quietly until I emptied my words. I began to regret my impulse. I said, Nine million people watched nine operas in nine years. It is wonderful. In the tenth year, there would be number ten. *Red Azalea*. I wanted to pronounce Cheer-

196

ing Spear's name but I could not continue. It hurt me to pronounce this name. My jealousy was indescribable.

You are not speaking your mind, he said. Of course I am, I said. He said, The model operas were created, let me remind you, by Madam Mao, Comrade Jiang Ching. Does that mean no one is supposed to criticize them? That's right, I said. He laughed, in a womanish silky voice.

He said to me that he had touched a sly mind. He said it was interesting to have a challenge. He had been bored. He took off the costume, the make-up, then put on an indigo Mao jacket. He was a delicate-looking man. I recognized the man I saw when I failed my performance. The Supervisor. He was the one who picked the thief who had stolen my Red Azalea. He liked Cheering Spear. I only wished that I could tell him what Cheering Spear did to me that day. But how could I make him believe me? How could I not sound ridiculous? Cheering Spear was fantastic when beating me. Cheering Spear was talented in making my work hers. If I spoke, how could I not make myself look more ridiculous than I already had? The Supervisor asked me if he could have a cigarette. His fingers were fine and smooth like a woman's. I lit a cigarette and gave it to him. The smoke we exhaled joined in the air.

The next evening he asked if I would sit with him until he finished his cigarette. I said, Fine. We sat in the smoking room. He asked where I lived. I said, On Shanxi Road in an apartment with my family. He asked, How many members? I said, Five at present. He asked, How many rooms do you have? I said, One room and one porch. He said, So you do not get to sleep alone? I said, No, of course not. He said, I see.

He asked again whether I liked the model operas. I replied again, How could anyone not like them? How would anyone dare not like something like that? He said, Can you explain? I said he would be bored with my answer. He said he preferred to hear a personal one. He said that he himself was not satisfied with the operas. He said that he craved revolutionary passion and many of the operas lacked it. I said that I agreed with him and that I would be interested in the private lives of the characters. I said that it was strange to me that the opera protagonists had no private lives. He said, You mean romance? I said, I didn't mean to say it, but yes, perhaps that was it. All right then, that *is* it. I don't have anything to lose now in voicing my opinion since I am only a set-clerk. I can't be put lower. He laughed silently. You don't have to be so panicked, he said, I am interested in your opinion. It pleases me. Go on. He said it was true that none of the model operas had romance. I said, I don't believe the protagonists have no lovers in their lives whatsoever. I don't believe any human's mind could be so free of deep emotions.

A cloud of scorn passed over the Supervisor's face. We should not use fantasy to deceive our young people, he said. His fingers carried the cigarette through the air. Romantic love does not exist among proletarians, he said firmly. It is a bourgeois fantasy. People will not forgive anyone who sells lies.

I stood up and went to take the mop. He rose and stepped on my mop. I stood quietly. You must have a lover of some sort, he said. Don't you lie to me. I do not, I said. You have problems, he stared into my eyes. That is not your business, I said, taking the mop, and went out through the door.

You forgot to ask me my name yesterday, he said to me the next afternoon in the smoking room. You can tell me now, I said impatiently. He said, I don't intend to. You will have to call me the Supervisor like everybody else. I said, I could find out from other crew members if I wanted to. Try it, he said.

No one knew his name. Everyone said that he was from Beijing and was an expert on opera and film. Everyone called him the Supervisor. His mission, Sound Of Rain once told the crew, was the most important mission of the century. Sound Of Rain himself knew nothing about the details.

Cheering Spear was brought to the set again and again to be

screen-tested for *Red Azalea*. I saw her dream in her eyes. Radiant faced. Cheering Spear didn't deign to glance at me. I mopped the floor and was burnt by envy. The Supervisor stood close to Cheering Spear, watching her being made up. Beautiful, he said wholeheartedly. He did not mind showing the crew that he adored her, so then everybody, except me, began to adore her.

I ate my rice cake in the dark in the smoking room. I felt like an animal who ate its own intestines. I could not eat any more. I could not endure watching Cheering Spear smile. I could not bear her happy singing. I could not escape from my jealousy of her success. Cheering Spear was working hard. Her performance was getting better and better. I was ordered to serve her. I had to remind her of her lines. I had to draw marks under her feet for the cameraman's purpose, to pass her a cup of water when she asked for a drink, to change her costume after shots, to button up her collar when she forgot.

Soviet Wong came to the set often. She would watch me as well. She watched me stand in for Cheering Spear when she was sent to fix her make-up. I stood under the spotlights for Cheering Spear. It was hard to bear. But I did not want to let Soviet Wong and Cheering Spear see my frustration, though Cheering Spear was too much into herself to notice me. I kept my face up there, between my shoulders, stuck on the front of my skull. I said good morning to Cheering Spear. I bent down on my knees to draw and redraw chalk marks for the camera movement. Sometimes my tears would come up without my being aware of it. Especially when Cheering Spear would say to me, Oh, you are so good at your job.

Though the Supervisor was the director, he came and went without announcement. He had a group of four associate directors working for him. They always whispered together. The Supervisor's voice would suddenly reappear behind the camera after a few days of disappearance. He seemed to like Cheering Spear more and more. One day he said to her, I want you to be prepared because the masses will want you so much that they could strangle you. Are you prepared? I was drawing chalk marks under Cheering Spear's feet when the Supervisor said this. My fingers broke the chalk.

You did not eat all day. Are you all right? The Supervisor's voice rose in the corner. You only have one stomach, can you afford to abuse it? I said, I am afraid that I'm not feeling too well. He said, Don't break your nerves, because it would not be worth it. No one really cares about what happens to you. Being egotistical is not a good idea. You can eat yourself up that way. He stood up and walked out of the door.

I was suddenly afraid of sitting in the dark all by myself. I had a strange urge to end the present, to end my life. To escape from this thought I took the mop and went to the hallway. As I mopped the hall I heard the Supervisor's voice over the microphone. Let me hear the key melody! Let me hear the key melody! he yelled. I peeked through a window on the stairs into the conducting room. With a set of headphones on, the Supervisor lay on a sofa. His feet were on a table. The orchestra played again. The Supervisor became furious. You group of rice-worms have no ears! he yelled, and stepped down on to the studio floor. He ran to a grand piano and played a fast string of notes. Turning his back he said, Take a break and we'll play it one more time. If you do not get it right, I'll make sure you all lose your rice bowls. The Supervisor came up the stairway. He saw me before I managed to step out of his way. He looked at me and said, Let out that bag of smelly gas in you. The day is bright. I made no response. He passed by and I heard his voice through the speakers singing the key melody.

I did not go to the smoking room that evening. I rode my bicycle around the city until midnight just to exhaust myself. I went home to sleep and left at dawn. I did not want to give my parents a chance to ask me questions. Their questions would spread salt on my wounds. I did not want to be talked about as a failure. I arrived at the studio by seven o'clock. I put out the call sheet and sat back in a corner. The pain of hopelessness rolled over me as I watched a costume designer dress Cheering Spear up. The Supervisor stood next to them making comments here and there. The costume designer asked if the foam she had stuffed into Cheering Spear's bra to make her breasts fuller looked real enough. The Supervisor nodded and said to Cheering Spear, Throw out your chest. Out! More! That's right. They went to the camera and Cheering Spear was shining like a high-wattage light bulb. Cheering Spear practised her lines. The lines that I was so familiar with. It was impossible to ignore her, impossible to ignore my pain.

I mopped the floor at people's feet. Foot by foot. My hopes withered. I constantly thought of escaping. I asked Sound Of Rain if he could assign me a job elsewhere. He said, I can't issue you permission because I know you have an impure purpose. I know leaving the studio is your true intention. You lied to me, you lied to the Party and that's that. I stood there. Sound Of Rain continued, How have you failed to see that you have serious work to do here? How can you possibly be so selfish as to put the revolutionary business second in your mind? He took out his schedule book and told me that I was booked with work for the next five years. He said he did not make the rules as he closed his book.

I smoked in the dark room. I had become a chain-smoker. After a day's work, the Supervisor came into the smoking room and sat by himself. We sat in silence as usual, about five feet apart, as if the other person were another prop. My senses sailed into a dark ocean. The dot of the Supervisor's cigarette reminded me of a buoy light.

The first rough cuts were highly praised by the upstairs. It was said that Comrade Jiang Ching was pleased. She wanted to show the cuts to Mao. The Chairman and his key men would view the cuts and endorse and promote the movie to the public.

Sound Of Rain and Soviet Wong came to the set and

announced that Comrade Jiang Ching would inspect the set and have dinner with the crew members in the evening. We were asked to keep the news secret for security reasons. The crew members became excited, so excited that they went into corners and whispered loudly into each other's ears, It's true! How lucky we are.

I cleaned the mop after everyone else had gone. I did not go to the dinner. I could only be reminded of my misery if I went. I decided to stay. I decided to be by myself. I went to the room to smoke. The Supervisor was not there. Strangely, at this moment, in darkness, I found my thoughts went to him. I wondered what kind of person he was, his background and purpose. I admired his devotion. If I had not been in such a bad situation, I would have made friends with him. I liked him. I liked his strange mind. I began to wonder whether, if we were friends, I would tell him everything. Would I talk to him about Yan? I wondered what made him, the creator of *Red Azalea*, so fond of Cheering Spear.

The doorknob turned. A familiar figure ducked in. Good evening, he said. You haven't had your dinner, have you? No, I said. The cafeteria is closing, he said. I know, I said. But I am not hungry. Why didn't you go to the dinner? he asked me. I am sure you were invited. Was it because you don't care to meet our greatest standard-bearer? Of course I care, I said. But I am sure no one would be bothered by the absence of a set-clerk. He said, You can never be too sure of that. Comrade Jiang Ching cares very much for ordinary people.

He smiled and sat down opposite me. He laid two egg rolls in front of me. Eat while they are still warm, he said to me. I took an egg roll and stuffed it into my mouth. I was starving. I did not know what made me so daring in front of him. Was it his praise of Cheering Spear that deadened my hopes, so I no longer cared to please him any more?

The Supervisor sat down and took the cigarette I passed him. It is a stifling world indeed, he exhaled. You are not a bad person.

202

Not bad? I sneered. What about not being bad? 'What about it' is not significant, he said. You are serving a purpose. I wanted to know what kind of purpose. He said, It's better if you don't know. I turned to him and said, I do not care to know anything.

That is very well, he said. Let the sun keep shining. Let heaven and earth share . . . share the myth and beauty of the unknown. You see, it doesn't make much difference, to know or not to know, he said as if to himself. It is the nothingness that makes the ideal state of things. He turned and looked at me. He looked at me, in the dark. I saw his glittering irises. He got up, switched on the light and left the room. He left me thinking about him.

Sound Of Rain and Soviet Wong came to the set the next day. A new document from the Central Party Committee was issued in which it said that the direction *Red Azalea* was going in had created some political problems. Comrade Jiang Ching was in the middle of decision-making. The shooting was not yet to be effected.

紅 杜 鵑

The last exterior scenes were to be shot in the West Lake district of Hang Chow province about two weeks later, in March. I came in just before the bus took off. The only seat left was the seat next to the Supervisor. I hesitated but decided to take it. I could feel a strange tension between us. He passed me a cigarette. We did not speak on our six-hour journey. Cheering Spear and Soviet Wong sat in front of us. They sang operas along the way. One after another. The bus broke down right before we entered the West Lake district. When the other crew members went out to stretch their limbs, the Supervisor and I began talking.

I carefully asked if he had a family. He said yes, but he had been basically alone all these years. I asked him where he lived. Here and there, I go where my job takes me, he said. He asked how I had been coping with my life and whether there was some happiness in it. I said no and asked him the same question. To my surprise he said that he was as dry as a fish lying on salty land. He said he was tired but obligated to a mission. What mission? To fight for the people, he said. People who have the same fate as mine, he added. I thought the statement was like some sort of slogan. I told him so. He laughed and said that he was impressed by my daring.

Why do you fight for the people? Who do you mean by the people? I asked. He said I should learn more about him. I said that I would like to. He began his revelation. His family was from the Mountain East province in the north. His mother was a maid before the Liberation. He never knew his father. Throughout his childhood he and his mother had been kicked around by the rich and had no roof over their heads. His mother had to prostitute herself to feed him. The rich kids beat him and had their dogs bite him. He had hated dogs ever since. His mother died of syphilis when he turned twelve. His mother could not be buried in her own village with her ancestors. A man from the village said that her bad spirit would chase the village's good fortune away. The man who said that had once taken pleasure from her body. She was buried right outside the village gate. Wild dogs raked her up and ate her down to the bones.

Though charged with anger the Supervisor was calm. After Mother died, I went to Shanghai, he said, to a relative, who was an underground Communist. He introduced me to a left-wing theatre organization in which I became the youngest opera singer. I joined the Party that same year. I missed my mother. She left with a great part of me. I have never escaped from loneliness since. In memory of my mother I produced and directed an adaptation of a western play called *The Doll's House*. It was the highest moment in my life. Raising his hand to touch the brim of his Red Army cap, he said, I played Nora.

Before I completed the picture he had painted in my mind, the Supervisor interrupted me. He asked me how I felt about being a female in this society. Seeing my hesitation he said that it should be every female's responsibility to promote righteousness. I disliked the question because in my experience there wasn't much righteousness being promoted. But I did not tell him so. I said, purposely, that I was confused by his question. I said that the Chairman had taught us everything about equal rights. Equal rights between men and women, equal rights among human beings. Such equal rights as Cheering Spear and I had been given. The Supervisor smiled vaguely. You again are not speaking your true thoughts. I said, Maybe, but, well, why don't you tell me your name? Why can't you announce your true identity? Have you ever spoken *your* true mind? He said, But we are talking about you. We are talking about how you feel, how you have been bothered by your own resentment. The resentment you often dip yourself in, like a dumpling being dipped in vinegar sauce. Sweet? Sour? He laughed. He touched my very unhappy nerves. I said, I am well and I am nobody else's business.

You are a poor liar, he said. You can't hide your feelings, which shows that you know nothing about the art of living. You are stressed. As stressed as a rabbit in a sack. Your eyes are telling me that you dislike everything you have been assigned to do. You are miserable. You hate Sound Of Rain and Soviet Wong. You hate them because they imprisoned your ambition. You are jealous of Cheering Spear. You can't face your ambition and you are tortured by it. You want to be somebody. You want to be history. You deserve to be capped as a bourgeois individualist. You can't be better described. Tell me if you disagree with my description. Tell me the truth, will you? The Supervisor noticed my quietness and said, Watch out, your mind is too complicated.

In the basement of the West Lake Hotel where we went to smoke every day after shooting, the Supervisor told me that Comrade Jiang Ching was being criticized for her creations. Her opponents say that when a female gets on a boat, the boat sinks right away. The Supervisor asked me if I was surprised. I said, with five thousand years of tradition I am not surprised. Ah, yes, history, he said. All the wisdom is man's wisdom. That's Chinese history. The fall of a kingdom is always the fault of the concubine. What could be more truthful? Why should Comrade Jiang Ching be an exception?

Comrade Jiang Ching needn't worry about her opponents, I said. She is the standard-bearer, China's modern empress. I am sure that the power she holds is beyond anyone's imagination. The Supervisor smiled. You really think so? His smile carried a message. The message was written in an unbreakable code which I could not interpret. How strange, I started to think. A supervisor who has no name, who swims in and out of the studio at will, who rounds his tongue with the country's most powerful names. Why was he interested in coming to the smoking room? Why did he speak with me? Why did he keep asking me to speak my true thoughts? I remembered that many people disappeared after they had exposed their minds.

We sat smoking. The streetlamp outlined the contours of the Supervisor's face. He stood next to the window, looking up at the moon. What thoughts was he burying up there?

My life greened. It greened because the Supervisor was taking an interest in me. Each day, I looked forward to provoking him. I kept telling myself that it was not going to change anything, but I would not let the attention I was getting slip away. The Supervisor began talking to me in public. He talked to me on and off the sets, in front of Cheering Spear, in front of Soviet Wong. We talked about the shooting board, the make-up, the costumes and the props. We talked in private as well, on the stairways, in the smoking room. I told him my version of *Red Azalea*. I showed him that I was a Red Azalea by nature. He looked at me, stunned. He was stunned by my craziness. I said that although I did not know how to ride a horse I knew how to drive a tractor. I told

206

him that a tractor runs faster than a horse. He must see that I have an engine and Cheering Spear did not. I said I would like to wind the ivy of my confidence around his nerves. I shouted at him, though in a silent voice, Don't you see I could be what you wanted?

The Supervisor went quiet on the set. He stopped talking to me. But I knew something was happening in him. I knew I had made him interested in me. I knew I was gaining a comrade. I sobbed at midnight, dreaming of Yan for the first time in a long time. I wrote to Yan and told her about the Supervisor.

The last of the shooting was done. Thinking of the coming farewell, I felt sick, as if a secret wish that had been cherished was going to be aborted. As I lay on the bed in my hotel room, the Supervisor's image kept appearing in my mind. I tried to chase out a mosquito-like shadow in my head. I warned myself that the crew would soon be dispersed. The movie *Red Azalea* would be done. The Supervisor would be gone. Cheering Spear would receive an award. Nothing more would happen to me. My effort would be wasted, like a ripple in that lake. A sudden sadness rained inside me. My heart became wet.

I was lying on the hotel bed wrapped up in thoughts of the Supervisor when the costume designer came in. She was a pleasant woman of about thirty who had the face of a Buddha. She told me that Cheering Spear had invited the Supervisor for a farewell dinner in a Russian-style restaurant near the lake. She then suggested that she and I go to visit a Buddhist temple hidden in the mountain range in the east of the province. My mind kept picturing Cheering Spear and the Supervisor sitting together chatting. The costume designer told me that the temple was best known for granting wishes. I did not care about the wishes, but I needed to get out of the room.

Looking up from the foot of the mountain, the temple was located in the middle of the clouds. A carved-stone stairway led up to it, so narrow that it could hold only one person. It felt like walking in a stone glove. The inscription on a memorial tablet said it took four generations of stone-carvers to complete the staircase.

Tiny old ladies, toothless, carrying food bags, were making their way up. They bowed low, heads hitting the stone stairway, at every step.

The costume designer and I finally arrived at the temple's gate at three o'clock in the afternoon. The temple was entwined in ivy. The air was chilly and filled with the smell of jasmine. The smoke from a huge bronze incense-burner lingered and drifted around the shoulders of the worshippers. Through a long hallway there was an altar, carved from sandalwood. In front of the altar a line of primitive-looking stuffed dolls, about three hundred of them, male and female, painted colourfully, sat under the feet of the Buddha statue.

An old lady, hairless, her body totally soaked in sweat, got down on her knees. Her face was coated with brown mud from the bowing ritual. She took out a red and green coloured stuffed doll and a ball-point pen, and wrote some characters on the back of the doll. She put the doll among the ranks and bowed to the Buddha statues endlessly. The sound of her head hitting the floor remained in my ear for a long time. I slowly approached her doll to take a look at what she had written. It said: Dear God of Birth. I have taken a doll from you and you granted me a marvellous grandchild. Now I have made another pretty doll to give back to you. I can never thank you enough. Your sincere follower, Mother of your child Big Bolt.

My fingers were trembling as I went to light the incense. For the first time, I sincerely bowed to the Buddha statues. I did not know what to wish. I rose to look at the statue. Tell me what to wish, I prayed. In the smoke I was shocked to hear my heart say, Please Buddha, make me strong, make me strong. At that moment, I realized my weakness. It was a weakness over the intrusion of a particular man. I got up in panic: I realized that my heart was longing for the Supervisor. I looked around and tried to find the costume designer but she had disappeared. I kept looking. Suddenly my eyes met his, the Supervisor's. He was in the crowd, his eyes following me. He looked away the moment our eyes collided. I made a move. Men and women with the stuffed dolls in their hands kept rushing in. They bowed, acting with abandon, as if no one was present. The sound of their praying spread and mixed with the sound of monks singing.

Another wave of people floated in. The number of stuffed dolls on the altar increased. The sound of worshippers going down on their knees was loud like beating drums. I was pushed by the human flow to the back of the altar where there was a wall of a thousand statues of the Buddha prophets. Painted ceramic clouds filled the scene, under the prophets' feet, on their palms, around their heads. A running deer with a red ribbon round the neck, a straw basket of peaches. A floor-long white beard swayed in the breeze. The prophets smiled obscurely. I turned as my whole being was absorbed by a gazing, a gazing from behind me, from him, the Supervisor.

I lost my mind in the clouds. My hand reached back towards him as if acting of its own will. I was dragged by it. It swam through the crowd's layers of flesh and suddenly was touched and tightly held by the other hand.

Without looking, I knew it was him. I looked at the statues of the Buddha prophets hearing my heart cry out in joy.

As the crowd moved through, the hand let go. I turned around to look. About four feet away he stood, as if nailed there, looking at me. He was deathly pale. Everything began to fade in front of me but his bright, almond eyes. The deer with the red ribbon began to run, the peaches swayed low on the branches, the prophets continued their smiling.

Two men in security-guard uniforms appeared. They rushed through the crowd and approached him. They spoke to him, looking around. They asked him whether he was well. He shook his hands impatiently and pointed them down the hill. The men were polite but refused to leave. They stood, locked. He turned towards the sky, chin tilted up. I saw extreme sadness in the almond eyes.

The costume designer reappeared. She complained about my slowness. She said she had made a wish for herself and felt much better now. She suggested we go to the dark underground cave. The Yellow Dragon Cave. It was said that millions of years ago a dragon died here and the narrow tunnel of the entrance was the shell of its intestines.

The cave was crowded, packed with humans who held jasmine in their hands, women who wore jasmine round their necks and in their hair. The Supervisor was following me, I suddenly noticed. And the two security guards were behind him.

The costume designer cheered when she saw the crowd. What fun, she said and asked someone where to pick the jasmine. She pushed into the crowd with her shoulder towards a light ray by the exit yards away. She said she must hurry and pick the jasmine before it was all gone. The passageway was so narrow that the unfamiliar bodies were jammed and squeezed together. The sour smell of sweat mixed with jasmine. I moved towards him. I hoped that he would hold my hand again. I hoped hard. I waited. The smell of jasmine grew stronger. He moved closer in the crowd. The two men disappeared. He was next to me. Our breath touched. I offered him my hand. He did not react. He did not grab my hand. Crushed petals of jasmine were all over me.

I blamed myself, my silliness. But my silliness was powerful. I was ruled by it, commanded by it. Yet there was my will. I purposefully avoided toasting with the Supervisor at the farewell dinner party, held on a large boat carved with images of dragons and phoenixes. I toasted with everybody else. I toasted with Cheering Spear and Soviet Wong. Farewell and take care, my lips opened and closed mechanically. I told myself everything would be gone for ever in a day, so stop hoping and snap out of it. I drank with the crew.

Cheering Spear was drunk. She began to sing a children's song. She sang 'Pulling the radish, pulling the radish' and she fell to the floor, laughing. Getting up, she vomited. Soviet Wong went to take Cheering Spear to lie down. The celebration continued.

The Supervisor acted as if our fingers had never touched. He smiled at the crew members. He faked it well. He unbuttoned his blue Mao jacket. He wore a white shirt inside. His long and fine fingers held a wine glass. His cheeks were red and the colour made his skin look like a young woman's. When the head of the lighting crew, Big Tai, challenged him to a drinking contest, he accepted.

The crew cheered and gathered around the table to watch. Big Tai was a huge, strong man of about fifty, a bachelor who had always adored the Supervisor. He praised him as the most beautiful man he had ever seen, and said that he would do anything to be close to him. People had warned the Supervisor not to get too close to Big Tai because he had problems. He always found excuses to make trouble with girlish-looking men.

The Supervisor took a glass of rice wine and drank it down as Big Tai took his. Their glasses were filled again by the crew members. I hid myself in a corner where the light failed to reach, feeling my mind getting stiff. Big Tai was a good drinker. The Supervisor's face, after three toasts, was as white as a Japanese paper doll. The crew members waited excitedly for a good time. They quietened down after the Supervisor and Big Tai emptied their fourth glasses.

Big Tai suggested they go fishing off the boat. The costume designer laughed on her way to borrow equipment from the man who drove the boat. Big Tai pulled out two fishing rods and gave one to the Supervisor. Shaking, the Supervisor took a small piece of food from his plate and stuck it on the hook. They threw the hooks into the water. The boat advanced smoothly.

In the distance a goose sang. The costume designer said it was mating season. The geese liked to mate under water and always at night. The male goose had beautiful feathers, magnificently coloured. But the female was plain, like a duck. They licked each other's necks after mating. It's disgusting, said the costume designer.

Big Tai leaned back in his chair, his face swollen. His eyes seemed so small, smaller than the eyes of a fat rabbit. He put his glass down and reached out his hand towards the Supervisor's face. He laughed showing his silver tooth. He said that he thought the Supervisor was more beautiful than a woman. He asked, Why are you a man? You shouldn't be a man – you ruin your looks when dressed as a man.

The Supervisor suggested a refill. Toast! Toast! The crew members encouraged. After the fifth glass, Big Tai began waving his arms and kicking his legs in the air. The Supervisor said there was a fish on the hook. He had heard a sound and was sure that a big fish was caught. Big Tai walked with difficulty towards the rod and fell into the water trying to pull the fish up. The costume designer got a huge net and the crew members helped to get man and fish out of the water.

The Supervisor turned around. He caught me watching him. He walked towards me. I found myself shaking, about to vomit. I smelled jasmine and was reminded of the afternoon at Yellow Dragon Cave. I went to the costume designer and helped pull Big Tai back on to the boat. He was sleeping soundly despite the pulling and dragging. Water came out of his mouth. The crew members laughed and laughed. Those almond eyes were fixed on me. I stretched the muscles in my face to laugh with the other people.

The next morning the bus was ready to take off back to Shanghai when the Supervisor stepped on. I lowered my head pretending that I was checking my notes. He came near, then sat down behind me. He asked for the total number of the takes we shot at the location. I did not reply. I knew I didn't have to. I knew he didn't really want to know the numbers. We sat in silence. The bus took off in the heat. The crew members sang a song about being a wanderer. Cheering Spear gave everyone farewell cards she made herself with paper cut-outs and pink ribbons.

We reached Shanghai in the afternoon. The bus stopped at the studio's front gate. The Supervisor stood up and shook hands with the crew members one after another. He wished everyone good health and a good life. The crew members wished him a safe trip to Beijing. When his hand reached out for mine, I did not give myself a chance. I refused to suffer this closeness. Letting his hand hang in the air, I stood up and got off the bus.

I quickly pulled my bicycle out of the parking lot. The back tyre was flat but I decided to put up with it and rode towards the gate. The wheels rolling over the dry maple leaves on the pavement made cracking sounds. Then something pulled me from behind. You've got a flat tyre. It was his voice. Never mind about that, I said, without turning my head. He refused to let go of the bicycle. I turned around. He made an effort to smile. Say a nice goodbye, he suggested. I looked away. People are watching us, the nasty, lusty pigs, he said.

I was suffering. I couldn't help myself. I began to pedal again. He let go of my bicycle and said, I want you to meet me at the Peace Park tonight at seven-thirty.

I sat by the window, my thoughts drifting. I did not hear my mother calling me for dinner. I did not hear anything but the crawling sound of my thoughts. I went to a desk and quickly pulled out a pen and a notebook. I tore a piece of paper from the notebook. I could not write what I wanted to. My mother came. She held my hands. You are hot, she said. She suggested I take off my sweater. I did. I looked at my mother and suddenly found that I was so much like her. I had inherited her stubbornness. I had inherited her passion. That I must live for myself was in my veins. Even if it were only a dream, so be it.

*

The Peace Park was located next to Dragon Sight Crematorium. It was a park with few visitors. Most people who came here were mourners, the relatives of the dead. I felt safe in the dark. Getting off the bus, I looked around. The smell of incense wafted over from the nearby cemetery. I made sure that I was not followed. I paid five cents at the gate and entered the park.

The quietness was extraordinary. Trees and leaves were thick as walls. I wandered between the trees as I fixed my eyes on the entrance. At eight o'clock I saw him. He came up to me from behind, dressed in black. We went into the shadow of the trees where the lights were like the eyes of ghosts. We stopped, facing each other against a big tree trunk. He said he had been here since seven. He was glad that I had come. I said that I was glad too. We ran out of words to say. We walked towards the thick trees and I could hear my heart beat.

Have you packed? I searched for words. Yes, he answered. His voice was unnatural. When does the train take off? Four o'clock in the morning. Well, I said. Well, he said. You must lead an exciting life in Beijing, I said, without knowing why. Exciting, true, where murderous intentions lurk behind charming smiles, he said, shaking his head. He slowed down his steps and said, You won't understand that part of me. No one would. I asked, Not even your wife? Oh, my wife, he said. My wife is a very lovely person. But she wouldn't be lovely to me if she knew the difference between the public self and the private self, the nature of my desires and my ambition. I want you to know me, though. He took my hands and said, I think you will. He stared at me. I could not see his eyes. I saw the shadow of his head. I was facing the light but he was cast in shadow. Looking at me, he put his arms around me and turned me round so that he was in the light and I was in shadow. I looked at him boldly because I knew he could not see my eyes. I looked at him. I looked at the contours of his face. It aged, second by second. He was penetrated by sadness. His expression sagged. I am a lonely person, he said. I thought I was used to it, but I am not. Can't you see?

My arms went around him. I felt, as I felt him, Yan's skin. I touched him and said, I am at your service. He quivered like a young tree in a storm. He embraced me. He said softly, Let me have it, let me have you.

His lips were tender. Tender like a naked lychee. My heart drank its sticky juice. Do you want to know my name? he said. No, I said. I do not want to know your name because we don't plan to see each other again.

He wet my cheeks. In his firm arms I found my thirst. We stood under the thick osmanthus tree, covered by its sweet smell. There was noise rising in the distance. A group of people with flashlights were coming in our direction. They were guards of the city criminal-control patrols. We split and retreated into the shadows. I leaned against a tree trunk when the sweep of flashlights passed me. To my surprise, as I followed the movement of the beam of light, I saw human figures in the bushes. Not a few, but many. Heads glued together, whispering in the dark.

The Supervisor and I walked around the park like wanted criminals. After the patrols passed, we went behind the park's bulletin board. The board was filled with pictures of criminals, thieves, men and women caught in the act of infidelity. Around the pictures were articles of public criticism.

He walked behind me and kept about ten feet away. We tried to find a place to sit down. But all the benches in the wooded area, next to the bushes, in the shadows where the ghost eyes did not gleam, were occupied by couples. Each bench had three couples, facing in different directions. Nobody bothered anybody. They were all busy minding their fiery business, whispering and cuddling.

We finally discovered a quiet spot behind the public restroom. We crawled into the bushes and lay on our backs on the grass. The darkness beckoned me. I asked him to sing to me from a favourite opera. He hummed in my ear:

215

Standing by the fence,
The woman is thinner than the withering flower.
She fabricated her love into weaving
The scarf she made worn out by a stranger.
She was an old woman when her love was young.

Suddenly he said that he sensed I had a lover. He asked if I could describe him. I sat up, dumbfounded. Facing my uneasiness, he whispered, rubbed the words with his tongue. It's all right, he said. He told me that ripeness was important to him, and anything I confessed would not change the way he saw me because he was boiling with desire for me. He desired to taste my hunger for passion.

He waited for my answer. He did not know that he was loading bullets in my gun. I smelled the smoke even before I pulled the trigger. I hesitated, then said that I'd had an affair but it was not with a man.

I heard a long silence. Slowly, I could feel him recover from the shock. Was she your choice? His voice was astringent. Yes, and no, I said, but it would not have made any difference if she had been a man. Where is she? he asked. At Red Fire Farm, I answered. I don't know exactly where. I owe her my life. Is that so, he said. I asked him whether I should confess the whole story but he said I did not have to. He would always be willing to listen but preferred to hear the story some other time. I told him I appreciated his understanding, but he answered that it was too early to appreciate anything. He couldn't predict our future, a great risk might be involved, but still he wanted to learn more about me, and to let me learn about him. Tea tasted the best at its second pouring.

A fever rose when hunger took its course. The hands, though forbidden to go under the clothes, measured intimacy in body heat. The skin radiated. Pleasure swept over our flesh and made our souls sing.

I asked him to tell me about Beijing, about his life. I asked if I could see him again. He said it would be very risky. I don't want you to get hurt because of me. Many people get hurt because of me, he said. It can cost a life to . . . He stopped, raising his hand to touch my face. My little friend, he continued, I am afraid of your questions. I held him and said, I would do anything you want me to. Be a sweet dream for tonight, he said. Why not for tomorrow? I asked. No, just tonight, he insisted. Because when the day breaks you will not know me. There will have been no tonight. Tonight never existed.

He said it would be like a moth trying to get to the filament of the bulb – I would only get burned if I insisted on keeping in touch with him. Any attempt to contact him was out of the question. Beijing is a square city, very square, he said. Because the sun rises there, it leaves nothing hidden.

I looked at him. I knew he was speaking the truth. Yet my senses refused to trust him completely. Who was he? His mystery intrigued me. I held him tight but still he felt unreal. I pasted my face on his neck, that beautiful feminine long neck. Still he carried the smell of jasmine.

Suddenly he told me to freeze and listen. Someone was hiding in the bushes watching us. Who could . . . could it be? The fright made my words knot. I hope he is not a secret cop, he said, still holding me. Let's not alarm him. Turn with me so that I can see his movements. As we slowly turned around, the shadow in the bush arched its back. What should we do? Who could he be? Have you heard about these lonely men and women, the masturbators? the Supervisor asked. He held me and began caressing me.

I have heard reports, not once but many times, he continued. Now he was drawing me into frightening pleasure. His voice at my ear aroused all my nerves: I am sure he is a lonely one. No, wait a minute, I see two people, the other one is hiding over by the evergreen pine. I am sure there are more out there watching. Yes, I see the third one, and the fourth now. Watch with me. Don't be afraid, because they are as afraid as us. Look behind

217

that mint tree, and there, behind the osmanthus trees. I can see them groaning silently, their fronts and rears exposed like animals in season, begging for touch and penetration. I see the hills of youth covered with blood-coloured azaleas. The azaleas keep blooming, invading the mountains and the planet. The earth is bitten and it groans, wailing nonsensically in pleasure. Do you hear it? The passion they had for the Great Helmsman has been betrayed. Oh, how grand a scene! I wish our greatest Chairman could see it. He would be shocked but impressed. Oh, now I know, this is a place where lonely men and women gather each night to experience the essence of drama. They meet their gods and goddesses here. They carry the spirit of the dead whose flesh has just been cremated. They masturbate and ejaculate their passion with criminal guilt. Calm down, my little friend, look at the gigantic chimney of the Dragon Sight Crematorium, look at the red smoke it sends to Heaven, look how it wafts away, look how it ascends. You must not close your eyes, you must watch, you must learn to appreciate the beauty given by nature. Watch with me, feel me in you, the excitement is far from over. The lonely ones are making their moves with us, struggling with a fright that is so deep it has blinded their inner-sight. They know they will be shot if caught, so do we. They regard this moment as their last performance, so do we. The fright sweetens the mood. We are near to death as well as to heaven. Do you feel it?

I begged him to leave the place. To leave the forest of the lonely ones. He supported me with his shoulder, the strengthless me, and we made our way off into the velvet night. The thorns of the bushes slashed my clothes, scratched my limbs leaving marks on my flesh. The shadows arched their backs. The bushes trembled in dense rhythm. The masturbators rocked, rising and falling monumentally and, as we passed, I heard the sound of them exploding one after another. I collapsed, half-unconscious, in ecstasy.

I looked back when I stepped out of the Peace Park gate. I saw the flashlights searching through the bushes. The patrols shouted slogans as warnings: 'Be aware of reactionary activities! Let's unite and get rid of bourgeois influences!' The park sank back to the sound of death.

I went to the train station at two o'clock in the morning. It was as crowded as a bees' nest. I turned sideways and squeezed my way into the Beijing Express zone, looking in carriage after carriage. Then I saw him. In carriage number twenty-four. The Supervisor was standing between two familiar men in security-guard uniforms. He kept looking out of the window. I came up to the train. But I did not wave my hand like all the other people did. Then he saw me, though his face was still expressionless. His eyes just stopped searching. He did not make a move to say goodbye to me. He could not. He was too important. We stared at each other. Then the train started to move. The men laid an off-white embroidered table cloth before him. A train hostess came with a mug of fresh tea. I tried to smile at him. He tried to smile back but one of the men rose and rolled down the blind.

紅　杜　鵑

The almost completed production was shut down suddenly. It was said that Comrade Jiang Ching had problems with the cast. We were given stacks of readings on the Party's policy on the arts by the National Cultural Bureau. Coming to the studio at eight in the morning we sat through readings, engaged in self-examinations, discovered each other's political errors and projected them for criticism. The meetings lasted until five in the evening. A cigarette, a cup of tea, a war of lips and teeth became the nation's lifestyle.

In addition to mopping, I was ordered to fill up the office hot-water containers, copy the records of everyone's speech and deliver them to the studio's Party committee. I had been a set-clerk for only a few months but the emptiness in me had become intolerable. It felt like an ulcer that grew larger each day. After the day passed, when I lay down in bed at night, I would feel the ulcer spread.

I never heard from the Supervisor, but wherever I went in the studio, I could see his shadow and hear his voice. The maple tree delivered his spirit. The memory of the night of his departure held me each evening. Alone in the emptiness, my body lay hopelessly on a field of desire, like a bird with clipped wings.

I missed Yan though she never answered my letters. We never spoke about our affair. We never dared to admit to ourselves and to each other that it was love that we shared. Instead, we shared the embarrassment and the guilt. We gave each other our deep shame. I had never thought of having her only to myself until the moment I saw Leopard touch her. It was in that moment that I realized my shame. Because it was at that moment that I wished to be loved so much.

Yan made it look like she had deported me. By doing so she gave both of us a chance. A chance for a new life. It was like what we did to the baby rice-shoots in early spring – break the intertwining roots, tear them apart to ensure the individual's growth in the future. Most of the rice-shoots survived, but a few of them died in the process. When I broke the roots with my hands, I would listen to the sound of tearing, and wonder if the roots felt the hurt. Yan never listened to this sound. She did what she thought was necessary without the blink of an eye. She was cruel. Her love was cruel. She had to be the way she was. She threw me out to save me. She sent me away to have me remember her. And I did. Yan had become a part of me. I knew this when

I touched the Supervisor. My relationship with the Supervisor, though it happened unexpectedly, was logical. Because I had experienced love before, it was within the realm of expectation. The difference was that I had been, strangely enough, aware of every move I made with the Supervisor. If it was love I shared with Yan, it was ambition I shared with the Supervisor, to exceed ourselves, our time, to reach beyond our spoiled minds.

The Supervisor had left without any promises. But my eagerness to excel made me want nothing but the impossible. Yan was the impossible. I could not escape from paying for it. And I was paying for it. I became my mother. Like my mother, I lived in the dream of a world I believed in. I longed for the return of the Supervisor. I longed for the moment of his presence. The endless longing; lonely, bitter, vaporous, so very vivid.

Cheering Spear became very sick. It was said that Comrade Jiang Ching's comments on the cast was a denunciation of her. It was said that Comrade Jiang Ching inspected the rough cuts and commented, 'All is not gold that glitters', meaning she had seen no real talent in the cuts. The phrase was printed on a red-headlined document. It was read in meetings at the studio. Cheering Spear went to Sound Of Rain and Soviet Wong for help. She poured out her tears. But they said nothing. Not a word.

Your name has been called, the guard One Ounce told me. Sound Of Rain and Soviet Wong were checking with Beijing to confirm the news. Whose name? Who was called, I asked as my heartbeat quickened, though I heard every word he said. For a moment I felt deafened as if by successive bangs of firecrackers. In the afternoon, I was called into the office of the studio heads. Sitting before a huge wooden desk, I was told by Sound Of Rain that I had been chosen by the upstairs in Beijing for an important assignment, a screen test as Red Azalea.

Soviet Wong sat next to Sound Of Rain, her eyes filled with

envy. Do you know anyone in Beijing? she asked. Her voice pronounced heavy suspicion. As I shook my head she said, You must tell the truth, nothing but the truth. The Party's needs are my priority, I replied. But I could stay as a set-clerk if the Party needs me to. Hypocrite! Soviet Wong shouted at me.

Strangely, it pleased me to see Soviet Wong acting like this. Why do I have to be a hypocrite? I said lightly. No! We can't let her go, Soviet Wong said firmly to Sound Of Rain. We are responsible to the upstairs. My instinct tells me, said Soviet Wong, that she is seriously corrupted, like a stone in a manure pit – smelly and hard! There must be a man, a lover of some sort behind the curtain! It is necessary to strengthen the dyke before the water rises!

But Sound Of Rain wore Soviet Wong down. The girl is bacteria-proof, we had doctors check her, remember? I don't think she has a crafty lover behind the curtain. She is virgin soil. She is a tough little shit, I agree, but maybe, who knows, that's what the upstairs likes about her. Our Chairman always praises the spirit of rebels. The upstairs always said they liked youngsters who carry the rebel flavour. Who knows?

Soviet Wong yelled at Sound Of Rain. You just don't want to go to the trouble of investigating her, you're being irresponsible to the Party. Don't you have any principle? Sound Of Rain sat down in his chair and said slowly, Always say yes to our Party, that is my principle.

I did not know where I was being taken. I only knew that I was in Beijing. I had been riding in different fancy cars. I had never been in a car before yet it did not make me feel nervous. All the drivers wore white nylon gloves. They did not answer my questions about directions. I figured that they were not allowed to. When they said 'Please' the accent was strongly northern, which revealed that they must be the sons of peasants. They had features like carved stones, sincere and tolerant.

I was in Yan's clothes, the washed-white army uniform. I

always wore it if I was either afraid or proud. Instinct told me that my being chosen by the Beijing upstairs had to do with the Supervisor. His secrecy excited me and frightened me at the same time. I did not like the fact that I was obsessed with him because I smelled danger in him. We were on an unequal footing. I could see the spell he cast over me and decided that if I were to see him again I would break the spell. I would count on myself. I knew I must. I was twenty. I had courage.

White nylon gloves guided me out of the car. I was surrounded by a park of peonies encircled by a forest. What a land! The streams under my feet sang through the stones. A clear path through the pink peonies led into the hills of green. The driver told me to follow the path and he walked back to his car, which pulled off like the shadow of a bird. I was left to an extraordinary quietness. Fields of grassland expanded to the end of the sky where the sun was setting. A breath of wind stirred the forest. Clouds swam in the mirror-like river. I began to walk, my steps light as if I were riding the wind. Although the nodding of peonies was pleasant, the flowers' splendidness reminded me of their owner's status. I suddenly remembered Yan's first order upon my arrival at Red Fire Farm: Act like a soldier! I forced myself on.

An old mansion appeared, draped with ivy and brightly coloured flowers. There was a dark narrow door. I stopped by the door. A young man with white gloves in a green army uniform opened the door for me. He smiled silently at me and guided me into the hallway. I failed at first to notice the other man in the hallway because he stood motionless by the doorway like a piece of furniture. Just like the first man he had a smile that was well trained. He gestured me to follow him to a tearoom where a row of black and white photographs was exhibited. I was seated on a sofa commanding a master view of the garden. The young man left the room with noiseless steps and another one, also pleasant-faced, appeared with a white tray. Trained smile. He offered me a warm wet towel. He left just as the fourth pleasant-faced young man stepped into the room and placed a cup of perfumed tea in front of me. Trained smile. Trained steps. White gloves. Shaved chins. Petal-like mouths. Carved-stone features. They swam in and out of the room like fish in seaweed.

As I sipped the tea, I began to look at the photographs. Most of the subjects were flowers and many of them were peonies. Peonies in fog, in rain, at sunrise, sunset, under the moonlight and in the dark. Peonies in snow, in white. Withering peonies, passionately shot. It touched me and for a moment I forgot where I was. As I looked carefully, I found the photographs were not exactly black and white. They were hand-coloured, slightly brownish. The colour of yawning petals was delicately handled. I was moved by the way the artist emptied himself in to these pictures.

From the tearoom an arched bridge led towards the garden. The brightness overexposed everything outside. I heard the click of a camera shutter. I heard a familiar voice, one I expected, but still it shocked me.

It's been a long time, hasn't it? the voice said. It made me tremble inside, just as before. I wanted to say something but my tongue failed me. Come and see my garden, the voice said.

The Supervisor was in a bleached-white cotton blouse, grass-green trousers and deep-blue straw sandals. His thin, young-girl-like arms folded over his chest. He turned to look at the heart of a peony. He was concentrating on the flower. The perfume he wore drew me towards him and the joy of seeing him again swept over me. His short black hair was combed back smoothly. He moved on to another peony. His elegance choked my breath with the desire to be close to him. When his fingers touched the petals of a peony, my whole being quivered inside, remembering the way he touched me.

I did not like my desire because it made me powerless in front of him. He bent to examine a roll-shaped flower. By speaking without a voice he attracted all my attention. I hated his tricks

224

but was so willing to be seduced. He spoke. Any comment on the photographs? I heard myself say, Were those taken by you? No one else is living here, he said. The photos were taken in this garden.

The pleasant-faced young men were swimming in and out. I felt I was being watched. Their brains are made of metal, the Supervisor said, pointing at the backs of the pleasant-faces. They have square hearts like robots. They do not understand emotions as you do. You are experienced. How is your lover? What's her name? No, don't answer that, I've changed my mind.

The way the Supervisor read me scared me. I asked the reason I was called here. I need you, he said. You are invited for an important screen test, a test which will change some fundamental ideas of our countrymen.

I almost dropped the tea mug in my hand. Am I to play Red Azalea? I asked, so scared for an answer. That's correct, he nodded. Remember, you would make me happier if you ask no questions. I began to see the logic of the events. My being brought to Beijing, to this place. He must have been the one who dropped Cheering Spear and replaced her with me for Red Azalea. He must have been the one who held the key for Comrade Jiang Ching. I began to see the importance of simply allowing the future to reveal itself. That's right, he said, reading my mind again. If you would like to play along, it will be a real adventure. Remember to strike while the iron is hot.

How are you prepared for Red Azalea? he asked me as he led me through the garden into another courtyard. We entered a room. I saw a white screen hung from the ceiling. The room had a dark lacquered wall carved with shapes of peonies. Four flower-shaped light fixtures stood in each corner. There were two big yellow sofas placed in front of the screen. The Supervisor pointed for me to sit down on one.

I sometimes sleep here when the night gets too deep and the dark chills me, he said. And I become the saddest person in the whole world after my favourite movie. I cuddle myself in the sofa and let my tears run like an infant. Shouldn't one let himself go when he feels weak?

A shadow passed by the screen. I turned and saw a projector in the wall. So this is a screening room, I said. It's a screen in which history is performed and re-performed, said the Supervisor. It is all in our will, he added. The perfumed tea was served quietly by the pleasant-faced young men. The Supervisor stared at me as he sipped his tea. I like the way your face is lit now. Don't move. Yes, that's nice. His hands were touching my face. Your face possesses the heroic quality I have been looking for. It pleases me so much to look at you. Are you pleased to hear what I say? Show me your appreciation like the others. Your quietness irritates me. I don't like to be confused. I observed that you would not laugh when other, silly, girls laughed hard. It impressed me, but I am not yet quite used to your character. Your quality is inborn. That is rare. The mopping of the floor made you learn. The saying fits: 'Swallow the bitterest in bitter, it makes one the finest in fine.'

He was telling me the story of *Red Azalea* as if it were his own life. She was a Red Army leader, a red goddess admired and loved by all. The story was about a long spiritual march. It was about an indelible faith in Communism, about the worship of Mao, but an incredible will in conquering enemies, about extraordinary military skills in conducting monumental battles.

The story did not hold me as much as the storyteller before me. He was an opening peony. A hand-coloured peony, like the one in his photographs. The almond eyes were as bright as ever. The porcelain-like fine skin spoke well of his elegance. He was a man and a woman. His story was bad liquor. It poured into my throat and made me drunk with heat.

This is what I want to see in your eyes, he said. A million bulls rushing down a hill with their tails on fire.

*

He waved his hand. The room turned dark. I want to show you one of my favourite films, he said into my ear. This is how I fill my nights. I asked what the film was called. It is *The Battle of Ancient Rome*. I said, I do not understand foreign languages, but he replied that that was why he was sitting next to me. He wanted to be an interpreter for me.

The film began to roll. The projectionist adjusted the lens. The blurred image came into focus. The round starting-cue looked like a huge eye spying on me from behind. The Supervisor's face was inches away. I could smell his perfume. He began his translation. His voice reminded me of bushes shivering in the wind.

The voice of the Supervisor had mixed with the soundtrack of the film. His voice filled with sorrow as he interpreted the ending of the story. It was about the falling of an empire and the suicide of its princess. The music was tragically austere. I saw the glittering in his bright almond eyes. Pearls dripped slowly down on his cheeks like a broken necklace. His interpretation became fragmented, and then his breath came harder. He stopped, unable to continue as the film went on.

The Supervisor sent me to a military training camp for three weeks. He said he wanted to see the blood of a soldier run in my veins. I was given a small room off to the side of the barracks. I threw myself into the programme. By six o'clock in the morning I was running with the company on a quiet road. The soldiers were the sons of peasants. Their steps sounded like the chopping of cucumbers on a board. I smelled the fresh air of the mountains. I smelled the manure along the side of vegetable fields. We were running towards the rising sun. The load on my back was heavy. It was a rifle, a blanket, a bottle of water and a pair of shoes. The backpack was falling apart because I did not tie everything down properly. It was impossible for me to tie them well in three minutes. I dragged on. My things were dropping. I waved at a commander who was running alongside the rank. I asked if I could pick up my things. He did not answer me. He pretended not to hear me. I asked again and he yelled, One, two, three, four! Then the whole company yelled, One, two, three, four! The young men's voices were as loud as thunder. The chopping of the steps forced me on. I kept running. The soldiers rushed me. They would not let me stop. I tried not to fall. My vision blurred. Their steps were chopping me. Yet my will kept me on. Then my eyelids fell. I fainted. The next day, the same ritual was repeated. I ran until I passed out.

Breakfast was served after running. I stood in a circle of soldiers. Everyone ate as he squatted on his heels. We ate steamed bread, porridge and pieces of salted vegetable. We ate in silence. The soldiers stared into their bowls. Then we practised shooting. I was given a human-shaped target with a US soldier's helmet. The instructor hung pieces of brick on my arms. My arms were shaking as I held the rifle. Every twenty minutes we changed position. I felt the dripping sweat crawling through my chest. Then we marched, baking in the sun and after lunch we lay on our stomachs and practised our aim. We changed position every thirty minutes. I thought that I would do anything to please the Supervisor to get out of here. The soldiers were lying next to me. As we changed position, I looked at them. They looked back at me despisingly.

We were lectured on Mao's book at night. The soldiers each held a book of Mao. They read aloud. We discussed what we learned from the book. The men talked with strong northern accents. They talked about sleeping on a woodpile and tasting gall. They talked about enduring self-imposed hardships. They told me that the most important thing was to be good at learning. I echoed the way they talked. I said we must learn from that foolish man who had moved the mountain with a shovel. Then we wrote down what we talked about and turned in the papers. It was after ten o'clock when we finished. I fell asleep before my head hit the pillow. Too tired to produce any thoughts, I dreamt about the Supervisor coming to save me. Yet I endured the training; my ambition gave me hope.

By the end of the three weeks, in the middle of a running

exercise, a jeep came by and picked me up. The soldiers watched me with deadpan faces.

A soldier with white gloves was driving the jeep. Another soldier was sitting beside me. They did not talk to me. The jeep stopped at a building like a hotel. The building had no name. There were soldiers on guard by the gate and there were cars going in and out. The cars were clean and shiny. White-gloved drivers saluted their passengers. I was led into a room where I slept for two whole days. I was served good food. On the third day, while I sat by the window, I recalled how the Supervisor had spoken with such sorrow and excitement about the film, how much he believed in it.

I learned not to ask questions. I only knew that what was happening to me was too important to be questioned. I was climbing high. To a height that my family could not even imagine. I waited anxiously in excitement.

Then I received a document with red characters on the cover. The characters said Top Secret Instructions. It was an order from the Supervisor. I was ordered to view one of the stage versions of *Red Azalea*. I was sent to see a local theatre troupe which had been rehearsing *Red Azalea* for years without being given a date of performance. I felt unwelcome as I arrived. The actress who played Red Azalea was three inches shorter than me and did not wish to talk to me. It seemed that all the troupe members knew who had sent me. Behind their politeness was distance and cold feelings.

Every morning at eight o'clock the actors began reading aloud, but they knew all the words by heart. The play had no energy. The actresses brought knitting to the set and the actors smoked packs of cigarettes. At lunchtime, I asked a troupe member why everything seemed so slow. He asked if I would allow him to escape from *Red Azalea* for a second. I was confused about what he meant. He nodded at me and then asked me to listen when he turned on his radio. He tuned back and forth exploring every station. It was opera, opera and opera. The operas we knew by heart for years. Children in the street joined in the music, singing. The man said, smiling bitterly, The revolutionary operas are what we breathe. He spat on the ground and wiped his nose with his fingers. I turned away. Excuse me, he said drowsily, and drifted off for a nap leaving the radio on. It was boredom he exhaled.

I was not bored by the operas, nor bored with Red Azalea. I paid a price at Red Fire Farm to get to play the role. Yan and millions of youths were still struggling with leeches. Just to think of it sent a chill through me. I no longer cared whether other people would enjoy Comrade Jiang Ching's opera heroines. Red Azalea had become my life.

I put on a respectful face each morning. I stepped into the rehearsal hall elegantly and sat down modestly. At lunch, I ate a bowl of rice topped with a few pieces of preserved sour vegetable. I did character studies. I ran through the lines until I could recite them by heart. I continued my waiting.

The Supervisor sent for me. He sent for me with a set of new army uniforms he wanted me to wear. Later in the afternoon I went to him in a new outfit. He smiled. He was a peony. He was in uniform as well. A piece of long hair lingered on his face. He greeted me by the gate and suggested that we take a long walk in his garden. We dipped ourselves in the green, into parks of peonies. We arrived at a stone boat beside a lake and he told me the fable of the boat. It was the gift of a son to his mother. The son was an emperor. He asked his mother what she wanted for her ninetieth birthday and she said she had always been fascinated by boating but was afraid of water. The son built the boat in stone right by the dock so the mother could be on a boat without water. The mother enjoyed her birthday boating party immensely and the fable spread through the nation as an example of piety.

We sat in the stone boat. I watched the reflections in the water. You should be thinking about the big picture, said the Supervisor suddenly, interrupting my scattering thoughts. The life of a true hero is like the life of acrobatic dancers on a string. You can never be fully prepared.

The sun dropped and the sky looked like a golden fan. The rosy clouds, as if painted with ink and water, were glowing and tinting the sky. We are the hands that should be writing history, he said, standing up and walking towards the edge of the stone boat. He stared into the water. The water had changed colour from dark green to deep black. I am not afraid of water, he said as he lifted his chin, gazing far into the sky. I looked at this gaze. I saw pure devotion. The gaze condensed the evening fog into dew. He asked me to abandon my old self to live up to the Party's expectations. Mao asked that his people totally forget the self. He told me that sacrificing one's life for the people's ideals expands one's life. He said that he wanted me to kill a devil in me. The devil that makes you yield to your emotional need, he said. He asked me to forget about my little self. He said he was asking for a full commitment. His religious tone scared me. I could not understand what he was talking about. Even though he loved me, and loved me partly for the independence of my mind, he wanted me to sacrifice my old self to his – and my – ambition for the film.

He asked me please not to disappoint him. He had been counting on me so much that his mission would not be complete without me. He said he never learned to take rejection well and asked me to be on guard. All his life he had been taught to hate individuality, even while he was attracted to it. He asked me to keep him from becoming harmful to me because no matter how much he loved me he would not let me stand in the way of his dream. He would replace me if he had to. He asked me to obey him, because to obey him was to obey my own ambition. Because he and I were inseparable now.

The Supervisor took me back to Shanghai. He said he would have had too much difficulty filming *Red Azalea* in Beijing. There was a political current that was against him, against the greatest standard-bearer Comrade Jiang Ching. Shanghai was a better place, he said. In Shanghai Comrade Jiang Ching's operas were daily spiritual meals. Radios all around the neighbourhood played operas. The Wu-Lee Hardware Workshop downstairs had their radio on all day. Most of the women sang along with the radio as they welded wires together.

> The insurrection after the harvest was a violent storm.
> The beacon lightened,
> Lightened my heart.
> It made me understand that
> To liberate our country we must depend on weapons.
> The only way to gain good life
> Is to join the Red Army and the Party.

On the flight he told me that one day I would remember him as a genius.

I was living at the Film Studio guest house during shooting and was allowed to visit my parents once every few days. I was fascinated with my costume, the Red Army uniform and coat, so I visited home wearing it. When I walked through the alleys, I knew my neighbours were looking at me through windows. Now they dared not speak to me. I had become too big for them to talk to. A few times when we did run into each other, they would speak to me in flattering tones. They would say, Oh, we knew a long time ago that you are going to be somebody some day. We've known that since you moved in to this district.

I found that I could not say much because I still remembered the days when they called me 'Flea'.

I spoke with Little Coffin when I saw her come to visit her parents. She had become a factory worker and married a colleague and moved away. Little Coffin never flattered me. She just looked at me with admiration. I knew she was proud of me and told her, I'll make you more proud.

232

紅 杜 鵑

From this moment on I want you to forget your family name.
You are Red Azalea now, said the Supervisor. Let me hear
your name please. I shivered and pronounced it loudly: I am Red
Azalea. He nodded with satisfaction. I want you to be aware of
what you are creating, he continued. You are creating an image
which will soon dominate China's ideology. You are creating history, the proletariat's history. We are giving history back its original face. In a few months, when the movie is all over the country,
you will be the idol of revolutionary youths. I want you to memorize Chairman Mao's teaching, 'The power of a good example
is infinite.'

Are you prepared? His eyes were red from lack of sleep, his
voice carried a smell of burned earth. We have begun our battle,
he said. Comrade Jiang Ching is with us. It is a battle of life and
death. A political power struggle. I nodded as if I understood what
he said. He moved towards me, stopped and used his middle
finger to tilt my chin up. He inspected me. He was a dragon
coming through the window of my eyes and permeating my
body with a silent force. Show me your determination, he murmured. I stared into his eyes. Yes, beautiful. You see, we are
going to go through a forest of guns and a rain of bullets to
pay respect to our mothers. Mothers who, for thousands of
years, lived their lives in shame, died with shame, were buried
and rotted in shame. We are going to tell them. Now it is a new
world. A world where being born female merits celebration and
salute. A world where a woman who is forced to marry a pig
can have an affair. He suddenly stopped. He stared at me,
narrowing his eyes. Well, enough for now. He pressed a bell
on the table and a pleasant-faced young man stepped in. Take

233

her to the make-up room. Your photo session awaits you, Red Azalea.

It was my first time posing. The photographer said printing machines in factories were waiting for this picture; the poster was to be out in three days. It was a political assignment from Comrade Jiang Ching. Red Azalea must live up to her earnest expectations.

I stared into the light bulb before me. I thought of Cheering Spear and Soviet Wong's hatred of me. I told the photographer I was ready. The sound of the clicks was unreal. I felt Yan under my skin.

The crew reshot the scenes. Cheering Spear and Soviet Wong were excluded. No one mentioned them. The ones who had served Cheering Spear now were made to serve me. The shooting went smoothly until one day when we were instructed to revise certain lines in the script. Red Azalea must not be too poignant. Her screen time must yield, meaning the male hero must appear dominant. The Supervisor made the changes. He was called back to Beijing several times. Each time he came back, he looked frustrated. He smoked four packs of cigarettes a day. His fingers had turned brown from holding cigarettes all the time. He explained nothing. He shot three versions of one scene with different lines. In the first one I was told to say, No, you can't take my dream away from me. In the second I was told to say, No, he is China's hope. You can never take that hope away from me. In the third I was to say, I'd sacrifice my life to follow him because he is the saviour of the world's proletariat. This was how the Supervisor fought with his opponents in Beijing. If the first one did not work, he would lay out the second or the third version. He negotiated. He fought for every inch of the film.

My face was painted. The costume designer dressed me up in a greyish Red Army uniform and straw shoes. My sleeves were rolled up, hair braided. A wide belt cinched my waist. Someone was binding a piece of long cloth on my leg. I rehearsed my lines. A new line had been added by the Supervisor. The line was, 'Chairman Mao!'

The Supervisor was sitting in the director's chair. His concentration ruled the set. An assistant measured the distance between my nose and the lens again and again, murmuring the numbers to himself while marking them down. Red Azalea's hands were tied back with ropes. She was about to be tortured in public.

Take two, take three. I want a big big close-up of her eyes, the Supervisor yelled. Frame her face! Camera move! Closer, closer! The camera crew moved around. Changes had been made. Production assistants began to sweat. One of them murmured his numbers. Four feet and five inches. Five feet and three-quarters of an inch. A light fixture burned. The wire was smoking. The director of lighting replaced it right away. The make-up man combed my hair once more.

I was suddenly afraid of not being able to satisfy the Supervisor. I had no feeling for my lines. The make-up man asked if I needed him to put water drops in my eyes. The Supervisor waved him off. The costume designer came and wet my back with water. The Supervisor called, Roll the camera! I spoke my lines: 'Chairman Mao.' The Supervisor called, Cut! He said, No, maybe it's the lighting. Yes, the lighting is not right. This is not the light she likes. Comrade Jiang Ching would not approve of this way of lighting. It has to be straight flat light. Comrade Jiang Ching wants to see no shadows under Red Azalea's nose. Our heroine must have no shadows on her face. None at all!

The lighting director was upset but he dared not talk back. He kept moving the lights around.

The camera rolled again. Everyone held their breath. I repeated my lines carefully. The Supervisor kicked down a lightstand. He was frustrated. The camera crew got nervous. The studio heads came down to the set. Everyone was ready again. The Supervisor raised his head, his almond eyes brighter than the lights before me. I saw anxiety burning in his eyes. His lips were cracked dry, and his fingers stretched in the air like an eagle's claws. He closed his eyes and moaned my line. 'Chairman Mao.' Opening his eyes he asked me if I could give him more than the three syllables. Leaning back he said slowly, Roll the camera.

I failed him. I failed to deliver what he wanted. My acting was surgical. He cut me off, his face twisted. He said, One more minute and you'd better have it. Now immerse yourself. I took a deep breath and spoke my line. I repeated, 'Chairman Mao.' 'Chairman Mao.' There was no magic.

The Supervisor called me an idiot. And I called myself an idiot. I could not concentrate. I even found the line funny. Chairman Mao *what*? You should be shot by the nationalists, the Supervisor yelled at me. Where is the spirit I once saw in you? I know you have it. What's wrong with you? Don't you get the meaning of these three syllables? I thought you had sense. I thought you understood everything.

The make-up man came to repaint the scar on my forehead. The costume designer sprinkled more chicken blood on my chest. I was still not able to say 'Chairman Mao' right. The Supervisor threw the main electric switch. The studio went deadly dark. I couldn't breathe.

I sat by myself in one of the studio's guest houses. It was about midnight. The maple branches outside struck my window as if someone was knocking. The whole dormitory was as quiet as a graveyard. I had had a horrible day. I was almost fired on the set. The lighting men began to speak of Cheering Spear, of how easily she handled what I could not. They suggested that the Supervisor tell me to go home.

I heard the sound of steps at the end of the long hallway. They were heading in my direction. They stopped in front of my door. Light knocks, like a woodpecker. It's open, I said. The Supervisor ducked in, shutting the door behind him. He was in a blue Mao jacket. I tried to move a chair for him but he stopped me. He came and sat down by me, touching my bare shoulders with his hands. He stroked softly. He asked me to trust him. He asked me to have faith in him. He said, Only by having faith will you see the future I see, and feel the power I feel.

I said that the new lines were awkward. The script was too dry. I said I did not know how to put those words in my mouth. He said it was not a matter of awkwardness. The awkwardness served a political purpose. The lines had to be in there, or there would be no *Red Azalea*. I said I knew no acting technique to get this right. I was incapable of filling the three syllables with emotion. He said that this was the point – I *must* have emotion. The syllables themselves carried no significance at all. The significance was beyond the words, beyond *Red Azalea* itself. I said that I didn't see it, but I did see that the new lines would ruin the movie. I said that people were going to laugh at it. He said, Who do you think people are? They are walking corpses. What do the people know? The only thing they know is fear. That is why they need authority. They need to be told what to do. They need a wise emperor. It's been this way for five thousand years. They believe what rulers make them believe. That is why there are intellectual formulas. The operas are a way to shape their minds, to keep the minds where they should be. You see? I am showing you what I know. I am giving you my power. You see? Now someone else knows exactly what I know. Someone else is using my power to get what she wants.

Looking at my confused face he said, You know, I envy you. I really do. I envy your naïveté, your pain and your doubts. Because I do not have them, any of them. I have no doubts, you see? My will is unbreakable. Are you listening?

I asked him what made him do what he did. He got up and went to pull the velvet curtains closed. As he turned towards me, he switched off the light. In the dark he grasped me against his chest. He embraced me. He made me want him. Then he told me in the dark, to my surprise, that he always thought that he knew women no less well than I did, because he carried a female part in him. It was this persona that drove him to do what he did, to work for Comrade Jiang Ching, who made women heroines; to work for himself. He said by having me play Red Azalea, he could play a woman whom he had been admiring himself.

I felt the spasmodic movement of fury and pain-like excitement run through his frame. Let's be gone, he whispered in my ear. A few moments later as we caught our breath, we heard the sound of steps in the hallway. The sound of wooden slippers. Though I was prepared, I still felt horror. They were the steps of the door-man, coming from the end of the hallway, coming closer. The Supervisor switched the light back on and quickly straightened his jacket. He went to open the door a slit and sat back on a chair opposite me. He pulled out a newspaper and pretended to be reading. I grabbed a pen and pretended to take notes. The steps stopped by the door. I looked at the Supervisor. He was as calm as a lake on a windless summer's day. The door was pushed open. The doorman's head popped in. He looked at us, then stepped in. He was carrying a teapot and two enamel mugs. He came by the table and poured the tea into the mugs. He did not speak. The Supervisor began to say to me, So I want you to memorize these new changes. You must be able to perform well tomorrow.

My pen made scratches on the paper. Yes, I said. I looked at the doorman from the corner of my eye. His face was expression-less. He filled up my hot-water container, then left the room and closed the door. We heard his steps disappear at the end of the hallway.

The Supervisor said that the doorman was a sign. A sign of urgency, a sign of danger. We were being watched. Now it is time for me to tell you something important, he said. Something I must tell you before it is too late. The Supervisor's voice trembled as the sentence landed. A strange light brightened his almond eyes. A religious lover's eyes. He took a sip of the tea and asked me whether I cared to hear a story, the true story of Red Azalea. I am waiting, I said.

*

She was the daughter of a woman who was abandoned by her husband, the Supervisor began. She was taught that to be born a girl was a thing of shame. She tried to believe this the same way her mother did. But she could not. She was sixteen. She was a Communist. She joined a local opera troupe and went to Shanghai. She played Nora. She was Nora. She heard about Mao and his Red Army. His ideals were exactly hers. She went to meet her hero in a remote mountain area, in Yanan cave. She carried nothing with her but her youth. She was twenty-three and she was an actress. There she met Mao, the heavenly dragon, the red sun, the hope of China, the hope of women. She met her soul-mate. He became her life and she never loved again after that. She could not forget him. She could not forget the passion in the midst of gunfire. She could not forget their bodies climaxing as a bomb exploded. She could not forget the smashed pieces of the roof showering down on their naked bodies at midnight. They saw through the roof. There was the black velvet sky. The sky of the Middle Kingdom.

She could not forget his laugh. He was a born poet, a born lover and ruler. He told her that it was the best performance he ever gave in his life. He did it again and again with her, amidst the gunfire. He told her that she was his war empress. He told her that she was his life, his goddess of victory. He said that they must unite spiritually and physically. She must grant him the wish to marry her for the sake of battling for a new China, a China where a girl's birth was cause for celebration. They joined together in the cave of Yanan. The whole Red Army celebrated the union with rice wine, peanuts and sweet potatoes.

It was the time of the Red Army in the 1930s. Mao's troops were few. He was recruiting men, women, and horses. The new couple fought together, side by side. They went through fire and water; braved countless dangers. She went through battles with him. Battles which almost cost her her life.

When she walked out of one long battle in the west, her

239

stomach was filled with leaves. Her thighs were the width of arms, her chest was a wash-board. Her horse was the size of a big dog. They killed her horse to fill the stomachs of the starving Red Army leaders. Soldiers died of wounds and hunger. They died on the road. Women and babies. She survived. She was so weak she could barely stand. It was the faith of her ideals that carried her out along the death-packed road. She could not describe her happiness on the day, the first of October 1949, when her man stood on the top floor of the Heavenly Peace Gate declaring to the world that China had come to the era of independence.

The Supervisor's tone changed. His voice became hoarse. His eyes looked like two red spiders. He continued. She did not know him the way she thought she did, however. When she was presented with a contract it was already too late for her to realize her naïveté. She was forced to sign a contract with the Party in which she was given no rights to take part in China's political decision-making. Her battles meant nothing to the Party. She was shocked. She did not want to believe it. She turned to Mao, to the source of her strength.

Mao said that it was the Party's decision and he must set an example for his comrades. He said that the individual must obey the decision of the group. It was the principle on which the Party was based. And she, as he emphasized it, should be no exception. She never understood his excuse. She only knew that he owned this kingdom. She began to realize that he was in the mood for a change. His love for her had faded with the smoke of the roaring cannon. She was thrown away. He moved out of their bed and never came back. She waited day and night for him, for the love she used to have. She never doubted his love. She wrote. He never answered. She went to see him but was stopped at the door by his bodyguard. His words were knives. She phoned because she did not believe his bodyguard. A young nurse, his mistress, answered the phone. She was polite but the words pierced her heart. The nurse said, Mao would like to see his wife rest quietly at the East Wing Palace. Mao said that you must remember to take your medicine on time.

She did not allow herself to cry. Her heart bled at midnight when she remembered the sky of Yanan. She could not bear to sit in the house going mad. She needed to work, to balance herself. She demanded to be with her people. But her mouth was shut by the Party's central bureau. She was sent to Moscow under the guise of recuperation. She never liked Moscow. The cold froze her breath. She ordered Hollywood movies shipped to Moscow. She watched them until the last winter leaf fell on the ice. She sang her favourite old operas to get through the white nights. She never stopped petitioning. Year after year.

One day in the early 1960s she was allowed to go back to her motherland. But her husband refused to see her. He did not care how her nights went. He did not care whether she would go mad. He did not care. He told the Party that she was mad and he would have nothing to do with a mad woman nor should any other members of the Party.

How *did* her nights go by? The Supervisor repeated the question with a voice of frightening sarcasm. The red spiders shrank in his eyes. It was like being buried, the Supervisor smiled, buried alive. But she did not accept what fate had brought her. She believed she was a heroine. She would crawl out of the grave with her bare bloody hands. Her one-time comrades had become her enemies. In fact they never liked her. They never liked the actress from Shanghai. They could never trust that woman. She was too wild for them. She was never tame, never quiet. She bothered Mao after she had seduced him, they said. She had seduced China. The country was at war with her. She was attacked but she never surrendered. She did not know how. She refused to vanish. She was a reed shooting up under a heavy stone. She learned the art of war. She began her public speeches with the phrase, 'I am bringing you greetings from Chairman Mao.' She held the Little Red Book and shouted, A long long life to Chairman Mao! A long

241

long life to revolution! She played it well. She was the greatest actress of her time.

The Supervisor lit another cigarette. His mind was far away. His hands were as cold as death. His voice swept through me and I was carried away. He continued. Time went by and an iron bar was shaped into a needle. It was hard for her to tell then whether she was a living human or the living dead, nor could she tell if she was a man or a woman. She just played the roles and changed colours like a chameleon. She was alive and dead. She had mansions all over the Middle Kingdom but she was scared to sleep in one bed, in one place, for too long. Each night she lay on the bed and was chewed up by deep loneliness. She was drowning. The waiting maddened her. She sharpened her teeth and she was ready to kill. She could wait no longer. She was truly mad. The operas she sang sounded shrill. She cursed. She prayed. She laughed. She cried and she was transformed.

One morning Mao woke up and realized that his political bureau had become a capitalist's headquarters. The dragon had become a bodiless creature. At an annual Party meeting, his five-year big-leap plan received no support because his communes had starved thousands to death. His old cadres were going to throw him out. He was absolutely foundationless.

It was in this condition that he turned to her. When he had no one else to turn to. She said yes to him. She had her own plan. Both of them appeared on the Heavenly Peace Gate, on a golden September day, in green army uniforms, inspecting millions of screaming Red Guards. It was here, at Tienanmen Square, that she felt her life come back to her. The old dragon was mad. It was something she had been praying for. Mao was feverish once again trying to make communism a reality in China. Now the Great Proletarian Cultural Revolution would reunite her with her past love. She asked for his support. She created eight model operas. The operas of heroines. The operas of her deep emotions. She told him that they would secure his red kingdom. She made the population of billions watch the same operas for ten years.

242

She made the children recite the lines and sing the arias. She allowed them to watch nothing but her operas. She tamed them, she had to, and they became her pets. Because she represented Mao. She was pleased to hear a popular slogan in Szechuan that said: Better to sing a model opera than to have a body full of bullet holes. A generation of youngsters attached themselves to her. She was almost voted in as the Chairman of the Communist Party of China. The masses, the millions of fans, worshipped her opera heroines. And her. She had become their religion. The masses started to say, Long live Comrade Jiang Ching! in their morning ceremony before work. She was the morning star hanging over the rim of the nation's world.

Mao became ill, his shaking tongue almost fell out of his mouth but Comrade Jiang Ching was the Yellow River overflowing. She stopped at nothing, destroying whatever was in her way. Mao's empire was shaking. It had become his party and her party. She rose above his men. When she disliked a man, he would be jailed and his family tortured. The old sun was setting helplessly. Mao appealed to the congress. He wailed, 'Unite and do not split, be open and above board, do not intrigue or conspire.' In his Forbidden Palace he gathered his men and issued an open telegram to the public. His appeal was desperate. 'Watch out, comrades. I am not in her eyes,' stated Mao. 'Jiang Ching wants to be the Party Chairman. I am not in her eyes. She respects no one. She will destroy everyone's peace. After I die she will cause the country trouble. She will, I am warning you, my beloved countrymen. I want you to know that she does not represent me. She does not.'

For half a century Mao ruled her. But she was stubborn. She was foolish that way. But she was such a heroine. Although her loneliness was thicker than the cocoon of a silkworm, she had no intention of giving up her ideal. She wanted to see it passed on, even if one day she would turn to ashes.

It must happen her way, for the people, the Supervisor said. Mao is over eighty-three. The mud is reaching his neck. His lower jaw hangs and his hands shake. We do not have any time. We must hurry. Comrade Jiang Ching is in a hurry. She must relieve the pain of her love for the people. We must lose no time. We must resurrect Red Azalea. You. The heroine. The fearless, the diabolical, the lustful, the obscene heroine, Red Azalea.

He drew away from my face with a nervous toss of his hair, then came again, darkly, near. The heat from his mouth touched my earlobe. As if in touch with a great power, his red-spider-like eyes glittered. Give yourself to the people, he whispered. Give yourself to Comrade Jiang Ching.

I never used to believe that the Supervisor worshipped Comrade Jiang Ching. But now I believed it. He was her spiritual lover. I believed his obsession with her, because she represented his female-self. Because she allowed him to achieve his dream — to rule China's psyche. Despite his public face, he too was an individualist. He wanted to give the people more than she had done; he wanted to exceed her.

I saw no line between love and hate. That night, there was no line between love and hate, between him and me.

紅 杜 鵑

The Supervisor had charged me with his lust the night before. I was like a bullet lying in the chest of a gun. I still felt his warmth inside of me. My ambition multiplied my strength. I looked at myself in the mirror in the make-up room under fluorescent lights. I saw Red Azalea. In her Red Army cap. Spicy Eyes. Equipped. Perfectly in control. She carried Yan's determination and the Supervisor's spirit. I believed my make-up. I believed that I was whom I was supposed to be. I was creating history.

I am Comrade Jiang Ching and the Supervisor's physical substance. I display their thoughts. I am my ambition. There is an energy that comes from heaven and earth and unites in me.

Tomorrow the name Red Azalea will be on the mouth of every person.

I am the embodiment of Red Azalea. I am my role.

The crew had been waiting. I was in costume and make-up. The lights were on and the camera was in place. We had been waiting for our director, the Supervisor, to show up. But he did not. My make-up was put on and was taken off.

The crew kept waiting. Maple leaves were still, as if listening to the unusual quietness. The members of the crew grew suspicious. Gossip started. The lighting crew made excuses to take off before the appointed closing time. The make-up crew followed. Then other departments began to make excuses. People said they had waited long enough and their waiting should be respected. I sat by the camera, waiting. The cameraman had been napping since lunch. No one was in charge. The atmosphere was strange. The way people talked, heads glued together as if biting each other's ears.

The studio went silent. Then the streets. The city and then the country. A sign of danger emerged with the Supervisor's absence. I was an ant crawling on a heated wok. I tried not to feel the surroundings. I tried not to notice that the explosion was near. I asked myself to remain in control.

Then the news of the century came. It was the ninth of September, 1976. The reddest sun dropped from the sky of the Middle Kingdom. Mao passed away. Overnight, the country became an ocean of white paper flowers. Mourners beat their heads against doors, on grocery shop counters and on walls. Devastating grief. The official funeral music was broadcast day and night. It made the air sag.

Like everyone else, I was given white paper flowers to wear. I wore them the way all the other women did, tied to my braids, on my blouse and shoe-laces. We looked like moving cotton plants. The studio people gathered in the main meeting hall to moan. The sound of sobbing stretched like a hand-cranked gramophone at its spring's end. I found it hard to behave correctly. I had no tears. I cupped my face with my hands to hide my face. Through the space between my fingers I saw Soviet Wong. She tossed her face in wet handkerchiefs. Her nose was a blower, she was crying so hard I wondered what she was crying about. Her faded youth, I was sure. She must be crying for her could-have-beens. She was celebrating too: her misery had finally come to an end. She glanced at me as she blew her nose. I felt she could see through me. She must have guessed that I was not thinking of the greatest loss of our nation. I was thinking of Comrade Jiang Ching.

It was said that the man was murdered by his wife. Mao was murdered by Comrade Jiang Ching. It was said that Comrade Jiang Ching had replaced Mao's doctor. Mao was poisoned. Comrade Jiang Ching pulled the air mask off Mao's face. She could not wait for the man to die. She ended him herself by asking him to sign a paper at his last breath. The gossip grew fat, greasy, like a dish of pork neck.

Men began to talk about hanging the bitch. The bitch who was running the country. The bitch who made the citizens' lives so miserable. How could we let the plague run China? Aren't we truly insane? Let's push the bitch into a jar of boiling water. Let's drown her. Slice her alive. And sacrifice her on the altar of our great ancestors.

The media published a photo of Mao's first wife, a young woman who was killed by the Nationalists half a century ago. They said the woman was Mao's only true wife. The photo was posted everywhere. Even in nursery schools, where the little babies were taught to say the woman's name and sing songs in praise of her.

246

During Mao's funeral on TV we hardly saw the face of the widow, the widow of the dead red sun. The camera showed the big heads of elderly men. The Long March cadres. Men with puffed faces whose eyes registered no emotion. The camera showed the faces of the closest associates of the widow. Those faces were thin and long. Pyramid-shaped mouths ready to say, Fire.

The Chairman looked dissatisfied lying on his death bed. The mourners, the representatives of the people, were wailing in sorrow. By morning the floor opened, the crystal coffin rose from the ground and the death was displayed. Hundreds of thousands of people met their beloved saviour. Each of them held a thick handkerchief. They wiped and wiped, then fainted, one after another, on TV. They were carried out and their loyalty was praised by the media. The people's beloved saviour was in a brand-new grey jacket, designed by himself. The holy body was wrapped in a national flag, with the face painted, the interior emptied and spread with anti-corrosive.

In the studio the crowd gathered in front of a new black-and-white TV set, watching. Behind the set a slogan still hung: 'A long long life to Chairman Mao!' The colours were as bright as roses in the summer time.

The words Comrade Jiang Ching no longer existed. She was called the whore, the worn slipper. The amplifier tied on the maple tree-trunk outside my window was re-broadcasting Mao's instruction. The dead's instruction. The male announcer's voice was smooth as a jellyfish. He repeated: I am not in her eyes. Jiang Ching wants to be the Party Chairman. I am not in her eyes. She respects no one. She will stir up everyone's peace. After I die she will cause the country trouble. She will, I am warning you, my beloved countrymen . . . I am warning you.

I refused to be frightened. The disappearance of the Supervisor had prepared me for the worst. At night I waited. Waited for a nightmare. It came in the morning.

It was brought by Soviet Wong. She looked incredibly fresh

and young. She gave me a stamped piece of paper. The paper said that the Party had decided to send me back to Red Fire Farm. The film crew had been dispersed. A van was assigned to take me back to where I belonged.

I did not say anything to Soviet Wong since I knew my words would only be wasted if I did. The train of history had changed its direction. I realized that I, regardless of the fact that I had never really chosen, belonged to the losing side. I wanted to see the Supervisor again, yet I knew it was impossible. I began packing for Red Fire Farm, where I would be imprisoned.

My doorknob turned. A note was dropped in. I opened it. It was the Supervisor's handwriting. I gripped a table-leg to hold myself still. The Supervisor wanted to meet me at the Peace Park. Immediately. Urgent. You do not have to come, the note said. Our meeting will be very dangerous. I am wanted. The nation will not forgive me, not my type of sin. But I want to see you. Come, please, if it is still possible.

I went. In the dark. Riding a storm.

He said he had never said sorry in his life to anyone, but tonight he must express his sorrow. I disappointed you. I disappointed myself. I am ashamed. I want you to keep my shame, carve it in the stone tablet of your memory.

I looked at him. I went to hold him. In his hands I experienced a strong convulsive quiver. He felt sad because he was too old for the coming hardships. He doubted whether he could survive. But he must live for his ideal, he said as he clenched his teeth. He said that he had no right to disappoint himself. He must not surrender. To kill oneself was to surrender. It was unacceptable to a true Communist.

I told him that the studio had put me on a list as a follower of Comrade Jiang Ching. Black stains splashed on my dossier. He embraced me and asked if I would forgive Comrade Jiang Ching. I said I did not know her. He insisted that I did. He said that Comrade Jiang Ching had been a spectator of my passion. She is proud of you and, at the moment, she is counting on you. Because she herself is going to be hanged by her Long March comrades one of these days and she must count on her Red Azalea. She must see her ideal passed on.

I asked what his position was. He smiled strangely. My best chance is to be on their list of mental patients. I am on the hanging rope, and I am becoming a black curse upon the Middle Kingdom, he said in a joking tone. My head is in the noose. That's why I must give you this last message. Listen, you have done nothing wrong politically. This means that you are politically innocent. You should be categorized as a victim of Jiang Ching, a victim of the Gang of Four. You must declare that to the public. You must declare that you do not know me. You have not killed, you have not done anything criminal. The only thing they can accuse you of is your looks, the looks that were favoured by Comrade Jiang Ching. As he said this he looked at me, under the bright moonlight. Gazing at every part of my face, his expression froze. But you knew nothing of her plan.

Do not fall into their trap, he continued. Remember there will be traps, excellently designed, well tested. But it will be nothing new. I have always outwitted them until this day. I lose to history, not to them. They will toss everything I praised in shit. Logically, of course. They will criticize you, but the day will pass if you clench your teeth and bear with the peeling of your skin. Tell me now you are a heroine. Promise me you can bear it. Don't disappoint me.

But I was already ordered to go back to Red Fire Farm, I said. What could I do? The order has been changed, said the Supervisor calmly. A friend of mine in the studio arranged this for me. You will be given a position at the studio. It will be a lousy position. But you do not have to go back to the farm. Your city residence number has been restored. I know you are not capable of going back to Red Fire Farm. I am sorry that I could not protect you more. I have brought you more harm than happiness. I only wish ... He stopped and looked at me for a long time. You are so

249

young, and beautiful. It is good that you do not know many things.

I asked about his relationship with Comrade Jiang Ching. I demanded to know. He said that it was better I did not know, that he was protecting me from being harmed. He asked me to remember the darkness of the night, to watch the marching steps of history, to watch how it was altered, to see how the dead were made up and put to speak, how they never complained about what was put in their foul mouths. He said that it was this power of history that had charmed him. He asked me to admire history. His voice pervaded my being. Red Azalea will be born in another time, another place, I am sure, very sure, he murmured. I love Red Azalea. Do you?

In the shadow of the bushes, the Supervisor told me that the operas were created out of Jiang Ching's unfulfilled desire. He said it was that very same desire that made ancient tragedies stir the souls and foster civilizations. And it was that very same desire that sparked the flame of the Great Cultural Revolution. He stopped and looked around, then said he was a little disappointed that there were not many secretive lovers and lonely ones present tonight. He said that the singing of the maple leaves should be fully enjoyed. He asked if I could imagine the green hills and pink peonies in his garden back in Beijing. He asked if I could imagine him and me sitting by the valley in the bosom of mother nature. He asked me to close my eyes to smell the fragrance of the flowers. He said, Let it remain with you all your life. Open the hidden path of your mind, experience it, be completely in touch with it. He asked me to tell him how the wind puffed away the clouds. I drifted in his warmth. I told him his hands were the wind, and in his hands my body became clouds. He said he was fierce and his passion was as strong as death.

He said he always liked to watch the smoke spiralling upwards from the chimney of the Dragon Sight Crematorium. He said death was never frightening to him. He had never trusted the Chinese history books. Because those books were written by

250

people who were empty of desire. People who were paid by the generations of the emperors. They were eunuchs. Their desires had been castrated.

He said that he expected it, expected the unavoidable sufferings, the martyrdom and infamy. But he wanted to see me live. He wanted to see me live his life. You know my secret wish, and now keep it and nourish it for me. I wept, shivering. I said, I will, I promise. He said, Let's hold each other and say nothing.

We held each other. I felt Yan, we were walking out of the darkness.

A week later, Jiang Ching, Madam Mao, was arrested and denounced. The arrest was conducted by the new Party Central Bureau in Beijing led by Hua Guofeng, a man appointed by Mao. It was handled nobly and with good manners. The arrest was swift and clean. The public was greatly satisfied. They celebrated, bought crabs and boiled them to go with wine. The female crabs symbolized Jiang Ching. She was eaten now. China was exuberant. Rallies, monster parades and fireworks all night long. Millions poured into the streets, beating drums and dancing like dumplings in boiling water. A year later Hua's government was taken over by Deng Xiaoping, a member of one of Mao's Long March cadres. More rallies, parades and fireworks. Hua's portraits were torn off the wall and replaced with the slogans that praised the new man. Jiang Ching was caged in the City of Ch'ing national jail waiting to be sentenced. People celebrated and shouted, Down! Down! Down!

I worked once again as a set-clerk at the Shanghai Film Studio. For the next six years I copied scripts, put up shooting boards, recorded sets in various locations, mopped floors and filled up hot-water containers in offices. In six years of severe loneliness and abandonment, my health broke down. I coughed blood and fainted on the set. I had tuberculosis but I was not allowed to take leave. In the Party's dossier I was executed permanently. At night I felt so defeated that I lost my courage. I missed Yan and the Supervisor. In six years I became a stone, deaf to passion.

One day in 1983, an overseas letter came from a young friend whom I used to know in film school. She was now living in Los Angeles and had left China three years before. She asked me whether I had ever thought of coming to America. The idea was as foreign to me as if I were asked to live on the moon, the moon as my father described it – icy, airless and soundless. Yet my despair made me fearless. Though I spoke not a word of English, though I hated to leave my parents, my sisters, my brother, and to fight for permission to leave would take all my energy, I knew that escaping China would be the only solution.

I fought for my way and I arrived in America on the first of September, 1984.

Chicago, Christmas 1992